DØ146090

Anxiety in Eden

Anxiety in Eden

A Kierkegaardian Reading
of *Paradise Lost*

JOHN S. TANNER

New York   Oxford
OXFORD UNIVERSITY PRESS
1992

Oxford University Press

Oxford   New York   Toronto
Delhi   Bombay   Calcutta   Madras   Karachi
Kuala Lumpur   Singapore   Hong Kong   Tokyo
Nairobi   Dar es Salaam   Cape Town
Melbourne   Auckland

and associated companies in
Berlin   Ibadan

Copyright © 1992 by Oxford University Press, Inc.

Published by Oxford University Press, Inc.,
200 Madison Avenue, New York, New York 10016

Oxford is a registered trademark of Oxford University Press

Library of Congress Cataloging-in-Publication Data
Tanner, John S.
Anxiety in Eden : a Kierkegaardian reading of
Paradise lost / John S. Tanner.
p. cm.   Includes bibliographical references and index.
ISBN 0-19-507204-9
1. Milton, John, 1608–1674.   Paradise lost.
2. Kierkegaard, Soren, 1813–1885.   Begrebet angest.
3. Anxiety in literature.
4. Sin in literature.
PR3562.T36   1992   821′.4 – dc20
91-35843

1 3 5 7 9 8 6 4 2
Printed in the United States of America
on acid-free paper

TO SUSAN

for

"Those thousand decencies that daily flow
From all her words and actions"

ACKNOWLEDGMENTS

The Concept of Anxiety has been called "possibly the most difficult of Kierkegaard's works" (Introduction, *CA*, xii). Explication alone poses problems aplenty, especially if one seeks to clarify the text for a nonspecialist audience, as I do. To this, I have assumed the additional labor of drawing apt comparisons between Kierkegaard's treatise and Milton's *Paradise Lost*. Because my project imposes on me the twin tasks of explicating and comparing these two highly complex deliberations on the Fall, I have not, except in the second chapter, encumbered my argument overmuch with in-text citations of secondary criticism. Nevertheless, at the outset I gladly acknowledge my indebtedness to the work of many Miltonists and Kierkegaardians; their influence, often implicit in my argument, I try to make explicit in my notes.

Further, in the years this work has been in preparation I have incurred many personal debts. At the risk of overlooking some who have taught me how to read Milton and Kierkegaard, I wish to single out for thanks Hubert L. Dreyfus, James E. Faulconer, Donald M. Friedman, and Arthur Henry King. In addition, I am indebted to dialogues with many students, especially Gideon Burton, Rebecca Piatt Davidson, and Andrew D. Olsen. But most significantly, I gratefully acknowledge special debts to John S. Anson, for first suggesting this project to me and then ably directing my doctoral dissertation, upon which this book is based; to John T. Shawcross, for reading both early articles and the entire manuscript and for encouraging me to overcome my own anxiety and publish it; to Linda Hunter Adams at Brigham Young University and her able assistants Lara Trammell, Carol Oertli, and Henry Miles for their valuable help in editing, source-checking, and proofreading; to Brian O. Call for preparing the index; and to Paul Schlotthauer and Betty Seaver at Oxford University Press for copyediting.

Finally, I acknowledge the debt I owe my wife, Susan, who from first to last has been a help blessedly meet for my venture through anxiety. I hesitate to dedicate a book about anxiety to her only because her life is conspicuous for its absence.

Parts of this book have appeared in significantly different versions as articles. Chapters 2 and 3 pursue parallel arguments to those I made in "'Say First What Cause': Ricoeur and the Etiology of Evil," in *PMLA*

103.1 (1988). Part of chapter 5 appeared in an earlier version in *Literature and Belief*, 7 (1987), and parts of chapter 7 appeared in altered forms in *Encyclia* 60 (1983), and in *Phenomenological Inquiry* 13 (1989). I wish to also thank Brigham Young University's Center for the Study of Christian Values in Literature for awarding first place to two essays incorporated in this study, Brigham Young University for summer grants and other research time, and the National Endowment for the Humanities for a grant to a Summer Institute on *Paradise Lost*.

Provo, Utah   J. S. T.
March 1992

CONTENTS

NOTE ON CITATIONS

Citations to *The Concept of Anxiety* and *The Sickness unto Death* are normally to volumes from *Kierkegaard's Writings* (Princeton: Princeton University Press, 1976–). Among its many other advantages, this series contains marginal references to the standard Danish edition of Kierkegaard's works, *Søren Kierkegaards Samlede Værker*. Occasionally, however, I refer to the older translations of these two works by Walter Lowrie. All references to *The Concept of Anxiety* and *The Sickness unto Death* are cited in-text according to the abbreviations below. Other references to Kierkegaard's works are included in the notes without abbreviations.

CA   *The Concept of Anxiety: A Simple Psychologically Orienting Deliberation on the Dogmatic Issue of Hereditary Sin*. Vol. 8 of *Kierkegaard's Writings*. Ed. and trans. with intro. and notes by Reidar Thomte, in collaboration with Albert B. Anderson. Princeton: Princeton University Press, 1980.

CD   *The Concept of Dread: A Simple Psychological Deliberation in the Direction of the Dogmatic Problem of Original Sin*. Trans. with intro. and notes by Walter Lowrie. Princeton: Princeton University Press, 1957.

SD   *The Sickness unto Death: A Christian Psychological Exposition for Upbuilding and Awakening*. Vol. 19 of *Kierkegaard's Writings*. Ed. and trans. with intro. and notes by Howard V. Hong and Edna H. Hong. Princeton: Princeton University Press, 1980.

SUD   *The Sickness unto Death*. Trans. with intro. and notes by Walter Lowrie. Princeton: Princeton University Press, 1954.

Citations to Milton refer to the following editions:

CP   *The Complete Prose Works of John Milton*. Ed. Don M. Wolfe et al. 8 vols. New Haven: Yale University Press, 1953–82.

PL   *Paradise Lost*. In *John Milton: Complete Poems and Major Prose*. Ed. Merritt Y. Hughes. New York: Odyssey, 1957.

All other citations to Milton's poetry are also to the Hughes edition. Bible quotations are taken from the King James Version.

Anxiety in Eden

1

Introduction:
Milton and Kierkegaard

In Hebrew, *Eden* signifies "delight" or "pleasure." Both Milton and Kierkegaard, however, detect something besides bliss in the Garden. "The profound secret" of innocence, avers Kierkegaard, is that "in this state there is peace and repose, but there is simultaneously something else" (*CA*, 41), something he calls *angst* — alternatively translated as "anxiety" or "dread." The psychological by-product of freedom, anxiety registers the pressure that future possibilities exert upon the present. As Merleau-Ponty remarks, "The future is not prepared behind the observer, it is a brooding presence moving to meet him like a storm."[1] Similarly, the future looms up before Milton's Adam and Eve. Across Eden falls the specter of fearful yet seductive anxiety-dreams and of a demonic rebellion prefiguring ominous but alluring human potentialities. Within the protective walls of paradise echo dread voices, warning of what may (and will) be. In myriad ways the future looms up before Milton's human protagonists, giving rise to anxiety in Eden.

In an indeterministic sense, anxiety may be said to motivate the Fall, for it describes the psychological condition from which sin arises. How sin emerges not deterministically from concupiscence but freely from anxiety marks this study's point of departure. In part I, I explore the relationship between anxiety and the potential for sin; in part II, I examine the relationship between anxiety and the actuality of sin. Taken together, the arguments of *Anxiety in Eden* attempt to delineate a coherent Kierkegaardian reading of *Paradise Lost*.

Before embarking on a closely focused study of *The Concept of Anxiety* and *Paradise Lost*, however, I shall outline a few broad biographical and ideological comparisons between Milton and Kierkegaard. These summary remarks lay no claim to comprehensiveness. Rather, they are meant to supply prefatory generalizations about similarities between the lives and thoughts of Milton and Kierkegaard, as well as to suggest

3

further areas for study. I have found no evidence that Kierkegaard ever read Milton;[2] affinities between their interpretations of the Edenic myth likely spring from origins other than direct influence, such as similar backgrounds and temperaments, common ideological commitments, and (no doubt) shared genius.

Though perhaps not the most important, certainly one of the more striking coincidences linking the biographies of Milton and Kierkegaard is the shared trauma of a failed romance.[3] One man suffered through a broken marriage, the other a broken engagement. In each case, the misalliance involved a seventeen-year-old woman with an intensely devout man much her senior. Kierkegaard was ten years older than Regine Olsen, Milton twice the age of Mary Powell. Further, neither young woman shared her older suitor's temperament, especially his religious intensity—a source of irritation to both men. Olsen also blessedly lacked Kierkegaard's debilitating morbidity and probable sexual anxieties and hence later enjoyed a normal marriage in a way he evidently never could. Both romantic crises played themselves out in melodramatic scenes of renunciation and reconciliation that Milton and Kierkegaard experienced as straight tragedy. These romantic traumas loom large in their psychohistories. Under the guise of fiction, Milton and Kierkegaard repeatedly seem to revisit their anguish. Hence, the Mary Powell and Regine Olsen affairs figure prominently (in my view, too prominently) in interpretations of Milton's and Kierkegaard's works.[4] These episodes also figure in the feminist questions that beset each author's current reputation.

More important than Powell or Olsen in forming Milton's and Kierkegaard's personalities were dominant, pious fathers. Neither Milton nor Kierkegaard had much to say about his mother, though in both cases the slender record is respectful.[5] Both men, however, both openly and covertly say a great deal about their fathers, whose new money financed their sons' intellectual endeavors and whose presence hovers over their sons' lives. Milton's musicality and Kierkegaard's melancholy are perhaps the most conspicuous patrimonies. In temperament, Protestant piety, and parvenu ambition, we often seem to hear the fathers speak through the sons. Although Milton appears to have remained his father's devoted, grateful son all his life, Kierkegaard suffered a well-known convulsive rift with his father. However, if William Kerrigan's oedipal reading of the poet is valid, Milton's deep relationship with John Milton, Sr., may also have been far more conflicted than appears on the surface.[6]

Both fathers took an active role in overseeing their gifted sons' educations, and both boys proved themselves ready students. As children, Milton and Kierkegaard equally reveled in Latin and Greek studies, all

the while remaining somewhat reclusive, especially the latter. A class-
mate many years later remembers the young Kierkegaard as having been
exceptionally capable in Latin composition, yet solitary, aloof, rather
severe in his relations with his fellows, and marked by an ironical vein
of humor.[7] The portrait resembles that of young Milton as it emerges
in early biographies, autobiographical reminiscences, and implied self-
portraits in works like *Il Penseroso* and *Paradise Regained* (1.201ff.).
Although more genuinely convivial than Kierkegaard, Milton apparently
shared with him a special fondness for the pleasures of solitude. The
following night piece by Kierkegaard, for example, begs to be set beside
Milton's eulogy to "divine Melancholy":

> Therefore I love thee, thou quiet of the night, when the inmost character
> of nature betrays itself more clearly than when it loudly proclaims itself in
> the life and movement of all things! Therefore I love thee, thou quiet hour
> of spiritual exercise here in my chamber, where no sound and no human
> voice sets limits to the infinity of thought. . . . Therefore I love thee, thou
> quiet of loneliness, rather than all that is multifarious, because thou art
> infinite![8]

As young men, Milton and Kierkegaard appeared equally destined for
the ministry. Both shared a keen sense of spiritual exceptionality that,
combined with their educations, pointed toward careers in the ministry.
Yet, as an adult, each emphatically rejected the ecclesiastical career for
which he had been groomed. What is more, each man bitterly attacked
the professional clergy of his day and the system of tithes and titles
that supported a state church: "Above all," Kierkegaard cries, "save
Christianity from the State. By its protection it smothers Christianity to
death, as a fat lady with her corpus overlies her baby."[9] Anticlericalism
is particularly pronounced in the polemical writings that occupy much
of Milton's no less than Kierkegaard's middle and later years. Both men
became strident controversialists, espousing many unpopular views and
stooping to give as good as they got in rough-and-tumble pamphlet wars.

For their attacks on the establishment, they took considerable abuse —
and both took it hard. Each was stung by public defamation of his
character and ridicule of his personal debilities and appearance. Milton
was scorned as a libertine divorcer and a wicked regicide smitten blind
by God; Kierkegaard was lampooned as a hunchbacked crank, the object
of children's catcalls on the street and satiric cartoons in the press. Pillo-
ried by (and scornful of) public opinion, both men learned what it was
to receive a prophet's reward: dishonor among their countrymen. Yet
public controversy appears only to have hardened each man's intellectual

independence from establishment views, especially in matters of religion. A graph of their religious sympathies would trace nearly identical arcs away from an established Christian community toward a church of one.

This brings me to ideological similarities. On the premise that every Christian must assume personal responsibility for his or her faith, Milton and Kierkegaard carried the logic of Protestant individualism to extreme conclusions. A shared commitment to Protestant individualism underlies many intersections between their beliefs. Thus, for example, in the preface to *The Christian Doctrine*, Milton justifies his experiment in personal theology-making in language that resonates with Kierkegaardian individualism: "I decided not to depend upon the belief or judgment of others in religious questions for this reason: God has revealed the way of eternal salvation only to the individual faith of each man, and demands of us that any man who wishes to be saved should work out his beliefs for himself" (*CP*, 6.118). In salvation, Milton concurs with Kierkegaard that the Christian stands "before God" as an individual (*SD*, 79–87): "built by Faith to stand, / Thir own Faith not another's" (*PL* 12.527–28). Faith is necessarily personal; secondhand Christianity belongs not to faith but to conformity.

This same spirit animates Milton's *Areopagitica*. In a passage whose terms and tone could have come straight out of Kierkegaard's *Attack on Christendom*, Milton decries the soporific effects of institutional religion:

> A wealthy man addicted to his pleasure and to his profits, finds Religion to be a traffick so entangl'd, and of so many piddling accounts, that of all mysteries, he cannot skill to keep a stock going upon that trade. What should he doe? fain he would have the name to be religious, fain he would bear up with his neighbors in that. What does he, therefore, but resolvs to give over toyling and to find himself som factor [agent] to whose care and credit he may commit the whole managing of his religious affairs; som Divine of note and estimation that must be. To him he adheres, resigns the whole ware-house of his religion with all the locks and keys into his custody; and indeed makes the very person of that man his religion. . . . So that a man may say his religion is now no more within himself, but is become a dividuall movable, and goes and comes neer him, according as that good man frequents the house. He entertains him, gives him gifts, feasts him, lodges him. His religion comes home at night, praies, is liberally supt, and sumptuously laid to sleep. (*CP*, 2.544)

Milton's Christian capitalist, who wants to make a commodity of his faith, prefigures the Copenhagen burghers of the 1850s, against whose complacent Christianity Kierkegaard inveighed all his adult life. Indeed

Kierkegaard satirizes such comfortable Christians, including (especially) their clergy, in very much the same vein as had Milton: "On Saturday a person takes out the religious (about the way a lawyer takes out his law books) and 'puts himself into it,' works out a sermon that he delivers on Sunday—but otherwise has nothing to do with the religious; it does not overwhelm him, never grips him suddenly—no, it is a business like the merchant's, the attorney's, the administrator's."[10] Once the task of a whole lifetime, Kierkegaard protests, faith had been debased by the present age; it was being sold cheap: "Everything can be had at such a bargain price that it becomes a question whether there is finally anyone who will make a bid."[11] Against such debasement of religion, Milton and Kierkegaard insist that faith is not a commodity one can buy from or consign to the parson. Rather, it is a high and holy religious passion.

This shared conviction gives rise to yet another saying from *Areopagitica* that forecasts a major development in Kierkegaardian thought. Milton asserts, "A man may be a heretick in the truth; and if he beleeve things only because his Pastor sayes so, or the Assembly so determins, without knowing other reason, though his belief be true, yet the very truth he holds becomes his heresie. There is not any burden that som would gladlier post off to another, then the charge and care of their Religion" (*CP*, 2.543). The assertion that "a man may be a heretick in the truth," echoed again shortly before his death in yet another plea for toleration (see *CP*, 8.421–24), moves Milton toward Kierkegaard's Christian existentialism. Consonant with Milton, Kierkegaard observes that "what is in itself true may in the mouth of such and such a person become untrue." In God's eyes, it may be preferable to worship an idol with full religious passion than to worship the true God insincerely. For "the one prays in truth to God though he worships an idol; the other prays falsely to the true God, and hence worships in fact an idol."[12] Admittedly, Kierkegaard pushes this position much further than Milton, boldly proclaiming that "subjectivity is truth." Nevertheless, neither Kierkegaard nor Milton is willing to reduce Christian truth to mere doctrinal correctness. Milton cites approvingly the ancient maxim *"Err I may, but a Heretick I will not be"* (*CP*, 8.423). Both men gauge faith not simply by *what* one believes but by *how* one holds the truth. After all, "the devils also believe and tremble" (James 2:19).

In *Paradise Lost*, the devils even dabble in philosophy and theology while conferring atop hell's equivalent of Athens's Mars Hill. Yet such speculation about fate and free will is not only an irrelevance in regard to the devils' salvation but a deliberate demonic dodge to avoid the only knowledge that might lead to repentance: true God-consciousness. The irony of hell's inhabitants' evading God by philosophizing about him would not have been lost on Kierkegaard. Indeed, he saw that form of demonic evasion all about him in modern Christendom, where "people's attention is no longer turned inwards . . . but turn[ed] to others and to things outside themselves, where the relation is intellectual." When the knowledge of God is reduced to an intellectual subject, pursued without passion or inwardness, as in Milton's hell, theology becomes mere soul-numbing talkativeness, "afraid of the silence which reveals its emptiness."[13] It becomes, as Milton says of hell's speculative theology, "Vain wisdom all, and false Philosophie" (*PL* 2.565). For Milton, the god of the philosophers is not the God of Abraham, Isaac, and Jacob — to echo Pascal's famous aphorism.

Kierkegaard is even more profoundly subversive of this false god. As theology, his work seeks to expose and overturn the Greek premises upon which Christian thought has been cantilevered at least since Augustine; as philosophy, his work seeks to reconstruct metaphysics, epistemology, and ethics upon genuinely Christian premises.[14] This double enterprise, destructive of the god of philosophy and recuperative of the living God of Abraham, is calculated to disconcert a misguided Christendom, which for centuries had taken its intellectual bearings more from Athens than from Jerusalem. Kierkegaard summarizes his life's work as "the task of translating completely into terms of reflection [philosophy] what Christianity is, what it means to become a Christian."[15] "Turning Hegelianism outside in,"[16] Kierkegaard's deliberately shocking conclusions about Christianity, expressed dialectically, invert the philosophical premises that prevailed from Plato to Hegel. Thus in epistemology, subjectivity rather than objectivity is truth (see *Concluding Unscientific Postscript*); in ethics, the single individual is higher than the universal (see *Fear and Trembling*). So it goes throughout his oeuvre. Kierkegaard translates authentic Christianity into the dominant contemporary philosophical discourse (Hegelianism) in order to disclose the vast gulf between philosophy and faith.[17]

A Christian-humanist, Milton likewise devotes his poetic career to co-opting paganism for Christianity. In the process, he "transforms theological tradition . . . by taking up a very Hebraic position in regard to Western metaphysics."[18] Though less radical in his critique than Kierkegaard, Milton, too, subjects his carefully acquired classicism to the scrutiny of scriptural truth — often finding the former wanting. From the "Nativity Ode" to *Paradise Regained*, Milton's work rejects much and transforms everything received from paganism within the poet's Christian alembic. To be sure, one strong Miltonic impulse is assimilationist: because his great epic is to be the story of all things, it must gather all other stories somehow into its wide net. Yet another even stronger Miltonic impulse is exclusionary: he remains profoundly skeptical of not only the moral but ontological status of his nonbiblical sources. Hence, as poet of the "true" story of all things, he characteristically casts a wary eye on his pagan sources in order to discern what is true and what "they relate, / Erring" (*PL* 1.746–47). The result is an epic determined not simply to retell but to reread — self-consciously and critically — pagan tradition in light of Christianity. Thus Milton and Kierkegaard learn to sing like Homer and reason like Hegel, respectively, in order to bear witness to Christianity's unknown God. They baptize epic poetry and dialectical philosophy and bring them, still dripping wet, to the Christian God.

What is more, their interrogation extends to paganism's replications within Christendom. Both believe that very early the church was wooed and won by siren muses. Consequently, both distinguish between an apostolic and apostate Christianity — or, in Kierkegaard's terms, between Christianity and Christendom — and each aligns his own beliefs with those of the primitive church. Like radical seventeenth-century sectarians, Milton suspected that Christianity went bad well before the Reformation. He insists that an apostasy began soon after the death of the apostles, when "grievous Wolves" succeeded as teachers, the truth was tainted with "superstitions and traditions," religious beliefs were enforced by "secular," "carnal" power, and religious leaders arrogated unto themselves "names, / Places and titles" (see *PL* 12.506–22).[19] Consequently, Milton distrusts all explanations of Christian doctrine based on tradition rather than scripture. In the preface to *The Christian Doctrine* he brushes aside *all* nonscriptural traditions (including, presumably, even the early creeds and church fathers) as "conventional opinions" and hence not binding upon Christian belief. At the same time, he announces his intent to provide his own views with an exclusively scriptural pedigree, unmingled with mere custom. Beyond even this Protestant ideal of *sola scriptura*, he glances wistfully back at the apostolic period before a written canon, a time when the gospel was delivered orally and heresy was a charge reserved solely for hirelings who maliciously caused divisions among the faithful while serving their bellies (*CP*, 6.123). This is an extraordinary comment coming at the beginning of *The Christian Doctrine*, a thoroughly Bible-based theology. It hints that, for all his strenuously Protestant commitment to the written word, Milton regards precanonical, primitive Christianity guided by living oracles preferable to religion based on rigid conformity to a written, canonical text.

Kierkegaard holds an even more pronounced conviction that one discovers authentic Christianity not in creeds but in its practice during the primitive, precanonical period. He believes that Christendom had done away with true Christianity and that his task was to reintroduce Christianity into Christendom.[20] For Kierkegaard, Christendom distorts Christianity not so much by adulterating pure but static ancient doctrines as by falsifying the dynamics of true discipleship. For Christianity is not primarily about creeds, says Kierkegaard in *Training in Christianity*, but about the *imitatio Christi*.[21] True discipleship finds its paradigm in the New Testament period when faith meant facing the scandal of the God/Man. Christ's first followers responded to a call not from a respectable, genteel minister of a successful world-historical institution but from a carpenter's son, without credentials, institutional sanction, or the weight of centuries of successful evangelism. Yet this lowly man was, nevertheless, God incognito. The God/Man was an offense to his contemporaries, a scandal; his kerygma, a stumbling block. True disciples recognize that Christianity still offends rationality and respectability. Yet, as Kierkegaard saw it, modern Christendom everywhere conspired to mask the affront. Its banality palliated the paradoxes of faith; its temporal triumph belied the difficulty of discipleship, seeming to underwrite the absurdity of belief with the testimony of nineteen hundred years' "success." Genuine Christians, however, are not lulled by the irrelevancies of history nor by Christendom's numerical successes. Rather, their faith makes them contemporaneous with the God/Man; they face the offense squarely. For authentic discipleship, whether ancient or modern, is found only within the possibility of scandal or "the offence."[22]

Judged by this standard alone, both Milton and Kierkegaard were faithful Christian disciples. They knew scandal, knew it intimately; indeed, they often courted it. To the end of their lives, opprobrium attached itself to their names: both men died in some disrepute (Kierkegaard perhaps more than Milton), leaving contemporaries unsure if England and Denmark had lost genuinely famous writers or merely notorious ones. The voices that echo from Milton and Kierkegaard down through the years remind us how strident each could be in matters of conscience. Sometimes their voices sound shrill—intemperate and petty, unlovely and uncharitable. But not infrequently they also sound prophetic—lofty, impassioned, indignant, ironic, dejected yet confident that God and history ultimately would vindicate them.[23] Each came to think of himself as a witness against a perverse majority—like John the Baptist or Milton's zealous angel Abdiel, lone voices crying in the wilderness. Moreover, each came to equate faith with the single individual who *qua* individual stands firm as:

> The only righteous in a World perverse,
> And therefore hated, therefore so beset
> With Foes for daring single to be just,
> And utter odious Truth.
>
> (*PL* 11.701–4)

No matter if none should heed their warning voices; they felt called to bear witness: "Thus much I should perhaps have spoken only to trees and stones; and had none to cry to, but with the Prophet, *O earth, earth, earth!* to tell the very soil it self, what her perverse inhabitants are deaf to" (*CP*, 7.462–63).

So writes Milton in a brave if futile defense of the "Good Old Cause." His witness is deeply enmeshed in a particular time and place in seventeenth-century England. The same is, of course, equally true of Kierkegaard, whose work is embedded in the controversies of nineteenth-century Copenhagen as well as couched in the special Hegelian idioms of his own philosophical system. The particularity of either author's work necessarily renders any resemblances inexact, including those I hereafter identify between *Paradise Lost* and *The Concept of Anxiety*, for though these texts share much in common, each possesses what Duns Scotus calls *haeccietas* ("thisness"), meaning unique individuality, which I have taken pains to honor and acknowledge. But such uniqueness characterizes in some degree or other any two texts. Dissimilarity does not obviate the enterprise of comparative analysis; rather, it makes the task profitable, for little could be learned from comparing clones.

Bound by similar temperaments and biographies as well as by common ideological commitments, Milton and Kierkegaard constitute a likely brace of Christian writers for comparative study. More especially, as among the most notable interpretations of the Edenic myth ever written, *Paradise Lost* and *The Concept of Anxiety* cry out to be read together.[24] Rooted in a seemingly simple story in Genesis, they conduct wide-ranging, brilliant investigations into the psychology of innocence, sin, and guilt, probing the nature of human fallibility and freedom. My task of comparison, made cumbersome by differences of time, language, and culture, is rendered practicable by the philosophic character of Milton's poetry and the poetic nature of Kierkegaard's philosophy.[25] By reading *Paradise Lost* through the lens of *The Concept of Anxiety*, I hope to reward Kierkegaard studies and Milton criticism alike: the one with a lucid explication and novel application of Kierkegaard's "most difficult" work, and the other with fresh perspectives from which to measure the complex artistry of Milton's masterpiece.

Notes

1. Cited in Taylor, *Journeys to Selfhood*, 177.

2. In a passage deleted from the final copy of *The Concept of Anxiety*, Kierkegaard admits he did not understand English (*CA*, 211). Though he owned a few works by English authors, citations to English literature are almost always from German translations. Moreover, Kierkegaard's library apparently contained no copy of *Paradise Lost* in either English or German ("His Library," *Bibliotheca Kierkegaardiana*, 12.92), nor have I found any references to Milton in Kierkegaard's voluminous writing.

3. A dated but still admirable introduction to Kierkegaard's life is Walter Lowrie's *Kierkegaard* in two volumes. The standard Milton biography is still William Parker's *Milton: A Biography*, also in two volumes.

4. For a critique of biographical approaches to Kierkegaard's works, see Taylor, *Kierkegaard's Pseudonymous Authorship*, 26ff.

5. Diekhoff's collection of Milton's autobiographical writings (*Milton on Himself*) lists only two comments on the poet's mother.

6. Arguing that "splitting the imago of the Father constitutes the major psychological strategy of Milton's life and work," Kerrigan explains how Milton simultaneously revered and rejected paternal authority: "His father first, then all the derivatives of his father in earthly authority—teachers, bishops, kings, parliaments, theologians—could be deposed and abused by a rebellious son, while Milton at the same time remained the obedient son of his divine father. This is the generative core of the strong poet" (*Sacred Complex*, 114–15).

7. *Bibliotheca Kierkegaardiana*, 12.45–48.

8. Kierkegaard, *Stages on Life's Way: Studies by Sundry Persons*, 307–8.

9. Kierkegaard, *Attack upon "Christendom,"* 140.

10. *Søren Kierkegaard's Journals and Papers*, 4.4557.

11. Kierkegaard, *Fear and Trembling: Dialectical Lyric*, trans. Howard V. Hong and Edna H. Hong, 5.

12. Kierkegaard, *Concluding Unscientific Postscript to the Philosophical Fragments*, 179–81.

13. Kierkegaard, *The Present Age*, 69.

14. For a discussion of the incompatibility between Greek and Christian thought, see Verdenius, "Plato and Christianity."

15. Kierkegaard, *The Point of View for My Work as an Author*, 103.

16. See ch. 2 of Hannay's *Kierkegaard*.

17. For important studies of Kierkegaard's relationship to Hegelianism, see

Crites, *Twilight of Christendom*; Taylor, *Journeys to Selfhood*; and Thulstrup, *Kierkegaard's Relation to Hegel*. Thulstrup provides a thorough examination of Kierkegaard's reaction to Danish Hegelianism, while the other two fine studies supply critical comparisons between the thought of Kierkegaard and Hegel himself.

18. Rapaport, *Milton and the Postmodern*, 19. Though I question a good deal of Rapaport's postmodernist reading of Milton (especially his chapter "Milton and the State"), I think he is right that Milton is "working out of a Hebraic tradition" (216) often at odds with the Greek tradition of philosophy.

19. On Milton's early dating of an apostasy, see Hill, *Milton and the English Revolution*, 84–87.

20. Kierkegaard, *Training in Christianity*, 39.

21. See 108–9. Also see Elrod (*Kierkegaard and Christendom*, 229–32) among many others who comment on the parallels between Kierkegaard and this famous medieval ideal.

22. Kierkegaard, *Training in Christianity*, 79–144.

23. See Kierkegaard, *The Point of View for My Work as an Author*, 99.

24. Apart from my own work, connections between Milton and Kierkegaard have gone little noted. Broadbent makes limited use of *The Concept of Anxiety* in *Some Graver Subject*, including adopting the term *anxiety* in a chapter subheading. Yet, as I explain hereafter, Broadbent often misconstrues Kierkegaard. In *Milton and the Nature of Man*, George is more accurate in his brief application of *The Concept of Anxiety* to *Paradise Lost*, which is not surprising because he is also author of a monograph on Kierkegaard's "aesthetic sphere." Brisman alludes often to Kierkegaard in *Milton's Poetry of Choice* but only to *Either/Or*, the central work of Kierkegaard's "ethical sphere." Brisman never even mentions Kierkegaard's treatise on the Fall. More recently, Kerrigan has made intelligent, sophisticated use of Kierkegaard in *The Sacred Complex*, though Kerrigan's comments are always made in passing, his primary attention clearly lying elsewhere.

25. On Kierkegaard as a "kind of poet," see Mackey, *Kind of Poet* (esp. ch. 6), and Taylor, *Journeys to Selfhood*, 93–99.

I

Anxiety and
the Potentiality
of Sin

2

The Fall as
Desire and Deed

"Say First What Cause": Motive-Hunting in Paradise

In *The Christian Doctrine* John Milton broaches what he must have known to be a delicate question: What motivates the Fall? As epic poet, he clearly thought long and hard about what led Adam and Eve to transgress—about their personalities, vulnerabilities, appetites, external circumstances, and all the various "causes" of the Fall that the poem develops at such length and with such care. As theologian, by contrast, Milton treats the Fall's human motivation only glancingly. Yet his analysis in *The Christian Doctrine* intimates Milton's awareness of the myriad perplexities entangling this problem. In the chapter entitled "Of the Fall of Our First Parents, and of Sin," Milton contends that all sin has "two subdivisions, whether we call them degrees or parts or modes of sin, or whether they are related to each other as cause and effect. These subdivisions are evil desire [*concupiscentia mala*], or the will to do evil, and the evil deed itself [*malefactum ipse*]" (*CP*, 6.388). At first glance, this division between desire and deed seems unremarkable enough. From its inception, Christianity has insisted on linking outward behavior to its inward sources in the heart. Christ announced that his new gospel would trace sin beyond murder to anger, beyond adultery to lust (Matt. 5:21–22, 27–28). He taught that corrupt acts spring forth from corrupt desires, as the evil fruits of a tainted root: "For out of the heart proceed evil thoughts, murders, adulteries, fornications, thefts, false witness, blasphemies" (Matt. 15:19). Likewise, he discovered the roots of good acts in the abundance of the heart: "Even so every good tree bringeth forth good fruit" (Matt. 7:17). Christianity thus seizes upon the appetite as well as its enactment, encouraging the excavation of the soul's deepest, most secret recesses; the disclosure of every hidden thought and buried motive. It presumes that good deeds derive from pure, regenerate hearts; evil deeds from depraved, fallen desires.

"It was this evil desire," Milton continues, "that our first parents were originally guilty of. Then they implanted it in all their posterity" (*CP*, 6.388). Here, Milton's simple dichotomy between desire and deed begins to become problematic, at least as it applies causally to Adam and Eve. If our first parents were originally guilty of evil desire, were they guilty of it *before* they were guilty of the evil deed? Milton seems to imply so here, but then qualifies this impression, for if in Eden concupiscence related itself to sinful conduct as cause to effect, then a psychological fall must have preceded the behavioral one. In other words, the Fall must have occurred as desire prior to disobedience; that is to say, Adam and Eve must have fallen inwardly before they fell outwardly.

Evidently sensing this theological conundrum, Milton quickly moves to reformulate the relationship between corrupt desire and corrupt deed in the case of Adam and Eve: "This evil desire . . . [that] is inbred in us . . . took possession of Adam after his fall [*post lapsum*], and from his point of view could not be called *original*." In this same vein, Milton asserts: "Thus *as soon as the fall occurred*, our first parents became guilty, though there could have been no original sin in them" (my italics). By "original" Milton means "inherited," the special definition Augustine develops as the concept of Original Sin. Since Adam and Eve inherit neither actual depravity nor even a propensity for evil, the first human sin cannot be explained by the notion of original (inherited) sin. Their evil desire (or "concupiscence") cannot be attributed, as ours often is, to prior corruption in-dwelling in the will, for it is, presumably, the very source of such depravity. Therefore, Milton speaks of concupiscence emerging "after" the Fall, or "as soon as the fall occurred" (*CP*, 6.389–90).

According to these formulations, desire and deed in Eden are not necessarily causally or even sequentially related. Concupiscence originates not prior to disobedience but either simultaneous with it or subsequent to it. Thus in Milton's theology, the visible enactment "Of Man's First Disobedience" does not necessarily presuppose an invisible, inward preenactment in guilty desire. Though Milton initially describes such evil desire as a precedent mode of sin—normally related to evil deeds as cause to effect—he ends the chapter resolving to treat concupiscence as a "consequence of sin." Rather than the Fall's cause, concupiscence is more properly considered, he concludes, to be its effect or "punishment" (*CP*, 6.390–91). Milton's position on concupiscence as alternatively the cause and consequence of sin resembles his remark about the place of poetry in education: "Poetry would be made subsequent, or indeed rather precedent" to rhetoric (*CP*, 2.403). Poetry is plainly crucial to

Milton's program of education, but it is unclear exactly where it fits — as the capstone or foundation or both. Similarly concupiscence vis-à-vis sin: Milton affirms that it is profoundly implicated in the psychology of sin, but its precise relation to the process by which sin first emerged remains ambiguous.

The same issues about motives and deeds with which Milton briefly grapples in *The Christian Doctrine* reappear in *Paradise Lost* as the problem of a fall before the Fall. Does *Paradise Lost* envisage an interior defection before Adam and Eve's outward disobedience? Or, to give the question its usual accusatory edge, does the poet motivate the Fall by surreptitiously borrowing motives from fallen psychology, in effect explaining the origin of concupiscence tautologically, *by* concupiscence? This is an old critical crux in Milton studies. Long ago Dr. Johnson impugned the poem's prelapsarian psychology: "To find sentiments for the state of innocence was very difficult," he demurs, "and something of anticipation perhaps is now and then discovered."[1] In the mid-twentieth century, the tone of critical opinion about what Johnson mildly labels "anticipation" changed sharply. E. M. W. Tillyard flatly calls it "faking: perfectly legitimate in a poem, yet faking nevertheless." Milton's sleight of hand, according to Tillyard, is that he "anticipates the Fall by attributing to Eve and Adam feelings which though nominally felt in the state of innocence are actually not compatible with it."[2] A truly innocent Adam and Eve could not speak, act, and feel the way Milton's protagonists do.

Tillyard's charges came near the beginning of a vigorous controversy in Milton criticism about the ethical status of Adam and Eve's prelapsarian actions and motivations.[3] If Adam and Eve begin to fall before they actually eat the fruit in Book 9, at what point does the break between innocence and sinfulness *really* occur? This issue polarized midcentury Milton criticism.[4] Many critics (often Milton's self-anointed champions) felt compelled to defend the traditional reading, which located the Fall in two specific, discrete acts of disobedience in Book 9. After all, it was argued, only such a reading retained the central ethical feature of Eden: its innocence. Others (often, though not always, Milton's self-styled detractors) felt that this reading denied significance to the drama leading up to the lapse. Never mind, it was argued, that flawed human protagonists may be scripturally untenable; the biblical myth of absolute innocence is humanly impossible anyway, and Milton's poetry often works at cross-purposes to his theology. Only readings that acknowledge his protagonists' flawed but therefore plausible human nature can account for Eden's chief interest for moderns: its psychological subtlety. The one side tended to view the Fall as a single, ethical event, a distinct deed marking a clear dividing line between innocence and guilt; the other, to regard it mainly as a psychological process, a gradual drama of defection spread out across time through various subtle stages.

The controversy over an inward fall before the outward Fall, though somewhat died down now, has scarcely been laid fully to rest.[5] I shall revive its mid-century arguments here in some detail because they most clearly define the contours of an enduring crux for Milton studies, one against which *The Concept of Anxiety*'s value becomes readily apparent. Through Kierkegaard, Miltonists can reinspect this literary issue as a splendid instantiation of perennial philosophical paradoxes about freedom — such as, how free acts can be at once enmeshed within a coherent historical process and yet irruptions from it; how free choices can be both situated by environmental determinants yet dislocations of them; how human existence can participate simultaneously in communal and individual dimensions, and so forth. Like Milton, Kierkegaard illuminates these paradoxes embedded in Genesis's seemingly simple but subtle tale of evil in Eden, for also like *Paradise Lost*, *The Concept of Anxiety* characterizes the Fall as both a psychological process and an ethical leap.

In this way Milton and Kierkegaard lay bare what Paul Ricoeur has called the "twofold rhythm" of the "Adamic myth." They affirm the myth of the "instant," which conceives evil's appearance as a sudden, irrational cleavage — a caesura about which St. Paul could say, "By one man sin entered into the world" (Rom. 5:12). And they subscribe to the myth of the "lapse of time" or "drama of temptation," which depicts sin's emergence as part of a gradual process that "multiplies intermediaries," spreading out the origin of sin "among several characters — Adam, Eve, the serpent — and several episodes." In other words, they endorse "the myth of the act and that of the motivation."[6] Kierkegaard reveals what is at stake in attaching motivation to act, not only for Genesis or for Milton's redaction of it in *Paradise Lost* but for freedom itself. His great value to Milton studies is to propose a philosophically sophisticated explanation of free yet motivated action, the very quandary that underlies the literary problem of a fall before the Fall.

This quandary is essentially one of causality. As such, it belongs to a larger inquiry into the etiology of evil, which Milton launches, after the pattern of Homer and Vergil, in the poem's opening invocation: "say first what cause / Mov'd our Grand Parents . . . to fall" (28-30). In reply, the muse supplies not a motive but evil agents: "Th' infernal Serpent," or Satan, and his "Rebel Angels," who seduce Adam and Eve to

"foul revolt" (33–38). These are the immediate causes adduced by the
muse as, again in the *Iliad* or *Aeneid* tradition, *Paradise Lost* initially
explains human misery by pointing to prior malice among the gods. Yet
as a Christian epic, *Paradise Lost* does not and cannot stop here, with
Satan. Unlike its pagan counterparts, it must wrestle with how Satan
became evil though created good; moreover, it must hold humans responsible for yielding to temptation. The motivation of both humans
and demons, therefore, must figure among the causes of sin, in addition
to the influence of external tempters. As Arnold Stein notes: "If the
motives and drama of Milton's version of Adam's fall are to be as profound as they are far-reaching in significance, then the essential conflict
must be internal."[7] Or, as Fredson Bowers observes, also invoking the
concept of dramatic motivation:

> Milton devotes many lines to what in the language of the drama would be
> called "motivating" the Fall from the point of view of Man. Indeed, if we
> are unwilling to accept his psychological analysis of the reasons that led
> Eve to fall a victim to Satan, and in turn Adam a victim to Eve, the poem
> will fail. . . . The actions, and their causes, must be credible, and even
> inevitable, at the level of the reader's human understanding.[8]

Stein and Bowers concur that the Fall cannot be explained, as older
critics were wont to do, as the result of disobedience. To them, as to
most modern critics, disobedience has seemed hopelessly tautologous:
"After all it is no explanation that our Grandparents disobeyed because
they were disobedient."[9] Modern efforts to ferret out the deeper motives
beneath disobedience began in earnest in 1917 and 1918 when two distinguished Miltonists, Edwin A. Greenlaw and James Holly Hanford, published separate articles on the motivation of the Fall in *Paradise Lost*.[10]
These articles initiated a critical vogue for motive-hunting in Milton's
Eden—an endeavor no doubt fueled by the burgeoning importance of
depth-psychology in the early decades of this century. During the twen-
ties, thirties, and forties numerous critics advanced opinions about what
"real" motive lay behind Adam and Eve's disobedience. For Adam, sensuality, uxoriousness, gregariousness, or idolatry were suggested; for
Eve, pride, injured merit, vanity, and curiosity constituted a likely list[11];
or as Maurice Kelley asserts, based on a passage in *The Christian Doctrine*, all of these motives (and more) rolled into one.[12]

Sleuthing for subliminally sinful desires in Eden focused extraordinary
attention on the human details of books 4–9. Milton's proleptic hints of
the Fall came to be seen as explanations of it. For critics like Bowers and
Stein, the success of the entire poem hinged on the plausibility of Adam

and Eve's dramatic motivation. But motivating truly innocent protagonists to sin poses acute logical difficulties, of which many early motive-hunters seemed blithely unaware. As Leon Howard presciently remarked in 1945, motivating the Fall by fallen motives is a "logical trap."[13] If certain desires may themselves be sinful, how can truly innocent beings be motivated by idolatry or vanity without being sinfully idolatrous or vain before they transgress? And how can motivated free acts be merely "credible" but not "inevitable," to adopt Bowers's language? Few critics, especially before the midcentury, confronted these issues head-on.

Then in 1947 A. J. A. Waldock published Paradise Lost *and Its Critics*. His critique forced Miltonists for the first time to grapple seriously with the problem of a fall before the Fall. Waldock saw the task of providing plausible motivation for Adam and Eve as insuperable: "There was no way for Milton of making the transition from sinlessness to sin perfectly intelligible. It is obvious that Adam and Eve must have already contracted human weakness before they can start on the course of conduct that leads to their fall; to put it another way they must already be fallen (technically) before they can begin to fall."[14] For Waldock, a fall before the Fall formed but one of many intractable conflicts between dogma and poetry that beleaguered the poem's narrator. In this case, the narrator had to assert Adam and Eve's innocence against the experience provided by his actual descriptions of prelapsarian Eden. Though others had glimpsed the dilemma before Waldock,[15] none had mounted such an aggressive critique of *Paradise Lost* for it; none had called Milton's human protagonists "technically fallen" before the Fall.

Waldock's bold arguments galvanized Miltonists, who felt compelled to reexamine the ethical status of Adam and Eve's purportedly unfallen motives. Nowhere is this process of critical revaluation more conspicuous than in Tillyard's shift between 1930 and 1951 on the issue of Adam and Eve's innocence before they ate the fruit. In 1930 Tillyard was one among many motive-hunters urging Miltonists to reject the traditional tautology of explaining the Fall by "mere unmotivated disobedience." For his own part, Tillyard identified the weakness that resulted in the Fall as "shallowness" in Eve and "lack of self-knowledge" in Adam, indicative in both cases of a certain "triviality of mind."[16] At no time, however, does Tillyard imply that Adam and Eve are morally culpable for triviality. In the wake of Waldock, Tillyard published a substantial revision of his position under the title "The Crisis of *Paradise Lost*." In it, he reappraised the motives of Adam and Eve, concluding that both are "virtually fallen before the official temptation has begun," meaning sometime in Book 9 before Eve meets the serpent.[17] "Virtually fallen," of course, echoes Waldock's phrase "technically fallen"; both phrases bolster a growing assault on Milton for "faking" Adam and Eve's psychology in Eden.

Both Waldock and Tillyard hedge their claims slightly by calling pre-lapsarian Adam and Eve "virtually" and "technically" fallen. Tillyard also implies that their inward fall is complete only by the separation scene in Book 9, not before. It is possible to push the Fall still further back. Two years after Tillyard, Millicent Bell carried the chain of reasoning, begun by Greenlaw and Hanford and recently given a new twist by Waldock and Tillyard, to its inevitable conclusion: "From the very first," she avers, "we are after the Fall."[18] Although Bell concedes that innocence is a necessary presupposition theologically, creation's pristine purity is retained for her only implicitly in the "formal symbol" of the Garden itself; humankind's innocent "past lies beyond our view in *Paradise Lost*."[19] For Bell, this mythic past is humanly inconceivable and therefore not properly available to poetic representation. Yet Milton was stuck with a myth that insisted on the impossible: namely, that a wholly innocent woman and man become sinful. In order to span the chasm "between perfection and imperfection, the unimaginable and the familiar, the fable constructs a bridge. This bridge is the temptation." Bell's analysis of this bridge reformulates Tillyard's charge of faking in much more sweeping language, so that Milton's dilemma is seen as a "fundamental difficulty in the story" he inherited:

> The temptation, [is] an event which could not understandably occur before the Fall, an event which must actually be explained by motivations characteristic of men as we find them now — ambition, curiosity, vanity, gluttony or lust. It is a bridge built of the material of fallen human nature, that is, from the substance of only one bank of the chasm, the one nearer us. From the farther bank, the anterior condition of unfallen perfection, the bridge takes nothing at all. For there is nothing in the Paradisal state that can furnish cause for man's lapse from perfection. What is commonly identified as cause is actually result.[20]

Subsequently, Davis Harding refined Bell's metaphor by labeling the temptation specifically a "psychological bridge."[21] For Bell, as for Waldock and Tillyard, the psychological content of the bridge derives improperly from humanity's fallen condition as we now know it. As Mark Van Doren remarks of Milton's attempt to characterize Adam and Eve: "Psychology itself is a consequence of the Fall."[22]

Bell's article still provides the most consistent and capacious argument for a fall before the Fall in *Paradise Lost*. She pointedly articulates what is often only implicit in other critics, as for example the close connection between a psychological analysis of Adam and Eve and a dramatic reading of the poem. For Bell, the poem enacts the Fall not as a single event but as a dramatic process; Milton's drama removes "the threshold of . . . transition to sin to some indefinite moment in the past,"[23] subtly obscuring any sharp division between before and after. For her, the drama of the Fall culminates in a recognition scene in which the characters, like figures out of Greek tragedy, discover the latent evil of their own natures. In a response to a critic, she wrote:

> I saw—and see ever more confidently as I go back to the poem—a drama. . . . In *Paradise Lost* we find, I think, the human creature becoming conscious of his own nature. . . . In *this* evolution, Milton isolates precise stages for both the Man and the Woman. . . . As the final stage in these two sequences, the technical Fall is not the sudden entry of Sin into the guileless heart, but the bursting forth of human, fallible nature into the external act which forces it to recognize itself for what it is.[24]

The timeless significance of *Paradise Lost*, as well as its relevance to modern readers, Bell insists, derives from the poem's engagement with the human predicament as we now know it, and not as it may have existed in some ineffable state of innocence. We identify with Adam and Eve because they are made out of the material of our common fallen natures. Hence it is with terror and pity that we witness them, like Oedipus, discover their sinfulness.

Predictably, such arguments in behalf of a fall before the Fall did not go unchallenged. The opposition began to rally, in fact, even before Waldock laid bare the implications of motive-hunting in Eden. For example, John S. Diekhoff presciently differentiated between the sinless "stages" that foreshadow the Fall and the fatal deed itself.[25] Unfortunately, Diekhoff fails to explain convincingly why the attitudes that lead to transgression are not themselves culpable. Indeed, Bell adopts his very term (*stages*) without feeling in the least obligated to accept his view of them as blameless. Likewise just before Bell's controversial article, Arnold Stein developed a nomenclature to describe the stages of the Fall. He calls them "preliminary gestures"—"pointing the possibility without prejudicing the case." A richly textured and finely nuanced discussion of the way the poem builds up momentum as it moves toward the catastrophe, Stein's account scrupulously maintains the innocent potentiality of Adam and Eve's behavior up to the Fall. Nevertheless, when explaining the importance of their "preliminary gestures," Stein occasionally borders on compromising the unforced freedom of their action. When Eve leaves Adam's side to work alone, for instance, Stein alleges that "the eating of the apple is as *good as done*"; likewise, when Adam resolves to follow his wife in sin, Stein asserts that "the eating of the apple is for Adam only a formal act . . . he is *as good as fallen*, and shows all the characteristics of fallen nature before he sets his teeth in the apple" (my italics).[26] Thus Stein inadvertently tilts his reading away from freedom and toward necessity. He accepts without qualification Adam's own (incorrect) view that his doom is irreversible after Eve's rash act, and edges precariously close to the notion that Eve is "virtually fallen" when she leaves her husband's side. I am confident the poet would (and does) reject both positions as deterministic (not to mention, in Eve's case, sexist).[27]

Clearly, Stein is at pains to avoid the deterministic implications of his argument. Yet my italicized phrases above seem to expose just such veiled connotations. Similarly, Stanley Fish notes: "The implication that the Fall must have antecedents is a denial of the freedom of the will. Watching Eve leave Adam's side in Book IX Stein comments, 'The eating of the apple is as good as done', thereby assuming, incorrectly, that neither of them can reverse the process their separation has set in motion."[28] Fish subsequently adds that "Stein would certainly not follow his analysis to this conclusion"—but others, such as Bell, would and did. And justifiably so, for Stein concedes the major point of the Waldock-Tillyard-Bell thesis when he explains that Adam is merely "theologically, and symbolically . . . innocent until he has to act. . . . Milton could not construct his fiction entirely from that perspective [that is, innocence]; he needed a scope of action sufficient for conflict, and he needed both direct and symbolic action that could borrow meaning, as it were, by anticipating human experience after the Fall."[29] Stein's argument proceeds from the familiar premise that Milton's art and dogma are at cross-purposes; consequently, the poet was forced to "fake" a resolution to the conflicting demands of myth and drama by dipping into postlapsarian psychology in order to color his prelapsarian beings. For all its marvelous sensitivity, Stein's reading proved sufficiently muddled to win approval from both Bell and her opponents.[30]

In an article specifically directed against Tillyard and Bell, H. V. S. Ogden urges the rightness of Stein's metaphor preliminary "gestures." However, Ogden insists even more strenuously than does Stein on the innocent potentiality of these gestures. We are told that Milton's foreshadowing of the Fall must not be thought to erode the "distinction between the liability to sin and the commission, between potentiality and actuality, between the beginnings of an evil will and the completion of an evil act."[31] Yet neither Ogden nor any of Milton's defenders, so far as I know, have successfully sorted out the theoretical perplexities involved in distinguishing between the innocuous beginning of evil and its baneful conclusion, though many since have concurred with Ogden that the notion of a fall before the Fall confuses liability to sin with actual guilt.

Ogden was also one of the first to call attention to the Tillyard-Bell misunderstanding of the concept of perfection.[32] Tillyard presumes, and Bell openly asserts, that perfection denotes an absolute category: "The mind cannot accept the fact that perfection was capable of corruption without denying the absoluteness of perfection."[33] Although this assertion sounds self-evident, many Miltonists have observed that absolute perfection has little to do with the kind of perfection that obtains in Milton's Eden. Absolute perfection belongs only to God, while Milton envisions relative perfection for all God's creations, whether fish, fowl, beast, or human.[34] As derivative creatures, humans are created perfect relative to their ontological status in creation; that is, they are perfect human beings, which is far different from the perfection of a Supreme Being. "Moving" rather than "static," human perfection allows mobility and scope for growth.[35] Miltonists have buttressed such arguments as these with evidence from theologians about the acknowledged limitations pertaining to Adam and Eve's *justitia originalis*.[36]

However, the real riddle is neither human mobility nor limitation. What baffles thought is the specifically human capacity to sin. A tree may evolve within its limited sphere of relative perfection, growing from a good seedling into a good tree, as it were. Only humans, however, "grow" in another way; only humans transgress, breaking out of a moral sphere by becoming evil. At issue is fallibility, which constitutes a special kind of limitation and movement—namely, the transition from good to evil. Diekhoff aptly labels this the "paradox of fallible perfection" in *Paradise Lost*.[37] Merely to label human perfection "paradoxical," however, does not take us very far into the paradox. Somehow the transition between innocence and guilt must be penetrated deeply enough to make guilt more intelligible while still preserving human innocence and freedom.

Efforts to explicate this transition predictably rely on the doctrine of free will. The arguments for a fall before the Fall, it is claimed, involve a post hoc fallacy; they deduce the Fall's inevitability from its occurrence, a false deduction if the Fall constitutes a free act.[38] Fish's *Surprised by Sin*, a virtuoso performance aimed directly at Waldock, provides perhaps the most elaborate free-will defense of the poem. Free will, however, offers only a partially illuminating, albeit crucial, proviso, for free will denotes the lacuna in the story of sin's origin; it posits a gap in the process by which sin emerges. As a principle of disjunction, it cannot explain the relation between the Fall and its precedents, except to say that they do not matter causally, for sin is uncaused — that is, free.

Yet if the events that seem to precondition the Fall do not determine it, how then are they related to it? What kind of a psychological relationship does exist between the "preliminary gestures" and the Fall, if not one of causality? To say free will mediates the relationship implies (or seems to imply) no relation at all, since a wholly spontaneous act is related to its antecedents as things indifferent to itself.[39] As Fish so pointedly remarks: "The decision of an absolutely free will cannot be determined by forces outside it, and, in a causal sense, such a decision has no antecedents. I would suggest that the point of the scenes in Paradise from Book IV to Book IX is their irrelevance, as determining factors, to the moment of crisis experienced by the characters."[40] But most readers would balk at an argument that dismisses more than half the poem as causally "irrelevant" to its principal action, or as relevant only as entrapment. Surely freedom, which is required ethically in Milton's theodicy, does not render the psychological conditions of sin utterly inconsequential.

This conceptual problem of free will becomes translated into specific questions of literary criticism in the debate between Bell and Shumaker following the publication of her controversial article. The two antagonists demonstrate between them the perennial problem of making either too much or too little of the Fall's antecedents. Founding his rebuttal on the doctrine of free will, Shumaker rejects Bell's implicit postulate that sin must originate from sinfulness. Correspondingly, he asserts the narrator's authority to describe Adam and Eve as innocent and to locate their falls as sudden events in specific instants in Book 9.[41] But Shumaker is hard pressed to account for Milton's proleptic characterization of Adam and Eve. Psychologically, the Fall seems to gather momentum from Milton's elaborate foreshadowing in books 4–9, not to mention from the direct pressure of temptation itself. Shumaker's argument seems to dismiss the dramatic motivation of *Paradise Lost* altogether, because the Fall is free. Understandably annoyed by this, Bell retorts: "Adam's and Eve's histories are given so elaborately and delicately in the poem, given with so much premonitory characterization, that I can only wonder what result Mr. Shumaker thinks this aspect of the poetry serves."[42]

In a conciliatory footnote Shumaker responds with an honest if inadequately explained concession: he does not dispute the "*importance*" of the dangerous impulses that lead to the Fall, only Bell's "ethical judgment" about their sinfulness. For his part, Shumaker sensibly wonders what Bell makes of the headnotes and narrator's comments that explicitly endorse a traditional reading of the poem by exonerating Eve from blame almost until the very moment she tastes the fruit. Shumaker finds "profoundly disturbing" a reading of *Paradise Lost* in which there is never "either a State of Innocence or a Fall of Man."[43]

Between these two positions—each alternatively overstating or understating the importance of Milton's "premonitory characterization"—there is no easily definable middle ground. The reason for this is that Milton's Eden occupies a borderland of becoming, a profoundly nebulous region located somewhere between innocence and guilt—"at the *cross*-roads, betwixt'n between past and future, beginning and end, Genesis and Apocalypse, creation and redemption."[44] A liminal world, Milton's Eden lies enshrouded in the mists of dreams and half-apprehended fantasies, an ethically ambiguous frontier that the language of criticism and theology seems too indelicate to describe. Of Shumaker's innocent but dangerous impulses (or we may add Diekhoff's "stages," Stein's "preliminary gestures," and so forth), Bell demands: "Can we give names to them except by reference to 'fallen qualities such as vanity, ambition, idolatry, credulity, or intemperance?'"[45] This is a demand that Milton criticism has yet to meet.

"But the Middle Terms!": Kierkegaardian Anxiety

It is little wonder that, almost forty years after Bell issued her challenge, Miltonists are still hard put to find the vocabulary she calls for. Milton himself cannot name the sinless conditions that precipitate sin without referring to fallen concepts. After Eve's dream-temptation, for example, he compares her emotions to "remorse," a patently postlapsarian sentiment. Then, in the same breath, he neutralizes the fallen connotations of this comparison by coupling remorse with "pious awe, that fear'd to have offended" (5.134–35). Similarly, in *The Christian Doctrine* he labors in vain to name the psychological condition that eventuates in the Fall. At first all sin appears to be the result of *concupiscentia mala*. Then concupiscence itself turns out to be the consequence of the first sin rather than its cause.

What is wanted to sort out these perplexities is a better theory of becoming, within which the problem of motivated free choice can be addressed. Criticism lacks a theory that is determinedly indeterministic about the transition and stoutly committed to the proposition that sin can break forth from morally neutral inward conditions. Ethically, the theory must explain Adam and Eve's motives without compromising either their innocence or their freedom. Yet psychologically, the theory must possess a certain elastic flexibility in order to follow the psyche's movements on its journey to sin; it must account for the way momentum can build inside free agents, inclining them toward transgression to the point that the transition to sin may seem almost inevitable. This is the delicate dilemma posed by the story of sin in Genesis and, *a fortiori*, by *Paradise Lost*.

It also is precisely the question Søren Kierkegaard sets about to answer in *The Concept of Anxiety*. In his "psychological deliberation" on the Fall, he proposes a middle way through the perplexities vexing the incipience of evil, in Adam and Eve, and in their posterity. Kierkegaard's treatise tries to chart an elusive *via media* between rigid necessity on the one hand and random spontaneity on the other.[46] It attempts to steer between the Scylla of making motivation to sin count for too much (as per Waldock and Bell, among others) and the Charybdis of making it count for nothing at all (as per Shumaker and Fish, among others). Thus, speaking of example's power to shape a child's character, Kierkegaard calls for "middle terms":

> A great deal has been very well said on this subject; but often there is lacking the psychological middle term which explains how it is that the example produces an effect. . . . Example is supposed to have had its effect upon the child. The child is represented as a regular little angel, but the depraved environment cast it into perdition. . . . Or the child is represented as so fundamentally wicked that the good example can do it no good. . . . But the middle terms! the middle terms! Let someone introduce a middle term which has the ambiguity that it rescues the thought . . . that the child in whatever "how" it was, can become both guilty and innocent. (*CD*, 67–68)

The middle term Kierkegaard himself proposes is, of course, *angst*. A concept developed specifically for a psychology of freedom, anxiety rescues motivational theory (as well as theories about the power of example, environment, history, and so on) from determinism. The notion of dramatic motivation, it is good to remember, entered literary discourse freighted with the baggage of nineteenth-century positivism. "Nineteenth-century faith in absolute causality," Shumaker shrewdly observes, sustains the Waldock-Bell conviction that "sin cannot arise out of sinlessness."[47] And as Harry Levin notes, "motivation" was imported into literary criticism via nineteenth-century German rationalist philosophy.[48] Waldock's and Bell's shared interest in dramatic motivation continues a special preoccupation of the past century. It is no wonder that Kierkegaard's *Concept of Anxiety* calls into question the deterministic assumptions sedimented in this now commonplace literary concept. His work was mounted against the very philosophy that first gave life to the concept of motivation and to the new science from which it derived — psychology.

Kierkegaard, like Milton, is hard put to find a vocabulary suited to a psychology grounded in freedom rather than determinism. He concedes, "If science has any other psychological intermediate term that has the dogmatic, the ethical, and the psychological advantages that anxiety possesses, then that should be preferred" (*CA*, 77). In the meantime, he offers *angst* as the cornerstone for a psychology of freedom. A familiar term in everyday speech, *angst* figures in many colloquial Danish idioms, which Kierkegaard frequently exploits in developing his esoteric definition (see *CA*, 42–43). This makes the term even more difficult to translate than it already is. From 1924 until recently, *angst* was commonly translated in English as "dread" (*CD*, ix–x); the new standard translation opts for the cognate, "anxiety." Either way, grasping Kierkegaard's distinctive usage of the term is essential.

As with any key term from a complex philosophical discourse-system, *angst* cannot be contained by a simple dictionary definition. I shall define it more fully hereafter. A good starting point, however, for understanding Kierkegaard's unique definition of *angst* may be found in a journal entry written two years before *The Concept of Anxiety* was published. In the journal, Kierkegaard's mature definition of *angst* is already embryonically present: "Anxiety is a desire for what one fears, a sympathetic antipathy; anxiety is an alien power which grips the individual, and yet one cannot tear himself free from it and does not want to, for one fears, but what he fears he desires."[49] This passage reveals that, though sometimes translated as "dread," *angst* is not synonymous to "fear" — not here, not ever in *The Concept of Anxiety*. Rather, anxiety signifies for Kierkegaard something akin to a conjunction of fear and fascination, of repulsion and attraction. His definition here, as later, makes anxiety sound similar to ambivalence: "a *sympathetic antipathy* and *an antipathetic sympathy*" (*CA*, 42). Yet, as we shall see, anxiety is also not exactly equivalent to ambivalence any more than it is to fear, since both these emotions presuppose a known, concrete object, while Kierkegaardian anxiety presupposes ignorance of its object. Anxiety's object is "nothing," for anxiety directs itself not toward actuality but toward possibility.

In the same journal entry, Kierkegaard writes that anxiety is a necessary though missing "primary category" of the Fall; it is Original Sin's "essential determinant."[50] Linking anxiety with the Fall, Kierkegaard's journal forecasts *The Concept of Anxiety*, which elaborates how anxiety constitutes the precondition of sin in Eden. It is not clear from the journal entry, however, why anxiety should have been "lacking" from explanations of the Fall. Kierkegaard later explains why: anxiety comes into view only when the Fall is regarded psychologically. This is specifically what Kierkegaard undertakes to do in *The Concept of Anxiety*, as Vigilius Haufniensis (Kierkegaard's pseudonym) announces in his cumbersome subtitle: "A Simple Psychologically Orienting Deliberation on the Dogmatic Issue of Hereditary Sin." A psychological deliberation means, according to Kierkegaard's rather romantic view of psychology, that his treatise will share with dramatic narrative a similar set of characterological questions about the Fall, such as What thoughts could lead Adam and Eve to transgress? What in their personalities and experience would make them susceptible to temptation? What in their interpersonal relationship might make them vulnerable? And so forth. Although Genesis is silent about all these human details—depicting, in essence, characters without character—the psychologist, like the dramatic poet, is naturally inquisitive about just such issues. Their common endeavor is to get inside human personality through a sort of negative capability: "The psychological observer ought to be more nimble than the tightrope dancer in order to be able to incline and bend himself to other people and imitate their attitudes. . . . Hence he ought also to have a poetical originality in his soul" (*CA*, 54–55).

For Kierkegaard, everything depends upon how nimble a psychological observer he is. Ultimately, the only confirmation to which he can appeal lies within each individual: "How sin came into the world, each man understands solely by himself. If he would learn it from another, he would *eo ipso* misunderstand it. The only science that can help a little is psychology, yet it admits that it explains nothing" (*CA*, 51). Kierkegaard's theory of becoming must be validated from our own experience with anxiety and sin. It follows that he believes Adam and Eve are recognizably human, as Bell believes Milton's protagonists to be. But for Kierkegaard their identity with the human family rests on entirely different grounds. The family resemblance arises not from their being fallen from the start but from their distinctly human capacity to fall freely. Their humanity consists largely in the fact that "man is the being *for whom* there are the future possibilities";[51] hence, human existence is marked by anxiety.

Kierkegaard's remark that psychology "explains nothing" hints at his esoteric definition of psychology — one that differs markedly from prevailing positivist ideas about the "science" of psychology then and now.[52] Unlike much that passes for psychological explanation, Kierkegaard's explanations never explain away freedom. We, by contrast, customarily look to psychology for full, rational explanations of even irrational human behavior. Psychology is the science that promises to make us transparent to ourselves by holding out the hope that our lives, however puzzling superficially, are governed in their deepest structures by law. Freud, of course, contributed immeasurably to the dream of making psychology a science. He brought psychology into the domain of "burgeoning nineteenth-century scientific naturalism" by giving us an image of man as fully continuous. Whereas Darwinian theory disclosed continuities between man and animal, Freudian theory uncovered continuities bridging child to adult, sleep to waking, unconscious to conscious.[53]

Kierkegaard, on the other hand, thinks of psychology specifically as the science of the human possibility for *dis*continuity; it deals in probability rather than determinacy. Its chief task is to describe the inner workings of a self constituted by a set of inseparable polarities, among which are freedom and necessity (see *SD*, 13–14 and passim). Psychology, according to Kierkegaard, should explore the interplay between these factors within human consciousness; therefore, a psychological explanation that disregards the disruptive factor of human freedom ceases to be, properly speaking, psychological:

> The science that deals with the explanation is psychology, but it can explain only up to the explanation and above all must guard against leaving the impression of explaining that which no science can explain [that is, sin or the leap] and that which ethics explains further only by presupposing it by way of dogmatics. . . . Psychology must remain within its boundary; only then can its explanations have significance. (*CA*, 39)

Or similarly:

> That which can be the concern of psychology and with which it can occupy itself is not that sin comes into existence, but how it can come into existence. Psychology can bring its concern to the point where it seems as if sin were there, but the next thing, that sin is there, is qualitatively different from the first. (*CA*, 21–22)

Kierkegaard's insistence on keeping his categories straight might seem excessive; it is undeniably characteristic. Yet, as we have seen in the controversy over a fall before the Fall, the whole issue turns on scrupulous distinctions between psychology and ethics. Only an explication of the text that explains "how" but not "that" sin exists can encompass both sides of the paradox: that the Fall is, somehow, both ethically free and psychologically conditioned.

Kierkegaard conceptualizes freedom through perhaps his most famous metaphor, the leap[54] — in *The Concept of Anxiety* regularly called a "qualitative" leap in order to signify its incommensurability. Sin as qualitative leap validates the scheme of the Fall as ethical instant. Kierkegaard thematizes the other half of the paradox, psychological motivation, by means of a much less familiar metaphor: "quantitative determination." "Quantitative determinants" measure the pressure in what might be termed a human anxiety-register; they gauge the way anxiety intensifies and builds. Quantitative determination provides Kierkegaard's account of the Fall with drama and process, in addition to the disruptive instant posited by the leap. It confers upon his psychological explanation "its elastic ambiguity, from which guilt breaks forth in the qualitative leap" (*CA*, 41).

The transition between anxiety and guilt is always mediated by the leap. Psychological explanation must not befuddle this point, though the temptation to do so is enormous. One must not be "deluded by determinants of approximation" (*CA*, 60) — imagining, for example, that because in retrospect we know Adam and Eve are careering toward the catastrophe, their sins are fundamentally any more explicable in Book 9 than they would have been in Book 4. In this sense, Kierkegaard agrees with Fish above. No matter how "near" an innocent individual draws to guilt, the transition never "becomes a simple transition" (*CA*, 60); that is, sin always remains a qualitative leap, inexplicable as the sum of quantitative determinants. Kierkegaard illustrates this point through a wonderful bit of word play:

> The understanding talks fantastically about man's state prior to the fall, and in the course of the small talk, the projected innocence is changed little by little into sinfulness, and so there it is. The lecture of the understanding may on this occasion aptly be compared with the counting rhyme in which children delight: one-nis-ball, two-nis-balls, three-nis-balls, etc., up to nine-nis-balls and tennis balls. Here it is, brought about quite naturally by the preceding. (*CA*, 32)

Kierkegaard's point here is that there exists no simple, numerical process by which to derive sin from innocence; no transition that bypasses the leap. True, anxiety may increase quantitatively, depending on the particular constitution of one's environment, culture, personality, and so forth. Individuals may be more or less susceptible to anxiety according to their background or their sensitivity to freedom ("spirit"). Yet no matter what quantitative "more" individuals experience, such "a 'more' cannot bring forth the leap." Nothing "can in truth make the explanation [of sin] any easier" (*CA*, 60), for the transition from innocence to guilt defines a quasi-ontolological transformation: "It is not a mere acquisition of knowledge, but a change in being."[55]

Strictly speaking, *innocence* and *guilt* are not even properly parallel terms in Kierkegaard's schematization. Guilt is a psychological concept like anxiety. Innocence, by contrast, is an ethical category, whose antonym is not guilt but sinfulness. Innocence and sinfulness are part of the juridical language of accusation; anxiety and guilt belong to a psychological discourse of observation (see *CA*, 22). Dividing anxiety from guilt and innocence from sinfulness is the disruptive element: sin. The binary pair for ethics is innocence and sinfulness; for psychology, anxiety and guilt (though, as we shall see, guilty people may also experience anxiety as they rediscover freedom vis-à-vis sin). The movement from one condition to the other is made only by a leap of sin, which occurs in an instant. The "instant" or "moment" (*øjeblikket*, blink of an eye) "is the *limen* or boundary forming the ambiguous, tension-filled frontier that is the passageway between past and future."[56]

As a leap, sin has no continuous existence: "the actuality of sin is an actuality that has no endurance" (*CA*, 53). In this sense, sin is unlike the conditions that encircle it: these are states in which one might abide, while sin is something "restless . . . that always either produces itself or is repressed." As a leap, moreover, "sin does not properly belong in any science; only . . . ethics can deal with its manifestation, but not with its coming into existence" (*CA*, 21). Kierkegaard's understanding of sin might be compared to Euclid's definition of a point: both are capable of dissecting a line yet in themselves possess neither spatial nor temporal dimensions. Further (to continue the geometric metaphor), the movement in anxiety toward sin could be plotted as an asymptotic parabola. The distance between unfallen anxiety and fallen guilt recedes *ad infinitum* as quantitative determinants multiply. This accounts for the way free actions seem determined, coherent, probable. Yet no matter how near to the line the parabola gets, its curve will never touch it. So too for free human acts, which may said to be "quantitatively determined" by environment, temptation, history, and so forth. Yet there is ever only one way to cross the threshold from innocence to sinfulness, and that is by a leap—namely, sin.

Sin is something genuinely new, arising out of anxiety but always "with the leap, with the suddenness of the enigmatic." The only adequate description of sin's origin and the true meaning of Genesis, according to Kierkegaard, can be distilled into one statement: "*Sin came into the world by a sin*" (*CA*, 30, 32). This seeming tautology offends reason because it retains the enigma of freedom, refusing to explain sin by prior sinfulness. Reason demands (as we have seen with Milton's critics) that "sinfulness precedes sin." Ultimately, this position disallows the possibility of anything new. It cannot countenance genuine freedom but regards transitions as matters of simple cause and effect: all is continuity and evolution; there is no qualitative leap. Scripture, by contrast, recounts a narrative about a bona fide origin. The "only dialectically consistent statement" one can make about the text is that "sin came into the world by a sin"—expressed (often thoughtlessly) in the theological commonplace that "by Adam's first sin, *sin came into the world*." Considered more carefully, Kierkegaard adds, Scripture also implies "that by the first sin, sinfulness came into Adam" (*CA*, 32, 33)—a position much like Milton's in *The Christian Doctrine*, that by sin humans acquired inward corruption of will or concupiscence.

It should be evident by now that Kierkegaard's treatment of the Fall resembles Milton's in many important respects. In particular, both men interpret the Fall so as to expose and accommodate a baffling paradox implicit in Genesis: sin erupts as a radically free act, yet as an act somehow conditioned by the Temptation, which confers upon it psychological probability. Both *Paradise Lost* and *The Concept of Anxiety* endorse Scripture's double vision of the Fall as coherent sequence and disruptive break. Milton's poem orchestrates this scriptural duality subtly and sublimely, but neither the poet nor his critics seem to have a theory of becoming that is adequate to his grand schematization. Kierkegaard's treatise provides such a theory of becoming, one specifically aimed at elucidating the philosophical and theological issues raised by Milton's main source-text, the Bible. Kierkegaard's psychological study of the Fall is precisely what is wanted to sort out the complexities posed by the literary crux of a fall before the Fall in *Paradise Lost*.

To be sure, crucial differences exist between Milton and Kierkegaard's specific treatments of the transition from sinlessness to sin. One of these I consider in the next chapter: their conflicting interpretations of the serpent's role in the Garden. Yet even within differences there are remarkable similarities. The commonalties arise, I suspect, from shared psychological approaches to the Fall as well as from similar sophisticated understandings of and commitments to the reality of human freedom. Common commitments to psychological probability and moral freedom—coupled no doubt with a generous dose of genius—yield two of the most remarkable analyses of Eden anywhere — two that are uncannily alike.

Notes

1. Johnson, "Life of Milton," 466.
2. Tillyard, *Studies in Milton*, 10–11.
3. An unpublished dissertation by George Louis Musacchio contains a comprehensive survey of the critical literature on the problem of motivating the Fall as it developed through the 1960s: "Fallible Perfection" (see esp. 1–24).
4. A useful summary of the way this controversy and others looked to midcentury critics may be found in Murray, *Milton: The Modern Phase*.
5. Significant contributions to this controversy from the late sixties and early seventies include (among others) those made by Blackburn, "'Uncloister'd Virtue'"; Bowers, "Adam, Eve, and the Fall"; Burden, *Logical Epic*; Diekhoff, "Eve's Dream"; Fish, *Surprised by Sin*; Lewalski, "Innocence and Experience"; Samuel, *"Paradise Lost"*; and Stein, *Answerable Style*. Contributions from the eighties include those made by Danielson, *Milton's Good God* (esp. 195–201); McColley, *Milton's Eve* (esp. ch. 5); Nyquist, "Reading the Fall"; Reichert, "'Against His Better Knowledge'"; and Tanner, "'Say First What Cause'" (esp. 49–52).
6. Ricoeur, *Symbolism of Evil*, 243–44; 252–53. For a full analysis of how Ricoeur's view of the Fall corresponds to *Paradise Lost*, see my article "'Say First What Cause.'"
7. Stein, *Answerable Style*, 76.
8. Bowers, "Adam, Eve, and the Fall," 264.
9. Bell, "Fallacy," 864. Cf. Mulder, *Temple of the Mind*, 121–27.
10. Greenlaw, "Aquinas"; Hanford, "Dramatic" and "Temptation." The Hanford essays are conveniently collected in Hanford, *John Milton, Poet and Humanist*.
11. Mills, "Logic of Milton's Narrative," 9, attributes these motives to Saurat, Diekhoff, Tillyard, Rajan, Lewis, Williams, and Hanford.
12. Kelley, *This Great Argument*, 148–49.
13. Howard, "Invention," 164.
14. Waldock, Paradise Lost *and Its Critics*, 61.
15. E.g., Willey, *Seventeenth Century Background*, 250.
16. Tillyard, *Milton*, 219–26.
17. Tillyard, *Studies in Milton*, 13.
18. Bell, "Fallacy," 867.
19. Bell, "Notes," 1195.
20. Bell, "Fallacy," 863.
21. Harding, *Club of Hercules*, 68.
22. Van Doren, *Noble Voice*, 140.
23. Bell, "Fallacy," 864.

24. Bell, "Notes," 1187–88.

25. Diekhoff, *Commentary on the Argument*, 54–56, 61–66.

26. Stein, *Answerable Style*, 92–94, 101–2.

27. Gallagher argues this point at length in *Milton, the Bible, and Misogyny* (esp. 93–96).

28. Fish, *Surprised by Sin*, 231.

29. Stein, *Answerable Style*, 99.

30. Bell, "Notes," 1188; Shumaker, "Notes," 1202.

31. Ogden, "Crisis," 8.

32. Shumaker also rather cryptically criticizes Bell's concept of absolute perfection without directing much attention to the issue or explaining the alternative, relative perfection ("Notes," 1185).

33. Bell, "Fallacy," 863.

34. See, for example, Shumaker, "Notes," 1185; Ogden, "Crisis," 5–8; Summers, *Muse's Method*, 71–86, 148–49; Diekhoff, "Eve's Dream," 5; Fish, *Surprised by Sin*, 226n; and Danielson, *Milton's Good God*, 164–201.

35. Summers, *Muse's Method*, 149.

36. See Musacchio, "Fallible Perfection," for a discussion of this term and Protestant theology; see also Steadman, "Man's First Disobedience," 180–97.

37. Diekhoff, "Eve's Dream."

38. Fish, *Surprised by Sin*, 231–32; Shumaker, "Notes," 1199–1202; Wright, *Milton's* Paradise Lost, 49.

39. For this reason, Kierkegaard rejects the conventional concept of *liberum arbitrium* (free will): "A perfectly disinterested will (equilibrium) is a nothing, a chimera"; or likewise, "*Liberum arbitrium*, which can equally well choose the good or the evil, is basically an abrogation of the concept of freedom and a despair of any explanation of it" (*Søren Kierkegaard's Journals and Papers*, 2.1241; 2.1249; cf. *CA*, 112).

40. Fish, *Surprised by Sin*, 346.

41. Shumaker, "Notes," 1201–2, 1198–1201.

42. Bell, "Notes," 1188.

43. Shumaker, "Notes," 1202, 1185.

44. Taylor, *Journeys to Selfhood*, 179.

45. Bell, "Notes," 1203.

46. Doubtless, many will be surprised that I characterize Kierkegaard's notoriously extreme individualism as a middle way. In fact, however, a number of recent studies share a "new . . . realization that Kierkegaard's theories are not as individualistic as has often been assumed" (Dunning, *Kierkegaard's Dialectic*, 254n) — or rather, in my view, that they are individualistic in a different way. Dunning's book argues, as do I in chapter 7, that Kierkegaard's self is "thoroughly relational," defined by a dialectic of inner/outer, self/other (242). Therefore, human existence cannot be so isolated and solitary as many suppose Kierkegaard thinks it is; e.g., Taylor, "The Solitary Self" in *Pseudonymous Authorship*; Mackey, "The Loss of the World in Kierkegaard's Ethics" in *Points of View*; and Thompson, *Lonely Labyrinth*. One contribution of *Anxiety in*

Eden is to buttress a somewhat less radical, less Pelagian, less Sartrean interpretation of Kierkegaard's individualism.

47. Shumaker, "Notes," 1202.

48. Levin, "Motive Hunters," 6.

49. *Søren Kierkegaard's Journals and Papers*, 1.94.

50. Ibid.

51. Mackey, *A Kind of Poet*, 110.

52. The positivist premises of nineteenth-century psychology are evident in an 1877 attack on *The Concept of Anxiety* by Harald Høffding. Høffding opposed Kierkegaard's notion of the leap precisely because "the sciences, including the science of psychology, are based on the assumption that there is an unbroken continuity in the passage from possibility to actuality and that every new state is thereby the simple consequence of a previous state" (*CA*, "Historical Introduction," xiv–xv).

53. Bruner, *On Knowing*, 153; see "Freud and the Image of Man," 149–58.

54. Actually, Kierkegaard did not invent the leap but borrowed the metaphor from Gotthold Lessing, who (like Kierkegaard) wielded the term *der Sprung* against Hegelianism (see Kierkegaard's *Concluding Unscientific Postscript*, 90–97; also Ostenfeld, *Søren Kierkegaard's Psychology*, 24–25). Observing how it yokes heterogenous notions of causality and freedom, Ib Ostenfeld remarks that the leap "stands as one of the most earnest attempts that has ever been made to combine apparently incompatible opposites" (22).

55. Turner, "Betwixt and Between," in *Forest of Symbols*, 102.

56. Taylor, *Journeys to Selfhood*, 124.

3

Satan and Sin

"Out of thy Head I Sprung": Satan's Sin as Leap

No discrepancy between *Paradise Lost* and *The Concept of Anxiety* is more conspicuous than their opposing treatments of the serpent. Kierkegaard, whose treatise aims at reducing Genesis to its essential philosophical position, all but dismisses the snake in Eden as a misleading human interpolation. For him, the malicious snake looks suspiciously like a rationalization for something that cannot be reduced — namely, the origin of sin. The snake's unexplained, subtle malevolence masks the problems posed by an absolute origin of evil by letting human iniquity arise out of antecedent evil. It insinuates that sinfulness precedes sin, making human corruption appear to be simply the effect of contamination — not something new, not a leap. Hence, Kierkegaard regards the serpent as posing as much a temptation for exegetes as it did for Eve. The serpent can easily beguile biblical hermeneutics into presupposing that sin's origin is explained naturalistically, unparadoxically, because depravity results so reasonably from the activity of a malignant tempter (*CA*, 48).

Milton, on the other hand, whose poem aims at adding *copia* to a slender source-text, makes a very great deal of the snake. Indeed, the Satanic episodes in *Paradise Lost* constitute most of books 1, 2, and 6, as well as much of books 3, 4, 5, 9, and 10. Almost half the text may be regarded, from this point of view, as epic elaboration upon a figure Genesis depicts in a few verses. To Milton, as to generations of exegetes, the serpent is a vehicle for Satan. It therefore imports into the human story of evil's beginning a prior history of demonic defiance in high places against God. When Eve and Adam disobey their Maker's "one easy prohibition" (4.433), they effectively enter into an ongoing saga of disobedience, recounted in great detail by the poet. Thus, just as Kierkegaard feared, Milton's epic exploits the serpent's potential to rationalize the etiology of evil. Adam and Eve's defection in Book 9 seems plausible, even predictable, because it is both continuous with an ancient

historical tradition of defection and actively brought about by the inter-
vention of a tempter. From this point of view, Satan may be regarded as
"the causal mainspring of the action," for he dominates the narrative
process, introducing into the poem an element of necessitarianism.[1]

Yet despite their seemingly disparate stances toward the serpent, Milton appropriates and Kierkegaard rejects the snake, respectively, in order
to endorse the same view of temptation and sin: that no matter how
powerful the inducements, sin is free. Neither author believes that temptation by the serpent truly explains sin. Both, in fact, root their interpretations of the serpent in a common commitment to St. James's doctrine
of self-temptation: "Let no man say when he is tempted, I am tempted
of God: for God cannot be tempted with evil, neither tempteth he any
man: But every man is tempted, when he is drawn away of his own lust,
and enticed. Then when lust hath conceived, it bringeth forth sin: and
sin, when it is finished, bringeth forth death" (James 1:13–15). Kierkegaard casts doubt on Eden's serpent because, "contrary to the well-
known classical passage from James" that each person is tempted by
himself, the serpent displays the temptation "as coming from without"
(*CA*, 48). *Paradise Lost* acknowledges that the temptation comes partly
from without: the serpent's "pleasing shape" and "glozing lies" play a
role in Eve's seduction. However, the poet protects his poem against the
misreading Kierkegaard fears by making the tempter's sinfulness point
back to the imperiled Jamesian doctrine of self-temptation. Milton's
serpent is infested by an evil that began in self-temptation; Satan's presence recalls the allegorical birth of Sin in Book 2 — an allegory constructed out of images rifled straight out of James 1:13–15. *Paradise
Lost* thus secures the poem against seeing the tempter as the sufficient
cause of sin. The snake's history (so to speak) reminds us that the
Woman and Man sin freely, inexplicably, just as had Satan in the beginning. Thus the serpent that Kierkegaard rejects because it threatens the
principle of self-temptation, Milton adapts to preserve the endangered
doctrine.

Actually, Kierkegaard never goes so far as to reject outright the biblical serpent. But he does seem to have it in view as he inveighs against
"myths of the understanding" (meaning rationalizations) that explain
human sin unparadoxically as the product of prior evil: "Insofar as the
myth of the understanding is supposed to contain anything it would be
that sinfulness precedes sin" (*CA*, 32). In other places he questions the
text's representing both the temptation *and* the prohibition as external,
calling these externalizations "imperfections" in the narrative (*CA*, 45,
47). His own preference obviously lies with a thoroughly internalized,

individualized Fall. Yet rather than dismiss the serpent, Kierkegaard simply shrugs, "I freely admit my inability to connect any definite thought with the serpent" (*CA*, 48). Perhaps, he opines, the snake makes visible symbolically the voice of seduction that primordial woman felt internally; this does not confuse thought as do pseudomyths of the understanding but accords to the nature of genuine myth because it "allows something that is inward to take place outwardly." Similarly, in a passage deleted from the final version of *The Concept of Anxiety*, he suggests that the serpent might symbolize the human capacity for language itself (*CA*, 47, 235n). Whatever the serpent signifies, the truth about temptation to which Kierkegaard holds fast is that of self-temptation.[2]

Milton's deference to Scripture's literal meaning is, obviously, much greater than Kierkegaard's. Although the principle of "accommodation" allows Milton some room to interpret problem texts figuratively, he could never dismiss so crucial a figure as the serpent — especially because long biblical tradition firmly identified the serpent with Satan, a fallen angel whom God had cast out of heaven along with a third of the heavenly hosts.[3] Milton believes unequivocally that Adam and Eve were tempted "from without." Indeed, the Father uses this fact to differentiate the human fall from that of Satan and his angels:

> The first sort by thir own suggestion fell,
> Self-tempted, self-deprav'd: Man falls deceiv'd
> By th' other first: Man therefore shall find grace,
> The other none.
>
> (3.129–32)

The Father's language echoes Paul's: the Fall is sin by deception. However, where Paul limits deception exclusively to Eve and uses her gullibility as an argument for perpetual distrust of all women (1 Tim. 2:14), Milton's God applies deception to cover the guilt of "Man" generically and reverses Paul's logic of accusation.[4] God's oracle discovers in deception a reason not for more blame but for less; that humans were deceived augurs hope for forgiveness. Deception makes redemption plausible for humans as its absence makes it impossible for devils. After this fashion *Paradise Lost*, unlike *The Concept of Anxiety*, insists that the beguiling serpent counts for something in the etiology of evil.

But not for too much. Despite the mitigating circumstance provided by temptation, on the deepest level Adam and Eve sin in essentially the same way as does Satan — namely, freely. As previously noted, the Father characterized the fallen angels as "self-tempted, self-deprav'd." Just before this, he characterized human rebels in similarly self-reflective terms:

> I form'd them free, and free they must remain,
> *Till they enthrall themselves*: I else must change
> Thir nature, and revoke the high Decree
> Unchangeable, Eternal, which ordain'd
> Thir freedom: *they themselves ordain'd thir fall.*
>   (3.124–28; my emphasis)

The oracle makes plain an essential parity between all free agents in Milton's poem, whether human or angelic. They are all formed free. This means they are endowed with power to ordain their own falls. It means that to sin in *Paradise Lost* is always at least partly to enthrall oneself; to be tempted is necessarily also to be self-tempted.

Self-temptation, then, lies at the root of both the human and angelic falls. Sin's birth from Satan in heaven, consequently, serves as a paradigm for its rebirth in Eve and Adam on earth. To the degree that Adam and Eve are self-enthralled, their sins are every bit as inexplicable as Satan's. One cannot say the devil made them sin any more than one can say what made Satan first sin; all one can properly say of either angel or human sounds tautological: "Freely they stood who stood, and fell who fell" (3.102). The difference is that Satan's sin exposes the nature of a self-ordained fall in a particularly clear, naked light because his fall enacts the transition between good and evil in a vacuum, without the obfuscation of prior sinfulness. The spectacle of Sin's leaping full-grown from Satan's head converts into shocking narrative what the Father's adverbs formulate more tamely as "self-tempted, self-deprav'd." Sin's birth startles us because it so plainly manifests the riddle of freedom latent in the language of self-temptation. Freedom posits the possibility of caesuras in human existence; it implies a deep human potentiality to reconstitute the self. Kierkegaard calls such acts of self-refashioning "leaps."[5] Sin's birth in *Paradise Lost*, so sudden and enigmatic, provides an uncannily exact equivalent of a Kierkegaardian leap, perhaps the best objective correlative anywhere in literature.

In summary, Milton's Satan falls paradoxically by a leap, and this leap acts as a paradigm for all subsequent sins in the poem. The implication of this is far-reaching for my study, for if Sin's birth is a Kierkegaardian leap, and if that birth functions paradigmatically — so that self-temptation forms a part of every origin of sin — then *Paradise Lost* concurs in principle with the fundamental thesis of *The Concept of Anxiety*: that the first sin began as a free leap and that, however trammeled human freedom eventually becomes, all subsequent sin continues to break forth as a leap. Much of what follows will work out the many complexities implicit in this position for both works.

My argument obviously lays great stress upon Sin's birth. Yet the text, I believe, not only sustains but invites such emphasis. Milton portrays Sin's birth very vividly, like a parallel scene from Redcrosse Knight's encounter with Errour upon which it is partly based. Her sudden birth and incestuous double rape by her Father and her Son remains fixed in the mind long after Book 2. More important for a work concerned with origins, Sin's birth occupies the key etiological position in the epic, for if we unscramble Milton's artful chronology, the history of evil ultimately begins the instant that the Goddess Sin, Minerva-like, leaps out of the sinister (left) side of Satan's head. Thus Sin's birth marks the Ur-fall in *Paradise Lost*, the anterior limit of any inquiry into the genealogy of evil.[6] Modeled on Hesiodic myth but fashioned out of James 1:13–15, the allegory fixes the doctrine of self-temptation at the text's most strategic spot, etiologically. At the headwaters of the stream of events whose course ultimately runs into the history "Of Man's First Disobedience . . . and all our woe" wells up a fountain of self-temptation—a spring of seemingly unfathomable depths, whose surface always reflects but one image: our own. Every explanation of evil in *Paradise Lost* must finally revert to this mysterious moment of self-fashioning, when Lucifer ("Light-bearer") transforms himself into Satan ("Adversary").

Milton marks the mystery of this moment by abruptly switching to allegory. Countless readers have, with Addison, Voltaire, and Dr. Johnson, balked at the poem's sudden shift in mimetic modes as Satan first encounters Sin and Death.[7] Against such Enlightenment literalists, I applaud Milton's decision to shift mimetic modes in telling of the birth of Sin. The story of an absolute Ur-fall does not lend itself to realistic narrative, since it is something with which historical men and women, whose guilt always locates itself within a compromised historical nexus, have no experience. Human evil always emerges in a context of prior evil; for us, there is always a serpent already in the garden, pointing back to a long history of fault that those with longer memories, like Raphael, stand ready to recount. Nevertheless, the dream of pure possibility, untrammeled by necessity, remains a permanent, if unelaborated, presupposition of human freedom. Milton rightly creates for this dream its own myth, thereby retaining within a persistently rationalized account of Genesis something openly paradoxical and irradicably mythic.

Milton's allegory is corroborated by Kierkegaard's practice. Like Milton, Kierkegaard can account for the enduring paradox of freedom only by way of a riddling metaphor: the leap. The leap resists assimilation into any simple discourse of cause and effect, just as does Sin's eruption out of Satan's head. Sin's birth, moreover, exhibits several remarkably

Kierkegaardian features. It highlights the suddenness and enigma of sin, qualities Kierkegaard repeatedly attaches to the leap: "The new quality [that is, sin] appears . . . with the leap, with the suddenness of the enigmatic"; or "Thus sin comes into the world as the sudden" (*CA*, 30, 32). It reifies Sin as Satan's offspring, sanctioning Kierkegaard's view that sin constitutes something utterly new, something the sinner brings into existence as by a birth. It brilliantly enacts the essential tautological meaning of Genesis: namely, that "Sin entered the world by a sin." And, most significantly, it thematizes the transition as a leap—a leap, moreover, specifically designed to recall James's doctrine of self-temptation. Kierkegaard would have found much to admire in every detail of this allegory:

> All on a sudden miserable pain
> Surpris'd thee, dim thine eyes, and dizzy swum
> In darkness, while thy head flames thick and fast
> Threw forth, till on the left side op'ning wide,
> Likest to thee in shape and count'nance bright,
> Then shining heav'nly fair, a Goddess arm'd
> Out of thy head I sprung: amazement seiz'd
> All th' Host of Heav'n; back they recoil'd afraid
> At first, and call'd me *Sin*.
>
> (2.752–60)

As Kierkegaard insists, Sin springs into existence not by degrees but full grown. That is, sin originates as sin—suddenly, in an instant, defining forever a radical division between an innocent "before" and a guilty "after." Sin is not simply a deliberative choice; rather, it is a fundamental reconstitution of the self: something which, as Kierkegaard frequently says, "breaks forth." The condition out of which sin breaks forth is anxiety, a state comparable to Satan's headache and, like it, produced by intense reflectiveness, which both Milton and Kierkegaard compare to dizziness (*CA*, 60–61). The object of this dizzy anxiety is not sin but nothing, for sin does not yet exist. Therefore, according to Kierkegaard, one cannot take full cognizance of sin before one posits sin, which emerges in a moment of psychological collapse, as a sort of faint brought on by the vertigo of anxiety. In the same way, Milton's Satan doubtless could not have known that Sin would be the offspring of his headache before she was born. He is "surpris'd" by what issues forth from the pain that dims his eyes and darkens his mind as he, too, delivers Sin in a sort of swoon. Once he has given birth to Sin, however, he recognizes her as his own "perfect image." Nothing can explain sin, in whose image the sinner discovers a new identity, for it explodes out of the self by the leap. Similarly, Kierkegaard suggests that before the leap, the individual reels and faints in the "dizziness of freedom"; after sin, he rises up to find that he is guilty and "everything is changed." "Between these two moments lies the leap, which no science has explained and which no science can explain" (*CA*, 61).

"Envy against the Son": Satan's Sin as History

Sin's birth, then, bears the defining traits of a Kierkegaardian leap. It is radically incommensurable, provocatively irrational, and profoundly world-defining. It also functions in the poem the same way the leap functions in Kierkegaard's treatise, attaching sin to such notions as freedom, self-temptation, caesura, instant, paradox, and so forth. Yet in the poem's economy of abundance, *Paradise Lost* does not recount Satan's fall only once, allegorically in Book 2. It also tells of the same event again, dramatically in Book 5.[8] Raphael's narrative, in contrast to the allegory, makes the Ur-fall seem somewhat more plausible, in several ways: it spreads out the transition over a slightly longer duration; it makes Satan's sin intelligible as a response to temptation (or, at least, provocation); and it intimates that the lapse begins as illicit desire before it becomes an (un)ethical deed. In these ways, Milton naturalizes what he had previously depicted allegorically, reconceptualizing Satan's first sin within a more realistic mode of discourse. As a twice-told tale, Satan's fall encompasses the same double scheme that generates the controversy of a fall before the Fall. Together, the text's two versions of Satan's original sin build into Milton's Ur-fall the complex duality Paul Ricoeur sees in Genesis: the allegory baldly schematizes the first sin as an "instant," while Raphael's narrative suggests Satan's defection occurs across a "lapse of time." Taken together, the two tellings enrich Milton's complex etiology of evil. This is not to suggest that accounts of Satan's fall in Book 2 and Book 5 are simply contradictory. Raphael's dramatic, psychologized narrative of Satan's rebellion never invalidates his ethical allegory of Satan's sin as an inexplicable instant. Rather, within Raphael's history of celestial rebellion Satan's fall still remains a leap.

Seeing humanity's peril, God sends the sociable Raphael to warn Adam and Eve against danger from without (Satan) and from within (their freedom to fall). Raphael is to modulate his discourse to human understanding: "as friend with friend / Converse with *Adam*" (5.229–30); he is to act as their "Divine Historian" (8.6–7). Raphael's history of the War in Heaven rehearses the same event told allegorically in Book 2, but it seems to envisage a different time scheme for the incipience of evil.[9] Where in Book 2 Satan's sin irrupts instantaneously out of nothing, in Book 5 it seems to emerge gradually as part of an unfolding historical process. Where the allegory told a frankly paradoxical tale of an endogenous birth, Raphael tells a humanly familiar story of filial hatred, sibling rivalry, envy, and rebellion. In the allegory, Sin's birth appears openly incommensurable; in Raphael's history, Satan's fall is contingent. If not caused, it is at least conditioned by an external factor — namely, the investiture of the Son. Upon closer inspection, however, we shall see that Raphael retains the leap even as he accommodates the story of the first sin to human understanding.

Raphael spreads the story of Satan's revolt through a sequence of dramatic incidents in much the same way Milton attenuates Adam's and Eve's falls. The Satanic defection "begins" the day the Father anoints the Son as "Vice-gerent" on the Holy Mountain; it is completed by the dawn of the next day when Satan's factious armies stand arrayed for battle at the foot of the Mountain of the Congregation. Filling the interim between these two scenes is Raphael's tale of nighttime sedition. Raphael outlines the following sequence of events: Lucifer first feels a sense of displeasure and then sleeplessness as he mulls over the Son's special investiture; subsequently, at midnight, his displeasure turns into "envy against the Son of God" and a firm resolve to rebel; he then seduces the other angels, who flee northward; watching the rebels flee, the Father utters a sardonic remark to the Son designed to mock his new enemies' folly; next, the apostate angels assemble at a counterfeit Mount of God, where Satan receives a counterfeit exaltation like the Son's; and finally, the zealous Abdiel defies the rebels and beats a solitary retreat back to God. Such are the multiple activities filling this decisive night of rebellion.

Book 5 ends with Abdiel turning his back "On those proud Tow'rs to swift destruction doom'd" (5.907) in order to make his way back to God's throne. Our normal sense of time would tell us that Abdiel's about-face comes very late in the night, if not in the first light of dawn. Yet, as the narrative continues in Book 6, Raphael jars ordinary expectations of how long all these events took, as he says of Abdiel:

> *All night* the dreadless Angel unpursu'd
> Through Heav'n's wide Champaign held his way, till Morn,
> Wak't by the circling Hours, with rosy hand
> Unbarr'd the gates of Light.
>
> (6.1–4; emphasis added)

"All night" contradicts our expectations. Surely the manifold incidents Raphael has just recounted have not left so much night for Abdiel's retreat. "All night" tends to collapse the whole scenario of rebellion and flight back to the poem's previous temporal indication, namely, midnight:[10]

> Soon as midnight brought on the dusky hour
> Friendliest to sleep and silence, he [Satan] resolv'd
> With all his Legions to dislodge, and leave
> Unworshipt, unobey'd the Throne supreme.
>
> (5.667–70)

Thus the same narrative that distributes the action historically across time also unobtrusively compresses it into a single moment: midnight. If this paradox reflects the problem of translating eternity into time, it is no wonder Raphael hesitates to "relate / To human sense th' invisible exploits / Of warring Spirits," nor that he begins his narrative cautioning Adam and Eve about the inadequacy of temporal discourse to represent eternal actions (see 5.563–82). Human language is necessarily sequential, while spiritual acts are swift as thought.

Beyond the compression of time registered in "all night," a great deal in Raphael's narrative heightens the impression of the rebellion's swiftness; a great deal preserves the leap within a historical process. Consider, for example, Satan's followers. As Satan wakes his companions uttering "ambiguous words and jealousies, to sound / Or taint integrity" (5.703–4), the conspiracy seems to spread as swift as thought, as if will and choice are nearly one in angelic beings. Surprisingly, there is never any prolonged choosing of sides, never a period of genuine deliberation and debate among all the angelic hosts. Of the cohorts who follow Satan north in the night, only Abdiel returns. Abdiel's defiant rebuke of Satan provides the only instance of the kind of discussion we might have expected to precede the rebellion. But by the end of this debate, the entire breakaway army except Abdiel applauds Satan's apostasy (5.872–74). It is not clear exactly when and why only these angels fall.[11] The text, however, gives a distinct impression that the fateful, eternally decisive division between good and bad angels occurs with blinding rapidity. It is as if sin erupts in an instant for Satan's followers as it did, in the allegory, for Satan. In fact, syntactically Raphael's first mention of the fallen hosts could refer to Satan's intent to beguile his troops, or to their simultaneous determination to rebel with him: "he resolv'd / With all his Legions to dislodge, and leave / Unworshipt, unobey'd the Throne supreme" (5.668–70). Thus the fallen angels' seduction and defection is collapsed into one.

In this fashion, Raphael ravels the precise instant of rebellion back-wards into a single midnight moment. Likewise, he knits together Satan's sinful motive with his sinful action, in effect making the internal and external sin synchronous.[12] Raphael's account of Satan's decision to break with God reads:

> but not so wak'd
> *Satan*, so call him now, his former name
> Is heard no more in Heav'n; he of the first,
> If not the first Arch-Angel, great in Power,
> In favor and preëminence, yet fraught
> With envy against the Son of God, that day
> Honor'd by his great Father, and proclaim'd
> *Messiah* King anointed, could not bear
> Through pride that sight, and thought himself impair'd.
> Deep malice thence conceiving and disdain,
> Soon as midnight brought on the dusky hour
> Friendliest to sleep and silence, he resolv'd
> With all his Legions to dislodge, and leave
> Unworshipt, unobey'd the Throne supreme,
> Contemptuous.
>
> (5.657–71)

As so often happens in Milton's verse, the complex syntax and shifting temporal indicators make the exact time of origin for Satan's sinful envy, pride, and malice extremely hard (if not impossible) to puzzle out. The general impression that the passage conveys is, of course, that Satan's motives precede his decision to revolt—though it is not clear by how much. The relative clause "That day / Honor'd by his great Father" seems to suggest that Satan's envy is coincident with the Son's exaltation. Yet technically, the passage declares only against whom Satan became envious, not when. The clause "that day . . ." functions adjectivally in apposition to "Son of God"; it does not modify the crucial preterits "yet fraught with envy," "could not bear through pride," and "thought himself impair'd." These verbal phrases, which describe Satan's sinful motives, are never firmly fixed in time. Rather, they are suspended indefinitely between a relative clause about the Son's exaltation and a phrase perspicuously marking the instant of sin: "Soon as midnight brought on the dusky hour . . . he resolv'd."

Envy, pride, malice, and disdain—though prompted by the Son's sudden preeminence—may materialize only with a midnight resolve through which Lucifer acquires a new name and identity: Satan or Adversary. Nothing in Raphael's description of Satan's fall (except our ordinary expectation that sinful motives precede sinful deeds) requires us to locate Satan's envy a few celestial hours before midnight—in spite of the illusion the narrative gives of an inward fall between the cue for action and the act.

From a Kierkegaardian perspective, Raphael's description of this interim between the Son's anointing and Satan's rebellion is critical. This interval before sin corresponds to the period of anxiety in *The Concept of Anxiety*. Raphael does not analyze Lucifer's temptation with the kind of psychological detail and specificity of Kierkegaard's treatise. (As an unfallen angel, neither experienced in evil nor privy to Satan's interior life, how could he?) Nevertheless, from the vantage of *The Concept of Anxiety*, Raphael's characterization of an unfallen but tempted Lucifer is philosophically tactful and psychologically suggestive. Raphael gingerly avoids reduplicating the problems of a fall before the Fall in his account of the Ur-fall by delicately characterizing evil's incipience in Satan's mind as some unfamiliar mental disturbance that keeps Satan awake while others sleep—and not, initially, as a fully conceptualized inward sin of envy. In Raphael's telling, Lucifer becomes anxious and restless after the Father singles out the Son for special honor. While heaven celebrates "In song and dance about the sacred Hill," he secretly broods, upset by the day's event (5.617–20). As night comes, he alone is wakeful while the other angels repose. Satan's moods through this decisive day and night correspond to Kierkegaardian anxiety. They show him to be afflicted not by sinful concupiscence but by a disturbing sense of alarm. Raphael is careful not to label these first demonic stirrings envy, just as he is not to call Lucifer by his fallen name, Satan, until the Adversary acquires that name by sin. Note Raphael's tactful phrasing of Satan's daytime mood: "All seem'd well pleas'd, all seem'd, but were not all" (5.617). To be "not pleased"—or, alternatively, to be not all (that is, entirely) pleased—denotes merely an absence, an absence of joy. It does not yet posit the presence of envy. To supply this void with a full-blown sinful attribute like envy is to mine the motive out of our own fallen condition.

Similarly, we may mistakenly read Satan's wakefulness as the sign of guilty conscience, in the tradition of Shakespeare's Henry IV or Macbeth. But here again, to do so is to construe the unfallen world from the world of fallen experience, to discover concrete guilt in attitudes that are left much less defined by Raphael. Satan feels upset rather than guilty. What, after all, could he feel guilty about before he sins? (Nevertheless, in the extremity of temptation, anxiety comes to feel more and more like guilt [see *CA*, 74–75, 103–10].) Satan's wakefulness is not like Henry's or Macbeth's, who are guilty of concrete sinful acts of murder and usurpation. Rather it is equivalent to the anxiety dreams that, according to both Milton and Kierkegaard, disturb Eden before the Fall. Eve's dream and Satan's sleeplessness equally register disturbance from what Kierkegaard calls sin's "alien reality." For both Satan and Eve, sin still exists only as dream — a "vague presentiment," a ghostly possibility that "disappears as soon as [one] seeks to grasp for it" (*CA*, 42).

A Kierkegaardian reading of Lucifer's spiritual condition from noon to midnight presupposes he does not — cannot — truly understand the new emotions that vex and seduce him, nor harden them into sinful resolve, until he breaks fealty at midnight. The contrary position, that Satan is inwardly fallen before he rebels, presupposes that Satan is already gripped by such sinful lusts as envy, jealousy, pride, and malice — so that after the Son's exaltation all that remains is for Satan to decide whether and how to act on his wicked desires. The Kierkegaardian interpretation of Satan's mood, I believe, better respects the studied nuances Raphael inserts into Satan's loss of innocence. (It also, I surmise, conforms far better to our own experiences with the loss of innocence, a rite of passage requiring an excursion through considerable anxiety before we arrive at full and knowing concupiscence.) In Raphael's version of Lucifer's passage, the mood shifts from amorphous *angst* to concrete concupiscence only as Satan makes his midnight resolve. It is as if immediately as Satan (and we) become fully lucid about the feelings set in motion by God's provocative action, those feelings turn into willful rebellion. Thus even in Raphael's accommodated telling, sin comes into the world by a sin. Before midnight, Satan experiences only the seductive but fearful disquiet of anxiety.

This reading of Raphael's narrative correlates it with the allegorical birth of Sin. Each account, in its own way, tells the same story. Satan's headache finds a counterpart in his restless wakefulness. Sin's leap finds an analogue in Satan's midnight rebellion, and Sin's origin in self-temptation finds a corollary in the rebellion's inception in envy. This last correlation (between self-temptation and envy) may be less obvious than the others, for unlike the allegory, Raphael's history provides sin with an external "cause": the Son's exaltation. Upon closer inspection, however, this cause only *seems* to make Satan's fall unenigmatic. In fact, the Son's elevation supplies Satan with a motive (envy) that, like the allegory, redirects explanation to the self.

Envy figures prominently among Satan's motives throughout the poem and not simply in Raphael's narrative. Indeed, from its first mention of Satan, the poem attributes demonic malice to envy (see 1.34–36). Envy is an apt choice for Satan's prime motive, one available in patristic and Protestant tradition about the devil but which only Milton works into so brilliant a portrait.[13] In discussions of Satan's envy, however, what is rarely acknowledged is that envy only seems to provide a sufficient cause for Satan's defection. In fact, it does not ultimately "explain" Satan's sin any better than does the *ex nihilo* birth of Sin. Or rather, envy explains sin the same way—as the offspring of self-temptation—for external temptation cannot explain a particular individual's response to that temptation, just as the opportunity to steal a fruitcake cannot explain why I would find the prospect utterly uninteresting while another might feel powerfully allured to commit an illicit act. It follows with respect to any temptation, as Kierkegaard observes, that "whoever yields to temptation is himself guilty of the temptation" (*CA*, 109). This surely applies *a fortiori* to Milton's Satan. The Son's exaltation obviously cannot be regarded as a sufficient cause of Satan's revolt, for many other angels felt joy instead of envy at the Father's proclamation. Having adduced envy or pride or any other similar "motive" as cause, one can still ask why. Why does Satan brood while others rejoice? Why does he feel God's love as an onerous burden instead of a blessing? Why does he alone convert God's goodness into an excuse for malice? (see 4.45–53). Faced with such questions, one is finally left with the mystery of freedom: the power that enables Lucifer to remake himself into Satan.[14]

Ultimately, the question of why Satan is envious is the same as why Satan is Satan. The answer to both questions is tautological, as God's language implies: "Freely they stood who stood, and fell who fell" (3.102). Satan is jealous because he is jealous. As Emilia observes of Othello: "But jealous souls . . . are not ever jealous for the cause, / But jealous for they're jealous. It is a monster / Begot upon itself, born on itself" (*Oth*. 3.4.159–62). Emilia's endogenous "monster," like Milton's demon Sin, reifies the idea of self-temptation; both reifications remind us that frequently adduced motives, such as pride and envy, mask etiological tautologies. As James 1:13–15 implies, such "causes" ultimately throw explanation back upon free self-determination. Beyond this we cannot go, for sin comes into the world by a sin. *Paradise Lost* thematizes this paradox of freedom in the figure of Satan and, through the Satanic paradigm, fastens the leap firmly to the etiology of evil everywhere in the poem.

"Who First Seduc'd Them": Satan and the Fall

As paradigm of the leap, Sin's birth discloses the essential nature of Adam and Eve's fall just as it does Satan's. In Eden, as in heaven, sin breaks forth freely from the self. As I have already argued, God's oracle applies the Jamesian doctrine of self-temptation to both demonic and human sinners; both sorts of malefactors are "Authors to themselves," both "enthrall themselves" (3.122, 125).[15] Thus the Father forbids our explaining human sin as simply the effect of seduction, compelling us to find the Fall's cause in freedom — for God ordained his angel and human creatures alike free; "they themselves ordain'd thir fall" (3.128).

Yet the Father also draws a distinction between the Satanic and Adamic falls: Adam and Eve sin in a previously corrupted universe and under active solicitation; Satan does not. Milton's God offers this fact as a mitigating circumstance: "Man therefore shall find grace, / The other none" (3.131–32). The poem thus assumes a complex attitude toward human sin and Satan's role in bringing it forth. Human sin is free yet conditioned, the consequence of external inducement *and* internal collapse. Satan, it turns out, points simultaneously to both these opposing features of Edenic evil: as the paradigmatic free sinner, he exemplifies human autonomy; as archetypal tempter, he embodies the concept of human captivity. Milton regards the seduction as relevant to but not determinative of the Fall; he sees Satan as the catalyst of sin in Eden, but not its cause.

Kierkegaard acknowledges a similarly catalytic function for the environment. Though he rejects the idea that the Fall took place in a garden already infected with a fallen angel's malice, he does recognize that all postlapsarian sin takes place in corrupt, seductive environments. "Subsequent" or "later" individuals (his terms for Adam and Eve's posterity) confront "quantitative 'more's'" in their particular history, culture, and personal makeup. Yet historical evil breaks forth by the "qualitative leap" just as it had in Eden. Kierkegaard's concept of historical sin obviously bears close parallels to Milton's view of Edenic evil; both accounts conceive of sinners as simultaneously responsible agents (because they are free) and victims (because they are seduced). A Kierkegaardian analysis, however, would suggest the following correspondences: Satan's fall in *Paradise Lost* coincides with Adam's fall in *The Concept of Anxiety* because both are thought to take place in a vacuum, as the absolute first sin. Milton's Adam and Eve, however, compare to Kierkegaard's "subsequent individuals," for they sin in an environment already defiled by the presence of evil. Their fall inaugurates the history of sin for the race while it continues sin's history in the cosmos. Therefore Adam and Eve's existential position in *Paradise Lost* is akin to that of the later individual in *The Concept of Anxiety* in that both bring sin into existence and also find it already there.

Viewing Milton's Adam and Eve as "later individuals," however odd initially, makes perfect sense of the place Milton assigns to them in his epic. From his first invocation, the poet locates human sin in a historical context of prior falls:

> say first what cause
> Mov'd our Grand Parents in that happy State,
> Favor'd of Heav'n so highly, to fall off
> From thir Creator, and transgress his Will
> For one restraint, Lord of the World besides?
> Who first seduc'd them to that foul revolt?
> Th' infernal Serpent; hee, it was . . .
>
> (1.28–34)

In *Paradise Lost*, human sin always already has a genealogy; its lineage reaches back well beyond "our Grand Parents" into a still more ancient history. This is a history *Paradise Lost* delights to elaborate, preeminently through the voluble Raphael. A "divine historian" (8.5–6), he instructs Adam and Eve in the antiquity of evil.[16] Through his lessons they become knowing participants in a historical process; however, we must remember this all-important caveat: When Adam and Eve hear Raphael's report of the War in Heaven, the topic is still one of foreign affairs; the subject becomes part of domestic history only when they themselves sin. At this instant, the first humans enter into the historical process they have heard so much about.

By historicizing the Fall in this sense of the term, Milton gives full expression to the intentionality of the biblical snake, as Ricoeur understands it: "The serpent represents the following situation: in the historical experience of man, every individual finds evil *already there*; nobody begins it absolutely."[17] If this is the meaning of the serpent—that historically no one begins sin absolutely—then *Paradise Lost* vastly embellishes what Genesis barely hints at in the figure of a subtle snake by framing the Edenic fall within a grand history of prior and subsequent falls, and by schooling Adam and Eve in that history. Not only this, but as mature adults, Milton's human protagonists appear to be exceptionally capable of understanding Raphael's history lessons and of making reasoned decisions based on their knowledge. In these ways, Milton's human pair seem very much like Kierkegaard's "subsequent individuals." Thus though Milton's Eden may be far better than our world, it is not wholly different from it.

Of course, this view of Eden takes us right back to Millicent Bell's objections. She, too, sees Milton's Adam and Eve as historical beings exactly like us, only for her this implies they are historically determined rather than free. Milton and Kierkegaard understand historical determination quite differently. For them, history, environment, temptation, and so forth, provide explanatory circumstances explicitly divested of final explanatory power; such nonexplanatory explanations can account only for the probability of possible irruptions of sin, *not* for their actuality. For Milton and Kierkegaard, sin is a leap; yet ever since the Fall brought sinfulness into existence, it is a leap somehow conditioned by past leaps. Otherwise, sinfulness could have no history in the life of either the individual or the community. Were sin only an instantaneous leap, disconnected from the past, Israel's prophets could not describe a nation as ripening in iniquity because this implies the possibility of sinfulness accumulating quantitatively across time and within a culture. Likewise, were sinners only autonomous individuals, Scripture could not declare that whole generations are victimized by the sins of the fathers. For the subsequent individual, then, sin remains emphatically a leap, but a leap from a particular history, environment, culture, and so forth — or, in the case of Milton's Adam and Eve, from a particular set of temptations in Eden. These constitute, in Kierkegaard's language, "quantitative 'more's'" from which sin breaks forth. They are "preliminary runs to the leap," which cannot, however, explain the leap (*CA*, 31n).

The middle path between freedom and determinism that Milton and Kierkegaard attempt to walk requires some fine distinctions and fancy footwork. Moreover, since both men strongly stress freedom, their positions are often misunderstood and misrepresented. Nevertheless, within their respective philosophies of individual freedom, both thinkers accommodate something more than individual will — something from the individual's community, genes, history, and environment. Indeed, Kierkegaard specifically subtitles *The Concept of Anxiety* "On the Dogmatic Issue of Hereditary Sin." The following passage illustrates just how much influence Kierkegaard is willing to yield to inheritance, a problem he dealt with elsewhere in anti-Hegelian polemics about historical determinism.[18] Here he takes up the problem of determinism in a scriptural rather than philosophical formulation, as the question of hereditary evil:

> What Scripture teaches, that God avenges the iniquity of the fathers upon the children to the third and fourth generation, life proclaims loudly enough. To want to talk oneself out of this dreadful fact by explaining that this saying is a Jewish teaching is of no help. Christianity has never assented to giving each particular individual the privilege of starting from the beginning in an external sense. (*CA*, 72–73)

This is an important concession for one often credited as the founding father of modern existentialism: as a Christian, Kierkegaard accepts that human freedom occurs within a world and not simply on the world. In fact, as I shall argue in chapter 7, to pursue absolute autonomy after a Sartrean model is, according to Kierkegaard, to enter on the high road to despair. No subsequent individual starts from scratch. Or, as Ricoeur observes, "Every individual finds evil *already there*; nobody begins it absolutely."[19] Human sinners always discover a snake already in the garden.

Like Milton's God, then, Kierkegaard concedes something to historical, environmental, and even genetic determination. These belong to the individual's collective identity as a member of a species, culture, and family; they express how individual existence participates in the larger life of what Kierkegaard terms "the race." But the individual is not simply his or her race. Of the individual's participation in the race, Kierkegaard observes: "The race does not begin anew with every individual, in which case there would be no race at all, but every individual begins anew with the race" (*CA*, 33–34). By this, Kierkegaard means that historical men and women somehow inherit the sinfulness of the race as their point of (free) departure. Although no individual in history begins sinfulness ("the race does not begin anew with the individual"), the sin of any particular individual constitutes itself a fresh beginning ("every individual begins anew with the race"). Individuals confront prior sinfulness as a condition of their existence, a feature of the landscape; sinfulness defines a "quantitative 'more'" from which every subsequent individual must begin afresh. Human beings, however, do not merely inherit their racial identity as members of a sinful family of Adam as if they were numerical repetitions of their first parents — as a vegetable inherits its color or a leopard its spots: "If the sinfulness of the race is posited by Adam's sin . . . in the same sense as a species of web-footed birds have webbed feet, the concept of the individual is canceled, and also the concept of the race" (*CA*, 186; cf. 57). Unlike plants and animals, humans are more than the repetition of their species; they are uniquely individual agents.

Kierkegaard formulates this paradox in the principle that human beings are at once themselves and their race. The significance of this for Kierkegaard's theory of history is that "as the history of the race moves on, the individual continually begins anew." Therefore "the sinfulness of the race does indeed acquire a history"; this "history proceeds quietly on its course, and in this no individual begins in the same place as another"

(*CA*, 33–34). But the individual participates in history by the qualitative leap.

Fancy footwork indeed. As he brings his theory near determinism's slippery slope, Kierkegaard holds fast to the freedom of the leap. The leap is easily missed by historical theories such as Hegel's, which attend only to history's collective, outward march rather than to its individual, inward movements. Hence, Mark Taylor is right to insist that for Kierkegaard "history is discontinuous, punctuated by surdity and novelty." But Taylor is wrong to imply that Kierkegaard sees history as entirely lacking the continuity and coherence Hegel attributes to it,[20] for if individuals were only themselves *and not also* the race, they would "fall apart from one another numerically" (*CA*, 29). So Kierkegaard admits that nobody begins from scratch; rather, "every individual begins anew, and in the same moment he is at the place where he should begin in history" (*CA*, 35). Viewed from a properly psychological perspective through the eyes of Vigilius Haufniensus (Kierkegaard's pseudonym in *The Concept of Anxiety*), each individual acquires his own history, appropriates his own environment. Therefore, while Hegelian and (its derivative) Marxian determinism correctly seize upon forces binding humanity together historically and societally, these theories of history actually express, at best, but half-truths — truths made potentially pernicious by their totalizing presumptions. They understand history only in its "external sense" (*CA*, 73).

A deeper understanding remains "firmly and unshakably convinced that never in the world has there been or ever will be a 'more' such that by a simple transition it transforms the quantitative into the qualitative" (*CA*, 72).[21] Kierkegaard's Christian view of the paradoxical relationship between the sinner and history — one that recognizes humans are the victims of ancestral evil and yet holds them responsible for their history — is summarized as follows: "Each individual begins in a historical nexus, and the consequences of nature still hold true. The difference, however, consists in that Christianity teaches him to lift himself above this 'more,' and judges [condemns] him who does not do so as being unwilling" (*CA*, 73).

Similarly, Milton's God condemns Adam as being unwilling — or more precisely, as *willing not* — to rise above the "more" of temptation:

> For Man will hark'n to his glozing lies,
> And easily transgress the sole Command
> Sole pledge of his obedience: So will fall
> Hee and his faithless Progeny: whose fault?
> Whose but his own? ingrate, he had of mee

> All he could have; I made him just and right,
> Sufficient to have stood, though free to fall.
>
> (3.93–99)

The Father's prophecy defines the relationship between the tempting environment and Adam's sin in a way that mirrors Kierkegaard's views on the subsequent individual's relation to history. Kierkegaard's subsequent individual participates in history by a leap that the quantitative "more's" provided by the race neither explain nor excuse; Milton's "Man" leaps into the unfolding history of cosmic disobedience through a sin that neither the prior sinfulness of angels nor the Satanic seduction explains or excuses.

Further, humans belong to a larger race of "ethereal powers and spirits" whose kinship rests in a shared capacity to obey or disobey. The Father continues his prophetic history of human sin by explicitly linking "Man's" sin with the sins of our spiritual cousins, angels: "Such I created all the Ethereal Powers / And spirits, both them who stood and them who fail'd. / Freely they stood who stood, and fell who fell" (3.100–2). Freedom designates the common racial characteristic that makes Man and Angel cousins in *Paradise Lost*. Yet the same trait that binds together two orders of God's creatures isolates each individual within those orders as either faithful or faithless: "Freely they stood who stood, and fell who fell." Freedom cannot supply a mechanism of automatic genetic inheritance, nor is it suited to biological models of cross-cultural contamination between the angels and humans. In Milton's Eden, although sinfulness gathers significant historical momentum as it spreads from the demonic to the human fall, sin begins afresh with Adam and Eve just as it began with Satan.

"So Will Fall His Faithless Progeny": Satan and Adam's Posterity

Yet for Milton the situation apparently changes after the Fall. Although biology does not explain how sin enters into Eden, it does, Milton concedes, explain in part how evil is transmitted from Adam and Eve to their posterity. Not once but several times, in both *Paradise Lost* and *The Christian Doctrine*, Milton lends support to a contamination theory of inherited sin. His view, ultimately attributable to Augustine's concept of inherited sin, seems on its face simply to contradict the leap. Examined more closely, however, *Paradise Lost*'s etiology of postlapsarian evil does not wholly abandon the leap. Rather, the poem intermingles

individual freedom (the leap) within its depiction of sinfulness as a con-
genital debility from which the whole human race suffers, will or nill.
Freedom still has a role to play in sin's origin in the fallen world, as it
had in Eden and in heaven—though freedom with respect to the Adamic
curse is considerably diminished, and to accommodate moral freedom
within a scheme predominantly of biological inheritance Milton must
stretch his poem to the breaking point.[22]

When God says of Man in Book 3, "So will fall / Hee and his faithless
Progeny: whose fault? / Whose but his own?" (3.95–97), it is possible to
construe his words as describing the *way* Adam's posterity becomes sinful (that is, they fall in the same manner Adam fell—freely, responsibly),
or the *effect* of Adam's sin upon his progeny (they fall automatically in
Adam's fall—genetically, by birth), or both. To understand these lines
in the first fashion is to align oneself with the Pelagian concept of imitation. For Pelagius, the human family becomes sinful by imitating the
fall of Adam and Eve; therefore, each sinner may be justly punished for
his own sins and not for Adam's transgression (cf. "whose fault? /
Whose but his own?"). To read these lines in the second way is to orient
oneself according to the Augustinian coordinate of inheritance. For Augustine, the entire human family acquires moral debility *per genera-
tionem*; therefore the human race is congenitally blighted simply by its
descent from Adam and Eve. With respect to the origin of sin among
Adam's progeny, *The Concept of Anxiety* and *Paradise Lost* position
themselves somewhere between Pelagian and Augustinian extremes—
with Kierkegaard leaning toward Pelagian voluntarism and Milton toward Augustinian determinism.[23] Kierkegaard, as we have seen, tram-
mels absolute individual freedom (presupposed by Pelagius) through the
concept of quantitative determination. Milton, I shall argue, opens up
racial determinism (presupposed by Augustine) through proposing a role
for self-determination even vis-à-vis the curse.

We can observe this unstable admixture of voluntarism and determinism already in God's oracle foretelling the common doom that awaits all
Adam's posterity. The Father's pronouncement "So will fall / Hee
[Adam] and his faithless Progeny . . ." blends individual agency within
the concept of racial victimization. "Faithless Progeny" binds humanity
together as a race of sinners, but it also isolates each of us as individually
responsible, according to the logic of accusation that immediately follows: "whose fault? / Whose but his own? ingrate." God's rhetoric seems
to place all human guilt generically under the sign of responsible freedom. We feel accused with Adam. Similarly, as the denunciation continues, we feel included among those created sufficient to stand though free

to fall, those who at once initiate evil and fall prey to temptation. As God disposes of Adam and Eve's sin, he seems to speak against all human sin. Their fall thus becomes not simply the source of human sin but its archetype. The entire human family seems to fall under divine accusation and to qualify for God's promised mercy. By such means, the Father's supposedly voiceless oracle masks in its subtle rhetoric the contradiction entailed in representing hereditary evil as somehow voluntary.[24]

Ricoeur's analysis of the Augustinian-Pelagian controversy clarifies both Kierkegaard's and Milton's positions on the question of inherited sin.[25] Ricoeur calls attention to the radical individualism implicit in Pelagianism. Pelagius, he observes, stakes out a "coherent voluntarism" according to which each man sins by himself; thus, God is just in punishing man for his own sin rather than for the sin of another. For Pelagians, the sinfulness that man acquires "in Adam" (1 Cor. 15:22) "can only mean a relation of imitation. *In* Adam means *like*."[26] To maintain such autonomy for Adam's posterity, however, Pelagianism has to presuppose an autonomy so radical as to cut human sinners loose from time, from place, from community: "For the Pelagians, freedom is without any acquired nature, without habit, without history and encumbrances. It is a freedom that in each one of us would be a unique and isolated instance of the absolute indetermination of creation."[27] To combat the singularity implicit in Pelagianism, Ricoeur continues, Augustine develops a "transhistorical," "transbiological" concept of original sin, a doctrine that welds the human family solidly into a race of sinners, who confess with one voice "we other poor sinners."[28] To achieve such solidarity, however, Augustine fuses inimical ideas into an inherently unstable dogma. He fastens a moral concept (guilt) onto a genetic one (inheritance). In the resulting dogma, Original Sin, "the concept of inherited guilt is crystallized, a concept that unites in an inconsistent notion a juridical category (voluntary punishable crime) and a biological category (the unity of the human species by generation)."[29]

Kierkegaard has nothing but contempt for the conflation of sinfulness and biology: "Sinfulness is not an epidemic which spreads like cowpox"; "If by Adam's sin the sinfulness of the race is posited in the same sense as his erect walking [posture] etc., the concept of the individual is cancelled" (*CA*, 38, 57; cf. 186). Kierkegaard shares Pelagianism's accent on individual responsibility. Yet he well knows the absurdities implicit in a freedom "without any acquired nature, without habit, without history and encumbrances." To counter Pelagian individualism and its heirs (*CA*, 28), he insists that the self is constituted such that one is at once both an individual and the race. The sin that we rightfully confess "before God" to be our own and none other's, belongs as well to a "corruption of the will which goes well beyond the consciousness of the individual. . . . For otherwise the question of how sin began must arise with respect to each individual" (*SUD*, 226).[30] Therefore, sin coheres within a particular historical moment, as the sinner coheres within a specific community of sinners, for although sinners act individually, they do not act ahistorically, in isolation from the individuals who surround them or from their past. If they enjoyed such absolute autonomy, Kierkegaard observes, there could be neither history nor race; instead, individuals would "fall apart from one another numerically" (*CA*, 29).

Because Kierkegaard recognizes that to be an individual is to be oneself and one's race, his concept of individualism differs markedly from that of Pelagianism; equally, his understanding of freedom differs from other strongman theories of human autonomy (such as Stoicism, Romantic individualism, and atheistic existentialism) with which it is regularly conflated.[31] Yet because Kierkegaard repeatedly urges an "imitation" theory of sin—that is, one in which the entire human family is held to enter the history of sinfulness by a sin comparable to the first sin of Adam and Eve—it is easy to regard him, mistakenly, as a nineteenth-century *Pelagius-redivivus*. Hence, Kierkegaard must repeatedly parry the charge of Pelagianism:

> Obviously this view is in no way guilty of any Pelagianism. The race has its history, within which sinfulness continues to have its quantitative determinability, but innocence is always lost only by the qualitative leap of the individual. (*CA*, 37)

> It hardly needs to be said that this view is not guilty of Pelagianism, which permits every individual to play his little history in his own private theater unconcerned about the race. For the history of the race proceeds quietly on its course, and in this no individual begins at the same place as another, but every individual begins anew, and in the same moment he is at the place where he should begin in history. (*CA*, 34–35)

Paradise Lost similarly orients itself paradoxically along the coordinates of race and individual, letting neither the communal determination of Augustinian inheritance nor the individual freedom of Pelagian imitation completely cancel the other out. Several times in *The Christian Doctrine* Milton accepts the principle of inherited evil.[32] *Paradise Lost* similarly supports a contagion theory of evil consonant with inherited sin. The vision of world history that Michael invites Adam to witness is one in which sinfulness infects the human family like some dark pestilence: "*Adam*, now open thine eyes," Michael commands,

> and first behold
> Th' effects which thy original crime hath wrought
> In some to spring from thee, who never touch'd
> Th'excepted Tree, nor with the Snake conspir'd,
> Nor sinn'd thy sin, yet from that sin derive
> Corruption to bring forth more violent deeds.
>
> (11.423–28)

This biological identification of evil gains further support from Michael's terrifying vision of the Lazar-house, whose manifold maladies are revealed to Adam in ghastly detail so that he may "know / What misery th' inabstinence of *Eve* / Shall bring on men" (11.475–77).

And yet the plagues of the Lazar-house are not visited upon humankind merely congenitally. Subsequent human inabstinence and intemperance (which reenact Eve's first sin) augment whatever debility her progeny may inherit from her. If Adam will remain temperate from this time forth, he is promised that he may "live, till like ripe Fruit thou drop / Into thy Mother's lap, or be with ease / Gather'd, not harshly pluckt, for death mature" (11.535–37), and thereby in a measure reverse the physical consequences of his fall. Similarly, Michael tells Adam that "Since thy original lapse true Liberty / Is lost," yet in the next breath blames fallen humanity for not governing passion by the rule of "free Reason" (12.79–101). In these passages (and many others like them), Milton works responsible, free self-determination back into postlapsarian racial guilt. The poem thus presents Edenic evil as something humans both inherit and imitate.

Let me cite just one example of Milton's strategic double accusation of fallen humanity as inherently and also imitatively guilty. Consider this description of how the human family participates in its Grand Parents' fall:

> Thir Maker's Image, answer'd *Michael*, then
> Forsook them, when themselves they vilifi'd
> To serve ungovern'd appetite, and took
> His Image whom they served, a brutish vice,
> Inductive mainly to the sin of *Eve*.
> Therefore so abject is thir punishment,
> Disfiguring not God's likeness, but thir own,
> Or if his likeness, by themselves defac't
> While they pervert pure Nature's healthful rules
> To loathsome sickness, worthily, since they
> God's Image did not reverence in themselves.
>
> (11.515–25)

Michael's "Inductive mainly to . . . *Eve*" places her posterity's sin under the sign of inheritance, acknowledging the tainted genealogy of human evil. But a great deal else in the passage places postlapsarian sin under the sign of imitation. Michael explains that fallen men and women inaugurate evil as well as continue it by personally defacing the remnant of God's image in themselves. This action recalls Satan's giving birth to Sin. So do the several reflexives that govern the complex syntax of Michael's outburst: "themselves they vilifi'd," "by themselves defac't," "they / God's Image did not reverence in themselves." These reflexive phrases do more than intensify the accusation, though they certainly do this. They spring from an even deeper imperative to develop a coherent theodicy justifying "the ways of God to men." The same impulse leads Milton to attribute sin to self-temptation in the Father's oracles in Book 3 and to construct an Ur-fall for Satan entirely out of self-reflexivity in Book 2.[33] The reflexives redirect etiology to the self, subsuming sin under the concept of personal freedom. Michael's answer infuses inheritance with imitation so that the poet, conscious of his theodicean purpose, may introduce the syntactically displaced "worthily" to vindicate God's "punishment" of fallen humanity. The tortured syntax of Michael's speech suggests the difficulty of his task. That Adam and Eve's descendants are worthy of their punishment is, of course, nonsense if they only inherit guilt and do not choose it. So Michael labors to recover voluntarism for necessary racial iniquity, to include self-determination within the "inconsistent notion" of biologically determined guilt.

Milton obviously concedes more than does Kierkegaard to inherited sin. Yet like Kierkegaard, he wants even Adam and Eve's blighted progeny to confess that God accuses them "worthily, since they / God's Image did not reverence in themselves." Likewise, justifying Original Sin in *The Christian Doctrine*, Milton insists that, apart from infants, "with everybody else, the explanation is that no one perishes unless he himself has sinned" (*CP*, 6.386). Both men recognize that the human race suffers under sin's collective weight so that by sinning, humans seem to incur the guilt of all sin. At the same time, both know that humans are held individually responsible before God and that guilt is by nature nontransferable—to the snake, to Adam, to Eve, to biology, to anything: "At last it is as if the guilt of the whole world united to make him [the subsequent individual] guilty, and, what is the same, as if in becoming guilty he became guilty of the guilt of the whole world. [But] Guilt has the dialectical character that it does not allow itself to be transferred" (*CA*, 109).

We do not—as Milton's God does not—condemn human sinners as

utterly responsible but, rather, find hope for repentance in the fact that human evil is never wholly contingent upon the individual; other influences always collaborate to bring about human guilt: "Man therefore shall find grace / The other none" (3.131–32). Nevertheless, as self-knowledge preparatory to repentance, we look for the sinner's recognition that personal sin ought not, and cannot, be blamed upon either a tempting serpent, wife, husband, or upon anybody or anything external, since "whoever yields to temptation is himself guilty of the temptation" (*CA*, 109). In *Paradise Lost*, forgiveness awaits self-accusation comparable to Adam's:

> all my evasions vain
> And reasonings, though through Mazes, lead me still
> But to my own conviction: first and last
> On mee, mee only, as the source and spring
> Of all corruption, all the blame lights due.
>
> (10.829–33)

or to Eve's:

> The sentence from thy head remov'd may light
> On me, sole cause to thee of all this woe,
> Mee, mee only just object of his ire.
>
> (10.934–36)

"Mee, mee only" Adam and Eve each confess in the time-honored language of true contrition. We poor sinners, like Satan, are the "source and spring" of sin. Evil has sprung forth from our freedom. Whatever the temptation, our sins are the result of self-temptation. This is clearly the primary lesson Milton wants us to read in the long saga of Satan and sin. But Milton knows that humans cannot absorb all fault within responsible freedom, for we are victims as well as agents. Therefore the Father responds to guilty Adam and Eve by sending his Son as "both Judge and Savior" (10.209), to condemn his fallen creatures, and to clothe them.

Notes

1. See Hunter, *Paradise Lost*, 62–64.
2. On Kierkegaard's reduction of all temptation to self-temptation, see Mackey's stimulating essay "The Loss of the World in Kierkegaard's Ethics" in *Points of View* (esp. 152–56). I disagree, however, with Mackey's conclusion that Kierkegaardian individualism "ends by isolating the individual not *within* but *without*

a world, just as effectively as if that world were not there" (157). My disagreements may be inferred from my views about Adam as both an individual and race (the third section in this chapter), quantitative determination (the third section and ch. 4), and demonic despair (ch. 7).

3. This derives principally from passages in Isaiah 14 and Revelation 12. From this scriptural base, the idea that Satan is a fallen angel gathered widespread acceptance: see Evans, *Genesis Tradition*, 75–81; Patrides, "The Breach Disloyal" in *Christian Tradition*; and Revard, *War in Heaven*, especially chapters 1 and 2.

4. See chapter 2 of Gallagher's *Milton, the Bible, and Misogyny* for how Milton exploits the "trope of deception" to exonerate Eve and women rather than to accuse them, as was customary in misogynist tradition.

5. For a wider study of this phenomenon in the work of various Renaissance authors not including Milton, see Greenblatt, *Renaissance Self-Fashioning*; for its application to Milton, see Grossman, *"Authors to Themselves."*

6. Readers may object that I slight the text's narrative order by tracing the absolute chronology of the etiology of evil, straightening out what Milton purposely convoluted. I am confident, however, that the poet cared as much about his narrative's *historie* as he did about its *discours du récit* (to borrow Genette's famous distinction in *Narrative Discourse*). I say this with no thought of disparaging the assertion that significant meanings are produced by Milton's disposition of his material and by the reader's experience with that ordering. For insightful discussions of the poem's narrative strategies, see "Narrative and Meaning" in Hunter, *Paradise Lost*, 31–56, and Nyquist's essays "Reading the Fall" and "Gynesis." For examples of various reader-response interpretations of *Paradise Lost*, see Fish, *Surprised by Sin*; Crosman, *Reading* Paradise Lost; and Quilligan, *Milton's Spenser*.

7. See Shawcross, *Milton: The Critical Heritage*, 152, 252–53, and Johnson, *Life of Milton*, 465–66.

8. Milton often tells the same story from two or more points of view. He presents the Creation, for example, alternatively from divine and human points of view through two raconteurs, Raphael and Adam. The accounts in books 7 and 8 correspond to a similar doubling in Genesis. As Evans (*Genesis Tradition*, 256) noted some time ago, Raphael depicts the Creation "from above," like the priestly creation story of Genesis 1, while Adam sees the events "from below," like the Yahwistic version of Genesis 2. More recently, Nyquist has offered a much more complex discussion of the ideological motivations informing Milton's disposition of the two creation narratives in Genesis (see "Gynesis," esp. 185–92). I suggest that the two narratives of Satan's fall are likewise ideologically motivated. For another discussion of the relation between ideology and the allegorized elements in Satan's characterization, see Kendrick, *Study in Ideology*, 148–78.

9. For a minute, indeed casuistical, analysis of exactly when Satan fell, see Gallagher, *Milton, the Bible, and Misogyny*, 84–93. Gallagher locates the instant of Satan's fall precisely at the moment Satan asserts he is self-begotten (5.859–63).

10. Milton regularly locates the important incidents in *Paradise Lost* at meridian hours. One of the traditions the poem draws on is that of the "noonday devil": see Cirillo, "Noon-Midnight"; Cope, *Metaphoric Structure*, 130ff.; Burden, *Logical Epic*, 134–36; Patrides, *Christian Tradition*, 107–8; and the Hughes edition of *Paradise Lost*, 273n. In addition, Fowler's edition, 482n, cites a medieval tradition that the Fall of Adam and Eve, their Expulsion, and the crucifixion of Christ all occurred at the hour of noon.

11. Not even the assiduous Gallagher can pin down the exact moment of their fall. He insists only that it occurs after the birth of Sin: "At some subsequent moment, however, they fall" (*Milton, the Bible, and Misogyny*, 92).

12. This leads Broadbent to complain of Milton's "failure to motivate Satan evilly" (*Some Graver Subject*, 223). But as Shawcross rejoins, "Satan may not be motivated by someone or something other than the announcement [of the Son's exaltation] . . . to be so would have required the existence prior to that inflection point of someone or something that was already fallen. It is difficult to understand how Satan could be motivated evilly in terms that would satisfy Broadbent" (*Mortal Voice*, 153).

13. Williams, "Motivation of Satan's Rebellion"; Evans, *Genesis Tradition*, 223–27; and Revard, *War in Heaven*, 67–85, all discuss how Milton uses various theological traditions about Satan's envy. Clearly, Milton is working in a tradition. Even so, I concur with Evans: "Milton's analysis of it [Satan's envy] is one of the most genuinely original things in the whole poem" (224).

14. As Fish observes about the cause of the Fall, all that can finally be said is that Adam and Eve disobeyed because they were disobedient: "Properly seen, . . . more sophisticated analyses of cause are merely amplifications of the word 'disobedience,' indicating, variously, what disobedience involves (presumption, ingratitude), what Adam and Eve commit themselves to by disobeying (lust, anxiety). . . . To any one of these we can still demand, why? (what cause) and receive no satisfactory reply. It is the habit of criticism to use one description of the Fall to explain another" (*Surprised by Sin*, 259n).

15. See Grossman, *"Authors to Themselves,"* for a book-length study of self-authorship in *Paradise Lost*. My characterization of human freedom as individual yet also communal, disruptive yet historically coherent, finds support in Grossman's analysis of Miltonic self-authoring. According to Grossman, self-authoring involves "historical consciousness" whereby "one must conceive of oneself as a subject moving through time, both self-consistent and capable of change . . . author of a particular sort of life story, and actor in the broader world history of which his personal story forms a part." Likewise, my characterization of Satanic freedom as constituting a false subjectivity (see ch. 7) conforms to Grossman's remark: "The inability to function *historically* is manifest in Satan. . . . Satan, unable to enter history except as an agent of providence, retreats into the false autonomy of the objectless or nondialectical 'subject,' the unchanging mind" (6–7).

16. See chapter 5 of Grossman's *"Authors to Themselves"* for a discussion of Raphael's role as "divine historian."

17. Ricoeur, *Symbolism of Evil*, 257.

18. See *Philosophical Fragments*, 89–110, and "The Historical Point of View" in *Concluding Unscientific Postscript*, 25–47. In the former work, Kierkegaard insists on the freedom of events that *come to be* in history: "If the past is conceived as necessary, this can happen only by virtue of forgetting that it has come into existence"; and likewise, "Knowledge of the present does not confer necessity upon it; foreknowledge of the future gives it no necessity (Boethius); knowledge of the past confers no necessity upon the past; for no knowledge and no apprehension has anything of its own to give" (95, 99). As Miltonists well know, these passages echo the similarly Boethian position on foreknowledge and necessity articulated by Milton's God (*PL* 3.117–19). The relevance of these passages on foreknowledge for Milton's and Kierkegaard's theories of history is this: historical knowledge (in advance by God or retrospectively by a human historian) does not abrogate the freedom by which events come to be.

19. Ricoeur, *Symbolism of Evil*, 257.

20. Taylor, *Journeys to Selfhood*, 127.

21. See Collins, "World History vs. Ethical Life" (*Mind of Kierkegaard*, 133–36), for a discussion of Kierkegaard's attack on Hegel's "world historical outlook." Hegel, Kierkegaard maintains, forgets the ethical situation of the individual *qua* individual.

22. See my discussion of Milton's problematic effort to weld freedom onto biological evil in "'Say First What Cause,'" 52–54.

23. Here and throughout I use *Augustinian* narrowly, to refer to hereditary evil. Augustine's full understanding of evil is clearly much more complex than this usage suggests. As is well known, Augustine's early conceptions of evil, which evolve within an anti-Gnostic dialectic, deny that evil possesses physical reality. Evil has no nature; it is not being but doing; it is a defect, an inclination toward nonbeing, nothingness. Against the Gnostics and Manichaeans, Augustine pursues a decidedly voluntaristic line of thought. Subsequently, however, he asserts his own "quasi-Gnosticism" (inherited guilt) in his battles against the radical voluntarism of Celestius, Pelagius, and Julius Eclanus (see Ricoeur, "Original Sin," 272–81).

For a different account of the relation between *Paradise Lost* and Augustinian original sin, see Fiore's *Milton and Augustine* (esp. 42–60) and his entry "Augustine" in *A Milton Encyclopedia*. Asserting that original sin is the "theological basis" for *Paradise Lost*, Fiore (*Encyclopedia*, 115) finds Milton much more thoroughly Augustinian than I do. I see Milton as willing to use patristic and Reformation theology when it suits his purposes, but in principle skeptical of all "received opinions" and bound only by Scripture (*sola scriptura*) and conscience (cf. Milton's epistolary preface to *The Christian Doctrine* [*CP*, 6.117–24]).

24. My reading suggests that the Father's speech may be subtly rhetorical as well as simply axiomatic. Similarly, Lieb ("Celestial Dialogue") vigorously challenges the view of the Father as voiceless logician—a view typified by this passage from Fish's *Surprised by Sin*: the Father "does not argue, he asserts, disposing a series of self-evident axioms in an objective order, 'not talking to

anyone in particular but meditating on objects'" (86). To the contrary, Lieb contends, Milton constructs the colloquy between the Father and Son "in what amounts to a five-act drama" ("Celestial Dialogue," 218).

25. The following paragraph summarizes Ricoeur's splendid analysis in "Original Sin: A Study in Meaning." Standard studies of the development of the doctrine of Original Sin are Rondet, *Original Sin*, and Tennant *Sources of the Doctrines*.

26. Ricoeur, "Original Sin," 278.

27. Ibid., 279.

28. Ibid., 282.

29. Ibid., 280; see also 270.

30. "Before God," of course, describes a category crucial to the Kierkegaardian concepts of sin and guilt (e.g., *SD*, 77–82).

31. See Croxall, *Kierkegaard Studies*, 31, 89–92, and Dupré, *Kierkegaard as Theologian*, 49–61, 91, for further discussions of Kierkegaard's anti-Pelagian position on the self as individual and race. As Dupré correctly notes, Kierkegaard's strongly ethical emphasis on freedom "forced [him] constantly to guard against Pelagianism" (91). Ricoeur identifies Pelagius with other philosophies of the "strong mind" ("Original Sin," 285). In chapter 7, I discuss how both Milton and Kierkegaard reject such notions of freedom.

32. See especially 1.11 of *The Christian Doctrine* (*CP*, 6.382–92). Original Sin's conflation of moral and physical categories poses a less acute problem to the monist Milton than it does to most Christians, who are dualists. If spirit and matter belong on a continuum of substance, and if souls are transmitted by the act of propagation (rather than "created daily by the immediate act of God" [*CP*, 6.319]), it is but one more step to believe that the soul's moral corruption also is passed down sexually into the race.

33. Note how Michael's language echoes the Father's: "they themselves decreed / Thir own revolt, not I"; "and free they must remain, / Till they enthrall themselves"; "they themselves ordain'd thir fall" (3.116–17, 124–25, 128). The point of the multiple reflexives in both cases is to attach human evil to individual responsibility.

4

Anxious Knowledge

That Obscure Knowledge of Sin:
Knowing Evil in *The Concept of Anxiety*

Strictly speaking, according to Kierkegaard, Adam and Eve do not choose evil but leap into it (*CA*, 49).[1] This essential distinction between a choice and a leap corresponds to the nature of their knowledge.[2] A choice is based on knowledge, a leap on ignorance. As with the snake, the contrast between the Fall as choice and as leap points to decidedly divergent orientations dividing *Paradise Lost* and *The Concept of Anxiety*. Milton stresses Adam and Eve's comprehensive knowledge of evil before the Fall, in order to make the Fall the result of responsible choice; Kierkegaard emphasizes their existential ignorance of evil, in order to portray the Fall as a leap into the unknown. Yet, once again, within this fundamental difference persist numerous similarities as both works probe the intersection between knowing and being posited by Genesis and by Judeo-Christian culture generally. This chapter explores Kierkegaard's and Milton's views of how innocence and guilt affect one's knowledge of evil.

As Kierkegaard uses the term, *choice* presupposes prior knowledge of the difference between good and evil. This distinction is not fully comprehensible to Adam and Eve, because it is "a consequence of the enjoyment of the fruit" (*CA*, 44). In its most important sense, the distinction can be understood only existentially—that is, only through the experience of guilt. A choice is a finite, concrete decision to act upon preference for a known end. Adam and Eve's fall cannot have been a choice in this sense, any more than it could have simply enacted lustful desire. And for the same reason. To choose evil, they would have had first to desire it sinfully. But such desire (or *concupiscentia*) is, as we have seen, a "determinant of guilt and sin antecedent to guilt and sin" (*CA*, 40). Kierkegaard therefore associates choice with concupiscent desire because both tend to envision sin as the externalization of something already inwardly present; both tend to make the Fall "something successive" rather than something genuinely new (*CA*, 40).

The leap, by contrast, presupposes that the Fall breaks forth out of ignorance. But ignorance of what? Ignorance of the sphere of existence into which one enters by sin.[3] In Kierkegaardian philosophy, one enters a "sphere of existence" only by a leap, and no one can truly understand a sphere unless he or she is in it or has passed through it. Spheres are known only from the inside—that is, through one's own existence. (Hence, though Kierkegaard can describe the Knight of Faith's movements, he repeatedly confesses that he cannot understand the Knight for he has not attained that kind of faith.) The leap redefines existence: "in that very moment everything is changed" (*CA*, 62). It constitutes a breaking forth beyond the bounds of what can be known before the leap. As a leap, the Fall defines a moment when the innocent individual "goes beyond himself" and apprehends the world with new eyes and a new consciousness (*CA*, 62).

That which precipitates sin in Kierkegaard's Eden, then, cannot be desire for a known end. Adam and Eve have never tasted the fruit in order to desire it. Instead, what provokes the Fall is anxiety, the most rarefied form of anxiety, which Kierkegaard labels "objective." Objective anxiety describes pure possibility, unattached to any concrete course of action: "freedom's reflection within itself in its possibility" (*CA*, 56); it is the sensation one would feel when first awakened to one's "possibility of [or for] possibility" (*CA*, 42). Possibility "does not tempt like a choice, but ensnaringly disquiets with its sweet anxiousness" (*CA*, 61). Innocence was first lost under a sweet and fearful anxiety that had itself for its object; hence, "objective anxiety." In a fallen world, however, anxiety attaches itself to possibilities figured in history, culture, one's environment, and so forth; these seem to give anxiety a subject, and consequently postlapsarian anxiety is called "subjective anxiety." Until one personally sins, however, the object of anxiety—whether subjective or objective—remains abstract, or in Kierkegaard's terminology, "nothing." Anxiety acquires a concrete object only through sin—and then, as "anxiety of evil," it is something else altogether (see chapter 6).

Thoroughly instructed in the difference between good and evil, capable of choice, and tempted by a specifically forbidden desirable object (the fruit), Adam and Eve in *Paradise Lost* seem not to experience the rarefied objective anxiety that Kierkegaard posits for the first sinners. (Of course, they are *not* the first to sin—Satan is. And his fall, appropriately, looks distinctly like a leap into the unknown rather than a choice among known alternatives.) I do not wish to deny or mask the conflicting orientation of Milton's text toward informed innocence on the one hand, and Kierkegaard's toward ignorant innocence on the other. But I hope to demonstrate that the divergence is not so absolute as it appears: Milton's human protagonists know less about evil than we might suspect, while Kierkegaard's know more. First let us see how Kierkegaard complicates the difference between objective and subjective anxiety, until the "nothing" that is anxiety's object becomes more and more of a "something." Then let us see how innocence veils abstract knowledge about good and evil for Milton's Adam and Eve, how they are drawn to the fruit not in order to seize a known good but in order to leap beyond themselves into unknown possibilities, and how sin breaks open the distinction between good and evil (which they had heard about in Eden) in an entirely new way.

"Freedom's possibility," writes Kierkegaard, "is not the ability to choose the good or the evil. . . . The possibility is to *be able*" (*CA*, 49). Since an innocent Adam and Eve cannot know exactly what they are able to do, anxiety fixes upon possibility itself as the object.[4] This, as I have explained, Kierkegaard calls objective anxiety. However, even pure objective anxiety requires some wrinkle in innocence that provokes the sensation of possibility. For this reason, Kierkegaard speaks favorably of Leonhard Usteri's view that the prohibition itself constitutes a "conditioning cause" of sin (so long as the prohibition is thought to awaken only anxiety and not evil desire), and of Franz Bader's view of the temptation as freedom's "'necessary other'" (*CA*, 39).

Milton, too, recognizes in both *Paradise Lost* and *The Christian Doctrine* that as a "Pledge of Obedience," the interdicted tree makes both obedience and freedom possible (*PL* 8.325; *CP*, 6.352). But for Kierkegaard, the interdiction opens up the possibility not of evil desire but of possibility itself. The danger of an explanation such as Usteri's, Kierkegaard demurs, is that it lets the prohibition awaken sinful desire, thus evading the leap by making the Fall into something progressive (*CA*, 40). Desire cannot explain the origin of sin because desire (*concupiscentia*) is sin. What is wanted is an intermediate determinant that brings about the transition from innocence to guilt without itself being sinful. This, of course, is anxiety.

As a sympathetic antipathy and antipathetic sympathy, anxiety has the "elastic ambiguity" lacking in desire (*CA*, 41). Unlike desire, "fear and similar concepts that refer to something definite . . . anxiety is freedom's actuality as the possibility of possibility" (*CA*, 42). Rather than impart knowledge to Adam, the dreadful prohibition would concentrate his ignorance upon the "enigmatic word"; it would impart a "higher form of ignorance":

When it is stated in Genesis that God said to Adam, "Only from the tree of the knowledge of good and evil you must not eat," it follows as a matter of course that Adam really has not understood this word. . . . . When it is assumed that the prohibition awakens the desire, one acquires knowledge instead of ignorance, and in that case Adam must have had a knowledge of freedom, because the desire was to use it. The explanation is therefore subsequent. The prohibition induces in him anxiety, for the prohibition awakens in him freedom's possibility. . . . the anxious possibility of *being able*. He has no conception of what he is able to do. . . . Only the possibility of being able is present as a higher form of ignorance. (*CA*, 44-45)

Thus the prohibition supplies the hint of a subject within Adam's rarefied objective anxiety. From a fallen vantage, we would say Adam has begun to learn about good and evil when he hears the dreadful interdiction. But for Adam, such knowledge is really a "higher form of ignorance" because the distinction between good and evil is not yet concrete enough to permit evil to become the subject of sinful desire. Evil is still a "nothing," yet "a nothing that communicates vigorously with the ignorance of innocence," a nothing that begins to look "more and more a something," as it will for Adam's posterity (*CA*, 61-62).

Like the interdiction, the word of judgment ("Thou shalt surely die") also supplies Eden with anxious knowledge; it, too, confers not knowledge but a higher form of ignorance, for "Adam does not know what it means to die. On the other hand, there is nothing to prevent him from having acquired a notion of the terrifying" (*CA*, 45). Similarly, Adam may even have been able to talk about death, good, and evil, but "from the fact that Adam was able to talk, it does not follow that in a deeper sense he was able to understand what was said. This applies above all to the difference between good and evil, which indeed can be expressed in language, but nevertheless *is* only [intelligible] for freedom" (*CA*, 45-46). Kierkegaard thus characterizes Edenic existence as grounded in ignorant innocence; nevertheless, he admits Adam and Eve know of and talk about realities they cannot fully understand, realities that focus their attention on their own anxious possibility for possibility—that is, on their freedom. In this way he allows objective anxiety to begin to acquire subjects (good-evil; death). Yet these subjects point to realities beyond Adam and Eve's ken before the Fall.

Kierkegaard deploys our experience with dreams as an analogue for how the knowledge of evil is known yet not comprehended in Eden: "Anxiety is a qualification of dreaming spirit" (*CA*, 41). As the pressure that possible futures exert upon the present, anxiety haunts innocent bliss as a shadowy dream of what may (and will) be:

> In this state [innocence] there is peace and repose, but there is simultane-
> ously something else that is not contention and strife, for there is indeed
> nothing against which to strive. What, then, is it? Nothing. But what
> effect does nothing have? It begets anxiety. This is the profound secret of
> innocence, that it is at the same time anxiety. Dreamily the spirit projects
> its own actuality, but this actuality is nothing, and innocence always sees
> this nothing outside itself. (*CA*, 41)

In these suggestive comments on anxiety and dreams, it will be noted, Kierkegaard attaches anxiety to "spirit." A technical term, *spirit* requires a detour through Kierkegaard's definition of the self, a topic he develops at far greater length in *The Sickness unto Death*. A rough but helpful initial synonym for *spirit* is *self-consciousness*. Humans differ from beasts in that they have spirit—which means, in Kierkegaard, not a quasi-physical soul but self-consciousness of the relationship between mind and body. "Man is a synthesis of the psychical and the physical," Kierkegaard writes; "however, a synthesis is unthinkable if the two are not united in a third. This third is spirit" (*CA*, 43). Spirit is a third factor in human consciousness because it is neither sensation nor thought but the way we take consciousness of the relation between the two. Full consciousness of oneself as a divided creature—that is, as a synthesis of body and mind—is not available in innocence, because innocence designates a state of immediacy or unity with the natural condition. Nevertheless, the possibility of a rupture of this unity projects itself into Edenic innocence dreamingly. Here is how Kierkegaard says this in several different ways:

> In innocence, man is not qualified as spirit but is psychically qualified
> in immediate unity with his natural condition. The spirit in man is dream-
> ing. . . .
>   So spirit is present, but as immediate, as dreaming. . . .
>   In innocence, Adam as spirit was a dreaming spirit. Thus the synthesis
> is not actual, for the combining factor is precisely spirit, and yet this is not
> posited as spirit. (*CA*, 41, 43, 48–49)

To summarize, *spirit* defines man's relation to two poles that constitute human existence: the somatic (the temporal, finite, and necessary)
and the psychic (the eternal, infinite, free). Spirit is not a combination
of body and soul but a synthesis of them—meaning the conscious relationship between them. Spirit distinguishes humans from other life
forms, which may be seen in the fact that humans alone face selfhood
as a problem—specifically, in Kierkegaardian terms, as the problem of
synthesizing one's free, unbounded imaginative existence with one's lim-

ited, necessary, finite, corporal existence. This crisis of spirit ejects humans from an immediate, innocent unity with nature and propels them through successive varieties of despair catalogued in Kierkegaard's *The Sickness unto Death*. No unparadoxical configuration of self—not aesthetic, ethical, or conventional religious—eliminates despair; only the paradoxical self capable of placing absolute value on both the temporal and eternal simultaneously (as does the Knight of Faith in *Fear and Trembling*) is not afflicted by this "sickness unto death." Only by attaining the paradoxical faith of an Abraham is the crisis of spirit begun by sin resolved.

An innocent being like Adam has spirit, too; otherwise human life would remain merely bestial or vegetal and could never rise to the level of the human (*CA*, 42, 44, 53). But in Eden spirit manifests itself only dreamingly, as a fearful yet fascinating future possibility. Qualified by spirit, Edenic existence seems designed specifically to be broken apart, and thereby revealing the problematic nature of fallen selfhood. "Every human life is religiously designed" (*CA*, 105) to be so broken and healed. This future possibility is registered as *angst*, and in the first instance specifically as "objective" anxiety or anxiety over possibility of being able. Beyond the inherent restlessness of spirit seeking to manifest itself, however, two external conditions in Eden point humans to the future, seeming to provide anxiety an external object on which to fasten. In Eden, anxiety focuses on the prohibition (which, in naming the tree, posits a distinction between good and evil that innocence cannot yet fully understand) and the threat (which, in pronouncing the doom of death, introduces a concept that also cannot be understood). As anxiety's focal points, spirit, the prohibition, and the threat all figure possibilities that envelop Eden in dreaming knowledge of its future. They point to reality outside Adam's and Eve's existence, reality that hovers just beyond the horizon of full comprehension, but "disappears as soon as [one] seeks to grasp for it" (*CA*, 42).

After the Fall, the nature of anxiety changes: "Anxiety as it appeared in Adam will never again return, for by him sinfulness came into the world" (*CA*, 60). In the fallen world, "subjective anxiety signifies the anxiety that is present in the individual's state of innocence and corresponds to that of Adam, but it is nevertheless quantitatively different from that of Adam" (*CA*, 56). The distinction between prelapsarian and postlapsarian anxiety (or objective and subjective anxiety) obviously belongs to the same distinction Kierkegaard draws between the first sinner and the subsequent individual. Subjective anxiety expresses how anxiety acquires a "quantitative more" for historical individuals than it had in Eden. The subsequent individual (to whom, remember, Milton's Adam and Eve are equivalent since they inhabit a universe in which sinfulness already exists — as an actuality in hell and as a possibility in their historically informed consciousness) experiences an anxiety that is increasingly "knowledgeable" of sin all the while remaining existentially ignorant of it:

> In each subsequent individual anxiety is more reflective. This may be expressed by saying that the nothing that is the object of anxiety becomes, as it were, more and more a something. We do not say that it actually becomes a something or actually signifies something; we do not say that instead of a nothing we shall now substitute sin or something else, for what holds true of the innocence of the subsequent individual also holds true of Adam. (*CA*, 61)

So concrete does the object of subjective anxiety become that it looks more and more as if the subsequent individual's anxiety is about personal sin itself, rather than about sin as a "foreboding presentiment" (*CA*, 53). Apparently forgetting for a moment his proviso that the innocent individual cannot experience anxiety about sin, Kierkegaard explains the apex of subjective anxiety thus: "*anxiety about sin produces sin*"; or similarly, "the individual in anxiety about sin brings forth sin — namely, *the individual, in anxiety not about becoming guilty but about being regarded as guilty, becomes guilty*" (*CA*, 73; 74–75). By these formulas Kierkegaard means to suggest that subjective anxiety can seem to have something so concrete as sin or guilt as its object, even though these conditions remain abstract until one has oneself become sinful or guilty.

Subjective anxiety acquires a "more" quantitatively greater than Adam's in two ways, according to Kierkegaard: (1) as a "consequence of the relationship of generation," and (2) as a "consequence of the historical relationship" (*CA*, 62, 73). The first "more" has to do with the subsequent individual's greater sensuousness; the second with his greater historical knowledge of evil, or the way that history and culture confer anxious significance on things innocence cannot understand — as, for example, sexuality. For the later individual, both these "more's" seem to fill in the object of anxiety with a content, though all the while the object is essentially nothing because the subsequent individual's knowledge of fallen realities remains bracketed by ignorant innocence.

That history and culture conspire to supply a sort of content for the subsequent individual's anxiety seems clear and compelling to me. But I frankly admit that I fail to see any logic behind Kierkegaard's first contention, that the subsequent individual acquires greater sensuousness through the process of generation. Upon this dubious premise, nevertheless, Kierkegaard bases his analysis of the supposed greater sensuousness of Eve and women generally. No doubt Kierkegaard's thinking about gender is determined in large part by fairly conventional sexual stereotypes, summarized in "Sorties" by Héléne Cixous as the polarities by which man has been differentiated from woman as subject to "other":

> Activity/passivity,
> Sun/Moon,
> Culture/Nature,
> Day/Night,
>
> Father/Mother,
> Head/heart,
> Intelligible/sensitive,
> Logos/Pathos[5]

Conventional though they may be at base, Kierkegaard's ideas about gender are also illuminating in the same way Cixous's oppositions are, especially for how gender and sexuality get inscribed in *Paradise Lost* and, more broadly, Western culture. So let me try to explain Kierkegaard's views on woman and sex as they appear in *The Concept of Anxiety*.[6]

For some reason, Kierkegaard believes that as "derived" individuals, Eve and women generally are necessarily more sensuous than Adam and men. Kierkegaard offers this judgment not as an empirical claim based on statistical averages but as a statement about a "dissimilarity in the synthesis" between men and women. Nor does he argue that this difference in synthesis makes women inferior; but it does, he asserts, render them more alive to freedom and possibility and, consequently, more vulnerable to anxiety. This, however, suggests potential greatness of spirit as well as susceptibility to sin, since "the greatness of anxiety is a prophecy of the greatness of the perfection" (*CA*, 64).

Kierkegaard "proves" this difference of synthesis largely by contrasting the aesthetic ideals of the female and male figure in Greek art. While his analysis fails to "prove" essentialist gender differences (since the evidence itself derives from artifacts produced by culturally constructed gender codes), it does shed light on Western gender stereotypes, including those in *Paradise Lost*. For example, the first time we see Milton's Adam, the text focuses on Adam's head: "His fair large Front and Eye sublime declar'd / Absolute rule" (4.300–301) and hair, which "manly hung / Clust'ring, but not beneath his shoulders broad" (302–3). By contrast, the narrator's eye fails to pause upon Eve's face but follows her hair as it flows "down to the slender waist," waving in "wanton ringlets" that imply "subjection" (304–8). This establishes a pattern for Milton's idealizations of Adam and Eve: Man is all head; Woman is a whole body — head, heart, and "swelling breast" (495). Milton's idealization of Adam emphasizes discourse and reason; of Eve, it emphasizes grace and beauty. Moreover, Milton's Eve is frequently associated with flowers and nature, blending her human existence into that of the natural world, her consciousness into a dreamlike world of sleep and mirrored reflections. To Adam, Eve appears more firmly and immediately grounded in herself and her world than he: "so absolute she seems / And in herself complete, so well to know / Her own" (8.547–49). Eve is capable "Of what was high" but prefers to attend to cares closer to the earth — "her fruits and flow'rs," "her nursery" (8.39–58).[7] In none of this is Eve morally inferior to Adam; indeed, according to Raphael's injunction that Adam should "Think only what concerns thee and thy being" (174), she may be superior. But she is a different human synthesis from Adam, as he is from her.

Kierkegaard endorses similar stereotypes, offering some unusual explanations of what might, in part, lie behind Milton's idealizations. Woman's "ideal aspect" is beauty, Kierkegaard observes; this conforms to her more sensuous synthesis. Beauty indicates the primacy of the sensuous over the soulish in the feminine ideal. To the extent that woman's existence is teleologically aimed at beauty, it tends to exclude spirit, gravitating rather toward immediacy with the natural world. Or as Kierkegaard says, "When beauty must reign, a synthesis results, from which spirit is excluded" (*CA*, 65). He demonstrates this difference by looking at the contrasting conceptions of male and female beauty evident in Greek representations of Venus and Apollo. Venus's beauty, he notes, concentrates on the whole body, often portrayed in repose or asleep so that the activity of her mind and force of her personality are suspended. Apollo's beauty focuses on the head, the center of spiritual activity, traditionally as well as in Kierkegaard's special sense of the term:

> The spiritual has its expression in the face. In the beauty of the man, the face and its expression are more essential than in the beauty of the woman. . . . Venus is essentially just as beautiful when she is represented as sleeping, possibly more so, yet the sleeping state is the expression for the absence of spirit. For this reason, the older and the more spiritually developed the individuality is, the less beautiful it is in sleep, whereas the child is more beautiful in sleep. Venus arises from the sea and is represented in a position of repose, a position that reduces the expression of the face to the nonessential. If, on the other hand, Apollo is to be repre-

sented, it would no more be appropriate to have him sleep than it would be to have Jupiter do so. (*CA*, 65)

Sleep blends the facial features into the totality of the physical form. This suits the feminine ideal of beauty, Kierkegaard says, which achieves its impression as a whole or totality. Male beauty, by contrast, depends on the face to make its impression. All else is forgotten so long as the countenance is "distinct and noble" (*CA*, 66). These gender-based differences in the aesthetic ideals of man and woman suggest, to Kierkegaard, that the spirit dominates in the masculine synthesis while the body (or sensuousness) is more important in the feminine synthesis.

Although both Man and Woman in Genesis are equally innocent, Kierkegaard notes, because she is derived and therefore more sensuous, Woman is constituted with "a presentiment of a disposition that is not sinfulness but may seem like a hint of the sinfulness" (*CA*, 47). Yet by the same token, her synthesis makes her that much more disposed toward faith. For though her synthesis is more sensuous than Man's, like him, she too is "qualified by spirit"—that is, she is a creature of freedom. Therefore, however much she may be blended into the physical world, she can never sink wholly into pure sensuous beauty, like a flower. Spirit discovers in Woman's sensuousness a "more" that gives anxiety "greater scope" (*CA*, 64). Woman's greater anxiety makes her more susceptible to sin, but also, according to Kierkegaard, more open to salvation.

Eve's sensuousness is emphatically not sinful, Kierkegaard insists. Nor, he continues, is sensuousness experienced by the later individual sinful per se. Rather, sensuousness becomes sinful by sin, in Eden and again in history (*CA*, 63). Likewise, the sexual is not sinful until the Fall, at which time sexuality came to signify sinfulness (*CA*, 67; cf. 48–49). Kierkegaard, unlike Milton, thinks that sexual intercourse did not occur before the Fall. Although Adam and Eve were sexually differentiated in the Garden, they were ignorant of the significance of the sexual until they sinned. Before the Fall, sexuality and sensuousness constitute mildly disturbing features of innocence, occasions for the possibility of sin.

After the Fall, sensuousness and sexuality function in precisely the same way, only now Christian culture attaches to them even more anxiety by identifying them with sinfulness. The later individual knows that the "sensuousness may signify sinfulness," and this imparts to him an "obscure knowledge" of sin, which functions as a quantitative "more" in his existential situation. This "obscure knowledge" of sin is deposited in the culture; everyone knows it, yet no one truly understands it until he or she has lost innocence. Such "obscure knowledge" is abstract rather than experiential; it is still "nothing." Kierkegaard elaborates how the later individual knows yet doesn't know the distinction between good and evil except by the experience of guilt and how sin renders the sensuous and the sexual sinful in an entirely new way:

> We do not say that sensuousness is sinfulness, but that sin makes it sinfulness. Now if we consider the subsequent individual, every such individual has an historical environment in which it may become apparent that sensuousness can signify sinfulness. For the individual . . . this knowledge gives anxiety a "more." . . . It follows as a matter of course that the innocent individual does not as yet understand this knowledge, for it can only be understood qualitatively. However, this knowledge is again a new possibility, so that freedom . . . as it relates itself to the sensuous, comes into still greater anxiety. (*CA*, 73–74)

Thus the knowledge of sin is "obscurely present as a more or a less in the quantitative history of the race" (*CA*, 53). This "obscure knowledge" of sin does not impart full understanding of sin and guilt because such knowledge is available only existentially, through personal sin and guilt. It does, however, provide a "more" that makes anxiety's object seem more concrete and the leap more like a choice. It follows that no matter how much the later individual is warned about sin, he will remain essentially ignorant of it. Indeed ironically, warnings may in fact serve to heighten his anxiety, generating even more "pressure" or "momentum" (understood nondeterministically) toward sin: "A warning may bring an individual to succumb to anxiety (it should be remembered that, always, I only speak psychologically and never annul the qualitative leap), although of course the warning was intended to do the opposite. The sight of the sinful may save one individual and bring another to fall" (*CA*, 74).

For Miltonists, this observation immediately recalls an effect of the many warning voices that echo in Milton's Eden. The same may be said of a great many observations Kierkegaard makes that I have outlined in this chapter — even though the similarities may yet be somewhat obscured by Kierkegaardian jargon. Following, I shall attempt to describe how Kierkegaard's views on the interrelationship among innocence, sin, and knowledge bear upon Milton's poem. Within the comparisons I shall draw, however, one should remember the fundamental contrast with which I began this chapter: *The Concept of Anxiety* interprets the Fall as an ignorant leap; *Paradise Lost* sees it as an informed choice. Milton employs the only concept of freedom available to him: free will. *Liberum arbitrium* (free will), Kierkegaard protests, finitizes freedom by making its object good and evil (*CA*, 112; cf. 49–50). In contrast, Kierkegaard conceptualizes sin as a leap motivated by freedom's infinite possibilities rather than as a finite choice between fully conceived alternatives motivated by evil desire for one rather than the other. As I said at the outset, this difference cuts deep, even to the very roots of each author's outlook on the Fall. Yet, as we have now seen, Kierkegaard concedes greater and greater scope for the knowledge of sin within an essentially ignorant leap; hence, in the title of his chapter on objective and subjective anxiety, he speaks of anxiety's "progressive" accumulation as the obscure knowledge of sin becomes ever more distinct. Inversely, as we shall now see, Milton brackets Adam and Eve's wide knowledge of evil within existential ignorance. No matter how much they know about evil, only sin can rip away the veil. Their sinful "choices" thus bear strong resemblance to world-defining leaps into the unknown.

"Innocence That as a Veil": Unfallen Knowledge of Evil in *Paradise Lost*

Milton believes that the Fall has epistemological consequences.[8] Twice in his prose — first in *Areopagitica*, then in *The Christian Doctrine* — he specifies the Fall's effects on human knowing in nearly identical terms:

> Good and evill we know in the field of this World grow up together almost inseparably; and the knowledge of good is so involv'd and interwoven with the knowledge of evill, and in so many cunning resemblances hardly to be discern'd, that those confused seeds which were impos'd on *Psyche* as an incessant labour to cull out, and sort asunder, were not more intermixt. It was from out the rinde of one apple tasted, that the knowledge of good and evill, as two twins cleaving together, leapt forth into the World. And perhaps this is that doom which *Adam* fell into of knowing good and evill, that is to say, of knowing good by evill. (*CP*, 2.514)

> It was called the tree of knowledge of good and evil from the event ["*ab eventu*"]; for since Adam tasted it, we not only know evil, but we know good only by means of evil ["*per malum*"]. (Sumner trans. in *The Works of John Milton* 15.115; cf. *CP*, 6.352)[9]

Both passages affirm that since the Fall humans know good by evil. In *Areopagitica*, however, knowing good by evil seems to refer principally to a mental process of comparative cognition (Psyche's labors); in *The Christian Doctrine* knowing good by evil appears to refer to an existential perspective acquired through personal guilt (*per malum*). It is this latter, existential interpretation of Adam's doom that best describes the epistemological effect of the Fall in *Paradise Lost*.

After all, Milton's Adam and Eve know good from evil cognitively before the Fall. Indeed, the whole point of Raphael's mission is to enable them to make an informed moral choice between good and evil, which presupposes they are capable of rationally distinguishing good from evil. The War in Heaven functions like "bad books" in *Areopagitica*, serving "to discover, to confute, to forewarn, and to illustrate" evil for "the discreet and judicious Reader" (*CP*, 2.512–13) — in this case, Adam and Eve. Yet no matter how much they know about good and evil, sin opens their eyes so that they know good by evil in an utterly new way.[10]

Obviously, *Areopagitica* does not recommend this means of knowing the good by evil, for Milton knows his readers' eyes are already opened by sin: "Assuredly we bring not innocence into the world, we bring impurity much rather" (*CP*, 2.515). Instead, *Areopagitica* endorses the notion that fallen humanity knows good by evil through the cognitive process of comparing and contrasting. It imagines the fallen world as constituted of intermingled oppositions, often difficult to discern owing to "cunning resemblances" between right and wrong. In such a world, one knows good by evil through strenuous deliberation, a necessarily slow and laborious endeavor. Contrastive knowledge requires the tedious culling out and sorting asunder of true seeds from false, like the labor Venus imposed on Psyche; or like Isis's effort to gather up "limb by limb" "the mangled body of Osiris" that had been hewn "into a thousand peeces and scatter'd . . . to the four winds" (*CP*, 2.549). By understanding Adam's doom through the Psyche and Osiris myths, Milton insinuates to Parliament that painstaking deliberation was unnecessary in Eden. These metaphors imply that sin cast humankind out of an intuitive, immediate, "angelic" mode of apprehension and into a wearisome world of ratiocination — a view corroborated in Christian tradition by the image of an intuitive Adam naming the animals.[11]

Although Milton tacitly subscribes to this interpretation of Adam's doom in *Areopagitica*, it is *not* the interpretation to which he later ascribes in either *Paradise Lost* or *The Christian Doctrine*. In *Paradise Lost*, the "Knowledge of Good [is] bought dear by knowing ill" (4.222) not because it is acquired through a tedious mode of cognition but because it is paid for by guilt. Milton's Adam and Eve are fully capable of comparative judgments (Psyche's labor) before the lapse; they already enjoy the liberty of scouting and scanning the verbal regions of sin and falsity, for which Milton lobbies Parliament. From Adam's own mouth comes testimony that he, like God, could have read unlicensed heresy in Eden without loss of innocence: "Evil into the mind of God or Man / May come and go, so unapprov'd, and leave / No spot of blame behind" (4.117-19). "Evil," in a narrowly cognitive sense as Adam employs it here, enters human consciousness even before the dream. In fact, God himself introduces the idea of evil by means of the prohibition. This lays down the foundational polarity between "ought" and "ought not," thereby enabling contrastive knowledge of good by evil. Milton's Adam and Eve thus know *of* good and evil innocently almost from the first moment of creation. When they transgress, however, they know good *by* evil in an utterly new way: they know evil existentially, through personal guilt.

This is the interpretation of Adam's doom that Milton urged in *The Christian Doctrine* when he recast the idea of knowing of good by evil first mentioned in *Areopagitica*. Milton's meaning, however, is blurred in Charles Sumner's widely used translation. Sumner, perhaps consciously echoing the famous purple passage in *Areopagitica*, translates Milton's text as "we know good by means of evil" — as if the Latin were an ablative of means, *mala*. In fact, however, the original carries a much more active, experiential sense than Sumner's translation connotes, for Milton employs the accusative *"per malum,"* or "through evil." Knowing good *per malum* suggests that since the Fall we, like Adam and Eve, know evil through our mutual sinfulness. Consonant with this, *The Christian Doctrine* holds that the fruit conferred knowledge of good and evil not from any inherent quasi-magical properties but from the experience of sin itself (*ab eventu*). To know good from evil *ab eventu* implies that sinning transformed an abstract, verbal distinction into something new and profoundly revelatory — the knowledge of good by the experience of guilt.

This existential explication of Adam's doom, though significantly different from the cognitive interpretation provided by *Areopagitica*, is clearly the view most fully endorsed by *The Christian Doctrine* and *Paradise Lost*. In these works of Milton's maturity, as in *The Concept of Anxiety*, the Fall marks an existential cataclysm, after which nothing is the same; a rupture that opens up the distinction between good and evil in an utterly new way.

That sin should be eye-opening at all might seem somewhat surprising, given all that Milton's human protagonists have both seen and heard about evil before their lapse. Nevertheless, after they transgress the narrator reports that Adam and Eve

> Soon found thir eyes how op'n'd, and thir minds
> How dark'n'd; innocence that as a veil
> Had shadow'd them from knowing ill, was gone,
> Just confidence, and native righteousness,
> And honor from about them, naked left
> To guilty shame.
>
> (9.1053–58)

Despite all they have learned about evil before the Fall, Adam and Eve are still characterized as having been "shadowed from knowing ill." Milton evidently believes that innocence constitutes in itself a kind of ignorance—just as, conversely, experience constitutes a kind of knowledge. Sexual knowledge presents a ready analogue to Milton's usage. However much the uninitiated may learn about sex, they remain fundamentally ignorant of the subject; thus all their knowledge may be regarded as but a higher form of ignorance. Likewise, the knowledge of "ill" remains "veiled" to unfallen Adam and Eve even though they receive an extensive education in evil for four books.

Cognitively informed but existentially ignorant, Milton's unfallen Adam and Eve know good by evil in one sense but not in another, deeper sense. Their "veiled" knowledge of ill equates to the "obscure" knowledge of evil identified in *The Concept of Anxiety*. Recall that, according to Kierkegaard, obscure knowledge of sin accumulates progressively—from the minimal awareness first conveyed in Eden through the prohibition and the threat, to the extensive knowledge deposited historically and culturally in fallen environments. For Milton, a comparable accumulation occurs within the course of Edenic prelapsarian life itself, as Adam and Eve are educated in the nature and history of evil and (what is more significant) in their own possibility for sin. They are increasingly knowledgeable about evil, yet their understanding is still veiled, obscure.

Disobedience changes this. I hasten to add, however, that in *Paradise Lost* the Fall does *not* alter the fundamental nature of human cognition. Having eaten the fruit, Milton's Adam and Eve are not suddenly transformed from intuitive into deliberative creatures.[12] Indeed as poet, Milton largely ignores the tradition of an intuitive Adam, whose "angelic understanding" is figured in Scripture by his naming of the animals. *Paradise Lost* alludes to this event only twice (7.493; 8.352–54), and each time only briefly and in such a way as to imply that Adam's sudden apprehension marks the exception rather than the rule for human epistemology.[13]

When telling Raphael how God enlightened his "sudden apprehension" as he named the animals, Adam attributes his instant comprehension to God's special providence rather than to his own powers: "I nam'd them as they pass'd, and understood / Thir Nature, with such knowledge God endu'd / My sudden apprehension" (8.352–54). Adam's recollection is filled with wonder at the event, as if he is still struck by the extraordinary, atypical nature of his sudden apprehension. Moreover, he attributes his knowledge to God's special providence rather than to his own powers, as if his extraordinary power to name the beasts were equivalent to glossolalia. Quite obviously Adam's "angelic" intuition is not the normal human mode of knowing in Eden. Raphael confirms this elsewhere by explicitly contrasting Adam's discursive knowledge to his own angelic intuitive knowledge (5.488–90; cf. 7.176–79). Furthermore, Milton implies that Adam's intuitive knowledge about the world is incomplete, for immediately after telling Raphael about naming the animals, Adam recalls his nameless, unaccountable sense of need (filled later by Eve), thus acknowledging that there is much about his world he cannot name, does not fully intuit, and in which he needs instruction.

Raphael's version of Adam's naming the animals similarly hints that Man's intuitive grasp of animal nature was far from complete. After cataloguing the beasts in his Hymn of Creation, Raphael acknowledges to Adam: "And thou thir Natures know'st, and gav'st them Names, / Needless to thee repeated" (7.493–94). Then in his next breath, as if to undercut this compliment, the sociable archangel calls attention to the nature of one particular beast whose nature, at least from a historical point of view, Adam's intuition has not penetrated fully:

> nor unknown
> The Serpent subtl'st Beast of all the field,
> Of huge extent sometimes, with brazen Eyes
> And hairy Mane terrific, though to thee
> Not noxious, but obedient at thy call.
>
> (7.494–98)

Adam cannot know, even with his intuition about the created world, how to value Raphael's ambiguous description of the serpent. For Adam has only the enigmatic epithet, "subtle," and the obscure angelic animus toward the snake implied in the phrase "though to *thee* / Not noxious" to heighten his dim sense of the snake as an object of possible concern.

Adam's naming of the beasts, then, does not imply that unfallen Man in *Paradise Lost* enjoys extraordinary powers of intuition. Rather the event exemplifies, if anything, the human gift of language itself. Lan-

guage, unlike intuition, typifies for Milton the logocentric character of
human existence before as well as after the Fall.[14] In good Protestant
tradition, Milton's Eden is full of the word. His Garden reverberates
with homilies, exhortations, moral exempla, and other utterances that
verbally fill out the contrast between good and evil established initially
in the prohibition.[15] The rich verbal profusion of Milton's paradise
stands in marked contrast to Kierkegaard's Eden, in which Adam's ability to speak is consistently minimized (see *CA*, 45–46). Linguistically, as
in every other way, Milton's Adam and Eve enjoy much wider scope
than Kierkegaard's primordial humans. Yet the difference remains one
of degree not kind, as that between the first sinner and the subsequent
individual. Innocent beings, Kierkegaard reminds us, may know evil less
well than appears from the fact that they talk about it. *The Concept of
Anxiety* invites us to scrutinize how Milton's prelapsarian protagonists
apprehend knowledge that is deposited solely in language, such as the
knowledge of evil.

Kierkegaard takes a minimalist view of Adam's power to speak, comparing Adam's utterance in naming the animals "to that of children who
learn by identifying animals on an A B C board" (*CA*, 46). In this view,
Adam has a lexicon but an imperfect grasp of what the vocabulary
means. For although primal man is able to talk about evil and death,
Kierkegaard observes, "in a deeper sense" he does not fully understand
the words he utters (*CA*, 45). In particular the threat of death imparts a
vague "notion of the terrifying" to Kierkegaard's Adam, though the
word *death* as yet lacks concrete signification (*CA*, 45).

Likewise, Milton's Adam senses something ominous in the word
death, though he cannot say what it means. He tells Raphael that God
"pronounc'd / The rigid interdiction, which resounds / Yet dreadful in
mine ear" (8.333–35), suggesting that the word *death* has left a strong
impression of something fearful and foreboding. Yet, when instructing
Eve in the significance of the tree, Adam discloses that he does not really
understand what death means; he knows only that it must be something
dreadful:

> of all the Trees
> In Paradise that bear delicious fruit
> So various, not to taste that only Tree
> Of Knowledge, planted by the Tree of Life,
> So near grows Death to Life, whate're Death is,
> Some dreadful thing no doubt; for well thou know'st
> God hath pronounc't it death to taste that Tree.
>
> (4.421–27)

Michael Lieb offers the following analogy to illustrate Adam's predicament: "To understand the full impact of what God has imposed upon Adam, we might render the situation in the following terms: 'Do not touch the tip of your left ear with your right forefinger, or else you will *squibbledydib*.' Our response, like Adam's, would appropriately be, 'what ere *squibbledydib* is, / Som dreadful thing no doubt.'"[16] Though Adam can talk about God's threat of death, to the point that he even sets himself up as Eve's tutor on the subject, his explanation reveals that ignorance circumscribes the understanding of both teacher and pupil.

Adam's phrasing is subsequently echoed by Satan, who overhears this speech, during the Temptation:

> Shall that be shut to Man, which to the Beast
> Is open? or will God incense his ire
> For such a petty Trespass, and not praise
> Rather your dauntless virtue, whom the pain
> Of Death denounc't, whatever thing Death be.
>
> (9.691–95)

Satan's rhetoric plays off the still vague and merely verbal notions of death and evil (cf. "if what is evil / Be real," 9.698–99) against the concrete "good" promised in the example of his empowerment by eating the fruit: "look on mee, / Mee who have touch'd and tasted, yet both live, / And life more perfect have attained" (9.687–89). Eve must weigh a future abstract evil against an immediate empirical good, faith against sight. To be sure, she and Adam are well informed *about* the prohibition and the punishment. Nevertheless, as Kierkegaard reminds us, it does not follow that they have understood the words "in a deeper sense." The fact they can talk about fallen realities before they transgress is no guarantee that they understand, fully, the language they employ.

Milton criticism needs to consider more carefully than it has how Adam and Eve's confinement to discourse affects the knowledge of evil they extract from Raphael's lessons. If it is hard even for readers who inhabit a sinful world to imagine the "fight unspeakable" that Raphael accommodates as best as he can to human discourse, it must be well-nigh impossible for Adam and Eve to fathom the War in Heaven, given their innocence.[17] We glimpse a brief reminder of their difficulty in a parenthetical aside within one of Raphael's similes about the Creation. Describing God's dividing of the waters from the firmament, Raphael explains through a military analogy how the elements obeyed the Lord's command:

> such flight the great command impress'd
> On the swift floods: as Armies at the call
> Of Trumpet (for of Armies thou hast heard)
> Troop to thir Standard, so the wat'ry throng,
> Wave rolling after Wave . . .
>
> (7.294–99)

Yes, Adam and Eve have *heard* of armies — from Raphael himself; but if war lies outside their experience in the first place, the comparison can hardly be very helpful.[18] The simile asks them to compare one unknown to another.

I do not mean to imply that the War in Heaven would be totally incomprehensible to Adam and Eve, only to suggest that they could not have understood Raphael's narrative in the same way we have — especially insofar as our comprehension depends upon the experience of such feelings as rebelliousness, pride, envy, and hate that Adam and Eve know only through language, not (like us) by experience. To them, the War in Heaven must seem even more surreal than it did to Dr. Johnson. Their difficulty arises, however, not principally from "the confusion of spirit and matter which pervades the whole narration of the war"[19] but from its depiction of a moral phenomenon "so unimaginable as hate in Heaven" (*PL* 7.54).

That "our great Progenitor" finds the evil of Raphael's history unfathomable and strange is evinced in the two parallel observations about Adam's reaction that frame the war narrative. Upon first hearing the tidings that some angels are fallen, Adam tells Raphael "though what thou tell'st / Hath past in Heav'n, some doubt within move, / But more desire to hear, if thou consent, / The full relation, which must needs be strange" (5.554–56). After Raphael's dreadful history is ended, the narrator thus summarizes what Adam and Eve have learned:

> He with his consorted *Eve*
> The story heard attentive, and was fill'd
> With admiration, and deep muse to hear
> Of things so high and strange, things to thir thought
> So unimaginable as hate in Heav'n,
> And War so near the Peace of God in bliss
> With such confusion. . . .
>   Whence *Adam* soon repeal'd
> The doubts that in his heart arose; and now
> Led on, yet sinless, with desire to know
> What nearer might concern him.
>
> (7.50–56, 59–62)

Though sin has more content for the sinless Patriarch and Matriarch in Book 7 than it had in Book 5, they remain more dumbstruck than comprehending at something so strange and unimaginable as hate in heaven. Moreover, far from removing Adam's initial "doubt" about disobedient spirits, Raphael's history merely increases his "doubts." Evil has become even more disturbing. The effect of Raphael's history is thus analogous to that of Eve's dream: both introduce into innocent minds a certain knowledge of evil; yet since this knowledge still lies outside Edenic experience, it constitutes a knowledge qualified by ignorance — or what Kierkegaard calls a higher form of ignorance.

I take Adam's "doubts" that frame Raphael's narrative of the War in Heaven to be the proximate equivalent of anxiety. His doubts register spiritual disturbances engendered by the obscure knowledge of evil. What is more, like Kierkegaardian anxiety strictly defined, Adam's doubts may refer specifically to himself and his newly discovered human possibility for transgression, and not simply to his difficulty understanding and believing the narrative. For although Kierkegaardian anxiety may be occasioned by the "obscure knowledge" of sin deposited out in the world, essentially anxiety is never really about the world but about the self — that is, about one's possibility for possibility. Kierkegaardian anxiety thus describes self-doubt about one's own capacity for freedom. Milton hints that the doubts provoked in Adam by Raphael's narrative are also self-doubts. Adam's doubts in Book 7, we are told, arise not in his mind but in his heart. This suggests that "doubts" here signifies something much deeper and more intimate than intellectual uncertainty (such as critics usually express about the narrative). It may be that Adam's uncertainty alludes, rather, to some uneasiness about his own possibility for sin; hence, the narrator insists that Adam is "yet sinless" (7.61) — the exact phrase used in the last stages of Eve's temptation.

The "doubt" Adam confesses to in Book 5 is even more clearly associated with anxiety over freedom rather than simple intellectual uncertainty. In Book 5, Adam's doubts are stirred first by Raphael's puzzling remark "If ye be found obedient" (499). His conditional phrase disturbs Adam because it points to heretofore scarcely imagined possibility:

> What meant that caution join'd *if ye be found*
> *Obedient*? can we want obedience then
> To him, or possibly his love desert
> Who form'd us from the dust?
>
> (5.513–16)

Raphael then instructs Adam in possibility, explaining that Adam's future progress as well as continued bliss rests solely upon the proper exercise of his freedom, which others in the universe already have misused by rebelling. This incites Adam's "doubt," and so follows the narrative of the War in Heaven.

A Kierkegaardian Adam would swoon with anxiety merely at Raphael's reminder of human possibility, would faint from anxiety's vertigo during the panorama of abused freedom that follows. Milton's Adam is notably steadier on his feet when contemplating his freedom. Yet he is not so self-assured as to be without self-doubts. Having assimilated Raphael's history lesson, Adam later warns Eve as Raphael had warned him that "within himself / The danger lies" (9.348–49); the real threat to their continued innocence is posed not by the "outward force" that assails them but by yielding from within. In the awareness of their possibility for sin, lies anxiety. Adam's debate with Eve reveals how much Raphael's warnings have focused their minds upon the possibility of transgression.

Thus Raphael's hortatory cautions and admonitory history, intended of course to prevent sin, ironically seem to hasten the Fall by heightening Adam's and Eve's awareness of their precarious capacity to disobey — just as Kierkegaard describes (*CA*, 74). By the end of Book 8, a fully instructed human pair seems more likely and capable than ever of sinning since they are more cognizant than before of evil and of freedom. I do not say that they are really any closer to sin than before Raphael's visit, only that the content of their anxiety becomes more concrete with every increase in consciousness of sin — "but here it is important not to allow oneself to be deluded by determinants of approximation: a 'more' cannot bring forth the leap, and no 'easier' can in truth make the explanation easier" (*CA*, 60). Nevertheless, each injunction not to abuse free will, not to partake of the interdicted tree, increases Adam and Eve's (as well as the reader's) awareness of their possibility for sin and of the looming presence of the tree.

Not only the tree becomes more an object of anxiety through Raphael's warnings; other areas of life in Eden also assume a more fearful and alluring aspect by their being identified as potential sources of divine displeasure. When Raphael arrives in Paradise, Adam and Eve know only one provocative object (the tree); when the garrulous angel leaves, his warnings have conferred the aura of prohibition upon love and knowledge as well. The Adam who bids Raphael farewell in Book 8 has been made to feel that his boundless love for Eve may be dangerous if he does not keep it within bounds (see 8.560ff.). Similarly, he has been cautioned that his curiosity must be kept "within bounds" (7.120). While

Raphael does not prohibit love or curiosity in the same way God does the fruit, Raphael's warnings extend the concept of boundaries beyond eating to loving and questioning. These admonitions make the Garden proportionally more full of anxiety. Raphael adds quantitatively more to Eden's anxiety:[20] whereas before, Adam and Eve knew only of an interdicted tree, they now know that sex and curiosity are potentially dangerous, thus making them resemble Kierkegaard's later individuals who find themselves in a world where the sexual is disturbingly linked to the sinful. Everyone knows this, but only the sexually initiated know it in the full sense.

Raphael's warnings about erotic love in particular strengthen the analogy between Milton's Adam and Kierkegaard's subsequent individual. In Book 4, Adam and Eve enjoy an erotic relationship that appears serenely unproblematic. By the time Raphael leaves Eden, although presumably still capable of innocent love-making, Adam could scarcely regard his wife with equally untroubled eyes. Ironically, the divisiveness vented in their subsequent debate and enacted in their physical separation seems somehow made possible by Raphael's lesson in patriarchal priorities. During his final colloquy with the visiting heavenly messenger, Adam for the first time has had to define his sexuality not as sinful *per use*, but as dangerous. The sexual has come to be tangentially related to the sinful. Just as the prohibition tinges appetite in general with a trace of anxiety, so Raphael's warning against sexual love taints the erotic with a trace of dread. Analogously, Kierkegaard's later individual obscurely "knows" that the sensuous and the sexual may signify sin; this "general knowledge" (*CD*, 66) laces sensuousness with possibility for sin, which in turn occasions new opportunities for anxiety.

Thus by the time of the Fall, Milton's Adam and Eve strongly resemble Kierkegaard's later individual. They no longer have merely the enigmatic word of prohibition and punishment to arouse anxiety but are fully instructed in their possibilities for sin. To borrow Kierkegaard's vocabulary, Milton's Adam and Eve have heard so much about sin that it has become almost a "something" (although the full "somethingness" of sin awaits the concrete experience of personal guilt). Furthermore, quantitatively more aspects of Edenic existence share the aura taboo than was true on the morning of Creation—including curiosity and sexuality. In addition, Adam and Eve have become more "reflective," not only about evil abstractly considered but also about their own possibility for disobedience (see 9.342ff.). Nevertheless, innocence still qualifies all they hear and feel and know about evil. Sin remains veiled to them by innocence; it hovers, dreamingly, like a phantasmagoria, on the borders of Edenic bliss, figuring an obscure knowledge of evil.

"Thir Eyes How Op'n'd": Fallen Knowledge of Evil in *Paradise Lost*

In his dense and frequently baffling chapter "Anxiety as Explaining Hereditary Sin Progressively," Kierkegaard advances another meaning for "objective anxiety," one very different from the one I have already explicated (that is, the fearful fascination over one's possibility for possibility itself). Kierkegaard also uses "objective anxiety" to refer to the effects of sin upon the objective world: "By coming into the world, sin acquired significance for the whole creation. This effect of sin in nonhuman existence I have called objective anxiety" (*CA*, 57). The Fall's effect upon nature is to render the objective world more polar than before. Sin thus accentuates the natural world's oppositions, just as it awakens human consciousness to the contrasts inherent in body and soul (that is, to "spirit"). In fact, Kierkegaard is far less interested in the objective effects of the Fall on the physical world (this belongs to dogmatics rather than psychology, he asserts) than in the way sin causes humans to *perceive* the natural world differently. Because of the Fall, all "creation *is placed* in an entirely different light" (*CA*, 58; my emphasis). By "objective anxiety," then, Kierkegaard designates the parallel consequences of the Fall upon nature and upon the way nature is perceived: the Fall cracks nature and dis-integrates the way we know it.

In *Paradise Lost*, too, the Fall rips apart nature, creating "hateful contraries" where before there was "grateful vicissitude" (see 10.650ff.). Eve eats and "Earth felt the wound"; Adam tastes and "Nature gave a second groan" (9.782, 1001). The world is broken by sin, fragmented, rendered dichotomous.[21] What is more, Milton links the Fall's effects on the nonhuman sphere with its effects on the sinner's cognitive world. Sin introduces Adam and Eve into newly dichotomous modes of perception, so that the external disintegration in nature corresponds with internal disorder in the psyche, as Kierkegaard also proposes. Notice how the weather imagery in the following description of newly guilty Adam and Eve links the physical and psychological consequence of sin:

> but not at rest or ease of Mind,
> They sat them down to weep, nor only Tears
> Rain'd at thir Eyes, but high Winds worse within
> Began to rise, high Passions, Anger, Hate,
> Mistrust, Suspicion, Discord, and shook sore
> Thir inward State of Mind, calm Region once
> And full of Peace, now toss't and turbulent.
>
> (9.1120–26)

Further securing the nexus between inward and outward weather, Milton puns by introducing Adam's lament: "From thus *distemper'd* breast" (9.1131; my emphasis).

For both Kierkegaard and Milton, then, sin rends apart the external world. Concomitantly, and at least as significantly, it tears asunder the self as well. Kierkegaard understands the consequence of sin for the newly sinful individual as an emergence of "spirit." This is to say, sin makes the relationship between body and soul suddenly problematic; the sinner instantly becomes cognizant of the dualities that define human existence as sin throws into sharp relief the contrasts both in the world and in the self. More specifically, according to Kierkegaard (who imagines sin as a leap into the "Aesthetic"), sin "degrades" the sensuous to signify sinfulness. That is, sin makes the sexual sinful.

Milton, too, believes that sin rends asunder both nature and the self and that this divisiveness transforms the sensuous into something sinful. His fallen Adam and Eve find selfhood newly problematic after they transgress. Their predicament, moreover, has everything to do with a new dominance by the sensuous ("appetite") over and against other human faculties:

> For Understanding rul'd not, and the Will
> Heard not her lore, both in subjection now
> To sensual Appetite, who from beneath
> Usurping over sovran Reason claim'd
> Superior sway.
>
> (9.1127-31)

Thus for Milton, as for Kierkegaard, the Fall degrades innocent sensuality. This may best be seen in the poem's two contrasting love-making scenes; these offer *loci classici* for measuring the effect of sin upon Adam and Eve against Kierkegaard's maxim that sin transforms the sensuous into the sinful.

Kierkegaard rejects the idea of unfallen sex in Eden. Yet although sex becomes possible only after the Fall (*CA*, 67-73), he concedes that sensuousness is present in Eden from the beginning: "Sensuousness in innocence is not sinfulness; nevertheless sensuousness is there. Adam of course needed food, drink, etc." (*CA*, 80). Like Kierkegaard, Milton also insists that sensuous pleasures are very much a part of innocent life in Eden. Moreover, as one of the great poets of pastoral luxuriance, he makes us *feel* the high sensuality of Paradise. One typically evocative passage from Book 4, which serves as the center of blameless sensuality in Milton's Eden, displays with what ardor the poet imagines what Kierkegaard rather anemically recognizes: sensuousness in Eden:

> They [Adam and Eve] sat them down, and after no more toil
> Of thir sweet Gard'ning labor than suffic'd
> To recommend cool *Zephyr*, and made ease
> More easy, wholesome thirst and appetite
> More grateful, to thir Supper Fruits they fell,
> Nectarine Fruits which the compliant boughs
> Yielded them, side-long as they sat recline
> On the soft downy Bank damaskt with flow'rs:
> The savory pulp they chew, and in the rind
> Still as they thirsted scoop the brimming stream . . .
>
> (4.327–36)

Books 4 and 5 are replete with such pastoral scenes — each filled with richly sensuous images of Adam and Eve, focusing particularly on gustatory delights. In these middle books, eating becomes a subtheme of sorts (extending even to epic talk of angelic digestion!). Adam and Eve's evident delight in the pleasures of eating and sex is innocent yet vaguely anxiety-ridden (especially for the reader), for eating a certain delicious fruit is the one thing they must not do.

The "blissful Bower" near the end of Book 4 culminates the sensuousness of Milton's Eden. Chosen and adorned by God "when he fram'd / All things to man's delightful use" (4.691–92), its chief delight is the sexual love that it was fashioned to harbor. Unlike Kierkegaard, Milton boldly insists that Paradise allows the full gamut of sensual pleasure, including sexual intercourse. Yet, knowing the terrible power of sensuality in our fallen world to subordinate everything else to the sway of erotic desire (including the love of God and charity toward humankind), Milton as narrator cannot but sense the potential danger of the desires protected by the bower of bliss.[22] Countering his readers' (and perhaps his own) anxiety, the narrator strenuously defends innocent "wedded love" against its sinful counterfeits:

> Hail wedded Love, mysterious Law, true source
> Of Human offspring, sole propriety
> In Paradise of all things common else.
> By thee adulterous lust was driv'n from men
> Among the bestial herds to range. . . .
> Here Love his golden shaft imploys, here lights
> His constant Lamp, and waves his purple wings,
> Reigns here and revels; not in the bought smile
> Of Harlots, loveless, joyless, unindear'd,
> Casual fruition, not in Court Amours,
> Mixt Dance, or wanton Mask, or Midnight Ball,

> Or Serenate, which the starv'd Lover sings
> To his proud fair, best quitted with disdain.
>
> (4.750-54, 763-70)

The poet's negations in this passage acknowledge the disturbing power of eroticism to err, to assume any of its countless sinful manifestations, such as harlotry and courtly love, with which he and his readers are so familiar. The narrator's aggressive defense of sexual love's innocence imbues it with anxiety—not for Adam and Eve (this comes later, through Raphael's warnings) but for us.

Conversely, Milton transforms one presumably opprobrious variety of pagan eroticism, Ovidian love, into something beautiful and blameless: "Here love his golden shaft imploys / His constant Lamp, and waves his purple wings, / Reigns here and revels." In like fashion, the poet repeatedly detoxifies terms associated with sinfulness as he creates a pastoral landscape that trembles with potential to turn into something fallen:[23] brooks run through Eden "with mazy *error*," the purpled grapevine "gently creeps *luxuriant*," and Eve wears her hair "*dishevell'd* . . . in *wanton* ringlets wav'd" (4.239, 259-60, 306; my emphasis). Here again, the sensuous is innocent yet dreadful—at least for postlapsarian readers who know full well the evil significance latent in Milton's language. Although Eden's luxuriance initially holds no special significance for Adam and Eve, it eventually comes to acquire anxiety as they are warned by the divine voice (about eating) and by Raphael (about loving). Thus the sensuous and the sexual are not sinful in Milton's Eden; they are, however, dreadful—to the reader and narrator from the first, and to Adam and Eve the more they learn.

That which protects the primal pair from experiencing their sensuousness and sexuality as sinful is their innocent integrity (or, literally, "wholeness"). "Then was not guilty shame," writes the poet of their nakedness,

> dishonest shame
> Of Nature's works, honor dishonorable,
> Sin-bred, how have ye troubl'd all mankind
> With shows of seeming pure,
> And banisht from man's life his happiest life,
> Simplicity and spotless innocence.
> So pass'd they naked on, nor shunn'd the sight
> Of God or Angel, for they thought no ill:
> So hand in hand they pass'd, the lovliest pair
> That ever since in love's imbraces met . . .
>
> (4.313-22)

Innocence is here felt to be a condition of wholeness. While the sinner has some shameful part of himself to hide or deny, an innocent person has, literally, nothing to hide. Hence, he or she "passes naked on" both physically and spiritually until sin cracks the seamless "simplicity and spotless innocence," enabling the self to seem other than it is by "shows of seeming pure." "Sin-bred" shame expresses the self's consciousness of its loss of integrity. Guilty persons shun the face of God and Angel not because they know about evil but because they think evil of themselves. The hand imagery in the passage above, pervasively associated with Adam and Eve, symbolizes another form of innocent wholeness. They are not only whole in themselves, they are at one with each other. Addressing his wife, Adam puns: "Sole partner and sole part of all these joys"; likewise Eve confesses to him, "Part of my Soul I seek thee, and thee claim / My other half: with that thy gentle hand / Seiz'd mine" (4.411, 487–89).

While they remain innocent, Adam and Eve are of one soul; their sexual union expresses an outward manifestation of inward unity. Milton signals this unity in their prayer just before retiring to their bed of "connubial love." Adam and Eve offer an apparently spontaneous prayer in perfect unison. The unity of their voices anticipates the blending of their bodies in sexual union and both denote the oneness of their souls. To secure this interpretation, the poet comments at the conclusion of their orison, "This said unanimous" (that is, "of one soul"). Then Milton continues, extending the sacramental imagery from prayer to sex:

> and other Rites
> Observing none, but adoration pure
> Which God likes best, into thir inmost bower
> Handed they went; and eas'd the putting off
> These troublesome disguises which wee wear,
> Straight side by side were laid, nor turn'd I ween
> *Adam* from his fair Spouse, nor *Eve* the Rites
> Mysterious of connubial Love refus'd.
>   (4.736–43)

In this high moment of sexual consummation, the Puritan poet, recipient of a long and deep Protestant tradition that deprecated externality both in religious ritual and in physical love, alchemizes sexual union into a pure sacrament. Innocent sexual love in the bower becomes a sacramental commingling of body and soul in perfect unanimity, a perfect rite, as it were. In their bower of bliss Adam and Eve form an earthly equivalent of complete spiritual interpenetration, alluded to in Raphael's comments about angelic love-making (8.618ff.). Although subsequently they will learn of the body-soul distinction through Raphael's lessons on temperance (see 8.561ff.), Milton's lovers enjoy the innocent integrity that allows them to be at one with each other in sexual intercourse as they are one with God and Nature in their oblations.

The whole and holy sexual union in Book 4 well exemplifies Milton's vision of innocence. To be innocent in the poem is to be fully integrated with the natural world and the Creator (as suggested by the bower and prayer), as well as with one's soul mate and within oneself. The latter wholeness, integrity of self, makes possible all the rest; as soon as sin fractures the self, the sinner becomes alienated from nature, God, and others. Guilt necessitates the "troublesome disguises which wee wear" — meaning not only clothes but all the wearisome pretensions, posturing, deceits, and hypocrisies that intervene between our naked selves and our outward appearances. Innocence, by contrast, makes dissembling impossible. Indeed, when accounting for watchful Uriel's failure to see through Satan's disguise, Milton explains that innocence cannot even discern hypocrisy because

> suspicion sleeps
> At wisdom's gate, and to simplicity
> Resigns her charge, while goodness thinks no ill
> Where no ill seems.
>
> (3.686–90)

In a curious way, innocent wholeness (from our fallen perspective) seems to await fragmentation by sin to open up its full value. A particular joy that the narrator attributes to Adam and Eve in the love scene illustrates this. Part of the lovers' bliss, as the narrator imagines it, is being "eas'd the putting off / These troublesome disguises which wee wear." However, never having worn clothing, Adam and Eve cannot fully enjoy the pleasure of having none to doff. By corollary, being incapable of shameful duplicity, they cannot experience their nakedness as the wonderful wholeness of having no "troublesome disguises." In this sense, their eyes are not yet opened, nor can be until they sin. Guilt, not knowledge about sin, alone has the power to strip away such veils from their eyes. Milton's lovers seem to "need" a broken self to feel the value of a whole one.

This is not to say that they do not experience paradisal bliss as a kind of fullness, only to suggest that they are happier than they know — as Adam expostulates upon awakening from his creation: "I move and live / And feel that I am happier than I know" (8.281–82). Our response to his innocent bliss is to want to reach into it and let him know how happy he is; like the narrator in *Paradise Lost* upon entering, so to speak, his pastoral book, we are provoked by innocence to cry, "O for that warning voice"! (4.1). Yet, paradoxically, the only knowledge that could fully educate innocent beings in our perspective on their joy is the knowledge that comes through sinning—and this, of course, is precisely the experiential knowledge that would violate the condition on which the joy we prize is founded. The narrator's parting intonation over the sleeping lovers voices our rueful admiration of Adam and Eve's innocent bliss that is more wonderful than they know: "Sleep on, / Blest pair; and O yet happiest if ye seek / No happier state, and know to know no more" (4.773-75).

In order to "know to know no more" in the same way the narrator and the reader know, Adam and Eve must have wholeness of innocence fractured by sin. Both *The Concept of Anxiety* and *Paradise Lost* conceive guilt as opening up Adam and Eve's knowledge in just this way—so that they "know to know." Sin makes selfhood suddenly problematic and dialectical. In neither work is this new knowledge of sin a matter of learning about good and evil: Milton's Adam and Eve, obviously, are supremely well informed about evil before they sin; Kierkegaard's ignorant Adam knows of the distinction between good and evil ambiguously adumbrated in the name of the interdicted tree, while his posterity resides amid quite specific, though still "obscure," knowledge about sin. Nevertheless, in both works, sin itself is an eye-opening experience:

> and each the other viewing,
> Soon found thir Eyes how op'n'd, and thir minds
> How dark'n'd; innocence that as a veil
> Had shadow'd them from knowing ill, was gone,
> Just confidence, and native righteousness,
> And honor from about them, naked left
> To guilty shame.
>
> (9.1052-58)

As so often in *Paradise Lost*, moral attributes acquire seemingly tangible essences in this passage. In this case, confidence, righteousness, honor, and innocence are reified as a spiritual clothing able to cover over the evil only sin reveals; guilt exposes the nakedness that was always there but only now becomes troublesome. Though surface appearance may remain unaltered, after the sinful leap "everything is changed" (*CA*, 61) because the self is changed.

The rupture sin effects within Adam and Eve causes a corresponding

fission in the very relationships that had formerly defined their wholeness—that is, with nature, each other, and God. I have already described, in brief, the sin-induced rift in nature in connection with "objective anxiety." This is a theme on which Milton loves to play, as he links
the microcosm (the sinful self) to the macrocosm (the natural world).
Thus, for example, Milton again links outward and inward weather.
Bridging a description of the sudden "fierce antipathy" of nature and
Adam's remorseful soliloquy, Milton writes:

> these were from without
> The growing miseries, which *Adam* saw
> Already in part, though hid in gloomiest shade,
> To sorrow abandon'd, but worse felt within,
> And in a troubl'd Sea of passion tost,
> Thus disburd'n sought with sad complaint.
>
> (10.714–19)

Similarly, God's punishment of Adam emphasizes a division between
the human and the nonhuman as the Lord curses the ground and situates
Man in a new adversarial relation to the created world. No longer will
boughs bend compliantly to proffer their luxuriant fruit; now Adam
must labor against opposing nature to win his sustenance (see 10.197ff.).
This outward opposition of the elements mirrors new oppositions within
the self. Milton's prelapsarian Adam and Eve were aware of the hierar-
chy of reason and appetite, but sin causes virtual war between these
faculties. Analogously, Kierkegaard's unfallen Adam and Eve are dimly
cognizant of their "soulish" and "bodily" natures, but sin exacerbates
the dichotomy and makes selfhood suddenly problematic.

Milton symbolizes a fallen relationship to the physical world by images
of domination and exploitation, in direct contrast to his former images
of innocent oneness and wholeness. Thus his fallen angels are consistently portrayed as those who exploit and seek to dominant the environment. They rip up the landscape of heaven to fashion their engines of
war and, as soon as Satan's legions arrive in hell, they rape its environment, exhuming from its womb baneful precious metals to construct
Pandemonium. Similarly, fallen humanity, by diabolic

> suggestion taught,
> Ransack'd the Center, and with impious hands
> Rifl'd the bowels of thir mother Earth
> For Treasures better hid.
>
> (1.685–88)

Guilt allows the earth to be viewed as an object for exploitation.

Likewise, sin allows Adam and Eve to regard themselves and each other as objects, thereby leading to the sort of mutual rape that follows hard upon tasting the fruit. After their indulgence in sinful sensuousness (eating the forbidden fruit) and sinful sexuality, Adam and Eve discover their nakedness. This discovery suggests a new consciousness of the body as object. For the first time they look upon themselves and find parts that seem less honorable than the rest; their shame implies self-alienation from their "lower" parts. Thus Adam to Eve:

> But let us now, as in bad plight, devise
> What best may for the present serve to hide
> The Parts of each other, that seem most
> To shame obnoxious, and unseemliest seen,
> Some Tree whose broad smooth Leaves together sew'd,
> And girded on our loins, may cover round
> Those middle parts, that this new comer, Shame,
> There sit not, and reproach us as unclean.
>
>   (9.1091–98)

The sin-produced self-alienation that estranges Adam and Eve from nature and from their bodies, also spoils their erstwhile mutual harmony. The consequence of a rupture in the self is to allow them to look upon each other as exploitable objects, as objects of lust. In a series of puns about tasting that interconnect the first sin of gratification by eating with the subsequent sin of lustful sex, Adam transforms Eve into a fruit, to be relished like any other object, nothing more (9.1016–33). Sin degrades sexual union, formerly defined the highest reach of human unanimity, into something partial, unfulfilling, manipulative, and ultimately an ironic sign of their disunity. Sex becomes a "seal of thir mutual guilt" that ironically no longer truly seals them but, like the unrestful sleep that follows, mocks its intended end by further alienating them.

Even before Eve becomes the object of Adam's lust, Adam is the object of his wife's machinations. The love she proffers him after the Fall is riddled by self-interest. Duplicity characterizes Eve's relation with Adam from the moment she sins. Indeed, her first question to herself after tasting is "But to *Adam* in what sort / Shall I appear?" (9.816–17). Such a question is possible only for a sinfully divided self; it would have been impossible a few moments before as Eve deliberates at the tree, for unlike the self-reflection that characterizes her internal monologue as she contemplates partaking of the fruit, Eve's question "to Adam in what sort shall I appear?" is itself guileful. Its rhetoric belongs to what Grossman calls the "fallen conditional." It constitutes a new sort of self-reflection. While her former queries concern what she should do, the latter concerns what she should seem to be. Sinning enables Eve to dissemble after the fashion of the arch-dissembler, Satan.[24]

The narrator's description of her first guilty utterance implies exactly what kind of self Eve now owns:

> To him she hasted, in her face excuse
> Came Prologue, and Apology to prompt,
> Which with bland words at will she thus addrest. . . .
> Thus *Eve* with Count'nance blithe her story told;
> But in her Cheek distemper flushing glow'd.
> (9.853–55, 886–87)

This is obviously the utterance of a divided self; sin has created a cleavage between appearance and reality by splitting a whole self in two. More specifically, Eve acquires a theatrical self through sin, as Milton deftly attests by the stage terms that precede Eve's first "speech": "Prologue," "Apology," "prompt."[25] These terms connect Eve to the center of speechifying in *Paradise Lost*, hell, and to its chief orator/actor, Satan (see 9.670). As something got up for its effect, Eve's speeches to Adam are diabolically theatrical. As one now self-consciously on stage, Eve must relate herself to herself. She has acquired problematic personhood in the root sense of the word *person*: "mask." Theatrical selfhood is a burdensome task, for who can be so cautious as always to find the suitable mask, or so self-possessed as not to lose the "real" self among the countless disguises. Now Eve "knows to know" the significance of "being eas'd these troublesome disguises which we wear."

Adam's acute awareness of his own nakedness forms a corollary to Eve's sin-begotten theatricality; his embarrassment about his nakedness, too, manifests a self that feels newly exposed — on stage, as it were. Eve's daring bravado and aplomb correspond inversely to Adam's stage fright (so to speak). Whereas Eve successfully masks her true motives from her husband, Adam feels utterly exposed before his all-seeing Maker because for the first time he, like Eve, has something to hide. Painfully aware of his "soil'd and stain'd" body (9.1076), Adam cries for the curtain to fall so that he might skulk offstage behind the darkest arras — but ironically, there is no offstage since an omniscient God is audience:

> O might I here
> In solitude live savage, in some glade
> Obscur'd, where highest Woods impenetrable
> To Star or Sun-light, spread thir umbrage broad,
> And brown as Evening: Cover me ye Pines,

> Ye Cedars, with innumerable boughs
> Hide me, where I may never see them more.
>
> (9.1084–90)

For the first time, Adam's speech even sounds theatrical. With its fine modulation of enjambment and caesura, the high poetry in Adam's moving complaint resembles rhythmically the strong lines of the Renaissance stage.

Of course, neither by hiding in the "highest Woods" nor by covering themselves with the pathetic apron of fig leaves can Adam and Eve truly avoid God's sight. Yet they would escape if they could, for the sin that rent the self in two and at the same instant alienated the sinner from the natural world and from human companions, similarly cuts off the guilty individual from God. Sin violates humankind's relationship with the Almighty, preventing free intercourse with heaven. Formerly, in "simplicity and spotless innocence," Adam and Eve "pass'd naked on, nor shunn'd the sight / Of God or Angel, for they thought no ill" (4.318–20). Now, by contrast, guilty Man bewails:

> How shall I behold the face
> Henceforth of God or Angel, erst with joy
> And rapture so oft beheld? those heav'nly shapes
> Will dazzle now this earthly, with thir blaze
> Insufferably bright.
>
> (9.1080–84)

As innocence insulates them from the knowledge of evil, so guilt obstructs Adam and Eve from the knowledge of God. However, here "knowledge" must emphatically be understood as something far deeper than purely intellectual cognition about God. In *The Christian Doctrine* Milton avers that spiritual death "consists, first, in the loss or at least the extensive darkening of that right reason, whose function it was to discern the chief good" (*CP*, 6.395). But "right reason" as Milton uses the term here and in *Paradise Lost* (for example, 12.83–90) designates a moral quality akin to conscience rather than ability to wield syllogistic logic skillfully.[26] "There is an old saying," Kierkegaard observes, "that to understand and to understand are two things" (*CA*, 142). Greek philosophy stresses one kind of knowledge (intellectual clarity), Hebrew prophets another (revelation and relationship). In the prophetic tradition, theological knowledge is only a small part of genuine knowledge of God, and indeed it may be a hindrance to it, for true knowledge involves standing in the right relationship to the divine. So, too, in *Paradise Lost*. The devils in hell are capable of theological disputation (2.557–61). Yet this is not the knowledge from which fallen beings are disbarred by sin. Moreover, theologically correct propositions about God's attributes would provide cold comfort to Milton's Adam and Eve, recently exiled from an immediate, intimate relationship with heaven. Intellectual knowledge is not what Adam and Eve lack after sin, nor what they simultaneously dread and yearn for. Kierkegaard's comparison between the lover and theologian is very much to the point: "Whoever loves can hardly find joy and satisfaction, not to mention growth, in preoccupation with a definition of what love properly is. Whoever lives in daily and festive communion with the thought that there is a God could hardly wish to spoil this for himself, or see it spoiled, by piecing together a definition of what God is" (*CA*, 147).

To be sure, Milton thinks of sin partly as an impediment to speculative knowledge; his images of sin-darkened minds and guilt-obscured reason (see 9.1054; 7.86) certainly may be understood through a Greek (essentially Platonic) filter.[27] But *Paradise Lost* understands the sin-induced epistemological rupture in an even deeper, prophetic sense as well. It describes sin as obstructing a far more important "knowledge" of God — the knowledge of companionship with the divine. Sin prevents not theology but theophany. This conception of sin moves the poem into the orbit of Hebraic rather than Hellenic thought. In Socratic tradition, "Sin is ignorance," so "when a man does wrong, he has not understood what is right." The Christian view of sin focuses on the will rather than on the intellect and is much less sanguine: if a person does wrong, Christianity teaches, it may well be "because he will not understand . . . because he does not will the right" (see "The Socratic Definition of Sin," *SUD*, 218–27).[28] Finitude constitutes the chief obstacle to understanding transcendent divinity in Athens; in Jerusalem, the greatest obstacle to communion with a terribly righteous God is impurity (see Isa. 6:1–5). Not for the absence of schoolmen and synods does Hosea lament when, in the name of the Lord, he condemns Israel for lack of knowledge: "My people are destroyed for lack of knowledge: because thou has rejected knowledge, I will also reject thee, that thou shalt be no priest to me: seeing thou hast forgotten the law of thy God, I will also forget thy children" (Hos. 4:6; cf. 6:6). For Hosea, to know the God of Israel is to stand faithfully in a sacred relationship with him, as with a marriage partner; to forget the Lord is to betray that relationship as though by adultery (see Hos. 1–2). Sin in *Paradise Lost* similarly marks an adulterous violation of a heretofore integrated relationship with God. This act has enormous epistemological consequences. But chief among these, both Milton and Kierkegaard agree, is that by sin humans know good and evil from the event (*ab eventu*) — that is through standing in a new existential relationship to themselves, the physical world, other people, and most significantly, to God.[29]

Notes

1. Most discussions of *The Concept of Anxiety* focus on it as a philosophical rather than a theological work. The following chapter looks at it as an interpretation of Genesis. The critics I have found most helpful are Cole, *Problematic Self*; Croxall, *Kierkegaard Studies*; Dupré, *Kierkegaard as Theologian*; Malantschuk, *Kierkegaard's Thought*; and Roberts, "The Concept of Dread."

2. This distinction is sometimes blurred or avoided by Kierkegaard's commentators. Cole, for example, redefines choice as it applies to Kierkegaard's work: "This *choice* is not the rational deliberation that is usually meant by the term, an objective decision between two alternatives. This choice 'does not tempt like a definite choice, but alarms and fascinates with its sweet anxiety.' Nevertheless it is a choice" (*Problematic Self*, 82). I have preferred to preserve Kierkegaard's term *leap* in contradistinction to *choice*, as I believe Kierkegaard intends.

3. Kierkegaard's philosophy is organized by a theory of "spheres" or "stages" of existence. Unfortunately, this study cannot treat Kierkegaard's stages at any length. The essential metadiscourse by Kierkegaard on his master theory is to be found in *Stages on Life's Way*, together with sections of *Concluding Unscientific Postscript* and *The Point of View for My Work as an Author*. In addition major studies of Kierkegaard's thought virtually all comment on the stages, though there is substantial disagreement about the nature and even number of stages. A fine recent contribution to this scholarship is Dunning's *Kierkegaard's Dialectic*.

4. A parallel may be found in C. S. Lewis's novel *Perelandra*. In a thinly disguised retelling of the Fall, Lewis's Eve-figure is prepared to disobey by learning to think about her own possibility for possibility: "what might be." The "might be" defines an utterly new category for her; it, more than the content of the forbidden action, proves at once fearful and fascinating (see esp. chs. 8–13).

5. Cixous, "Sorties," in *New French Feminisms*, 90.

6. See "Kierkegaard's View of Man and Woman" in Malantschuk, *Controversial Kierkegaard*, 37–61, for a broader overview of the subject in all Kierkegaard's writing.

7. Similarly, Judge William says in *Either/Or*, "A woman comprehends finiteness, she understands it from the bottom up . . . therefore she is in harmony with existence (as no man is or should be)" (2:316).

8. For book-length studies dealing extensively with knowledge in Milton's Eden, see Schultz, *Forbidden Knowledge*; Madsen, *Shadowy Types*; Jacobus, *Sudden Apprehension*; and Swaim, *Before and After*. Burden's chapter "The Contention about Knowledge" in *Logical Epic*, 97–123, is also useful and more

directed to the question about specifically what kind of knowledge is forbidden to Adam and Eve in Paradise.

9. I have cited Sumner's widely used translation because it echoes *Areopagitica* in a way that tends to efface the difference I want to call attention to.

10. As Blackburn says, the Fall supplies "experiential knowledge of an actuality rather than any intellectual enlightenment or increase in moral acuteness" (cited in Swaim, *Before and After*, 15–16).

11. St. Thomas refers to Adam's intuitive understanding as "angelic" (see MacCaffrey, Paradise Lost *as "Myth,"* 37–38). MacCaffrey typifies many critics in ascribing to Adam's naming the animals far more scope than I believe Milton's few allusions warrant.

12. Hill remarks, "In his conversation with Raphael Adam's mental processes are not different from those in his postlapsarian discussion with Michael. In each he is enquiring, anxious to be informed, very human" (*Milton and the English Revolution*, 379).

13. It may be objected that in *Tetrachordon* Milton writes: "But *Adam* who had wisdom giv'n him to know all creatures, and to name them according to their properties, no doubt had the gift to discern perfectly" (*CP*, 2.602). Milton's remark here, however, constitutes little more than forensic exploitation of a commonplace. *Paradise Lost* simply fails to sustain the assertion that "before the fall the model of language occurs in Adam's naming of the animals" (Swaim, *Before and After*, 51) or to picture Adam as characteristically intuitive rather than discursive (con. Fish, *Surprised by Sin*, 113–14).

14. For extended discussions of Edenic language, see Fish, "Language in Paradise" in *Surprised by Sin* (107–30), and Swaim, *Before and After*, chapters 2 and 3.

15. See Lewalski, *Rhetoric of Literary Forms* for a masterful study of how Milton deploys multiple genres in his epic.

16. Lieb, "Myth of Prohibition," 242.

17. My argument is meant to direct attention to a significantly different problem of accommodation from the one that usually preoccupies Milton studies. Raphael's subject is unknowable to Adam not primarily because it treats transcendence but because it treats moral evil, with which Adam has no personal experience. See Jacobus, *Sudden Apprehension*, 92–97, for an analysis of Adam's understanding of the war along these lines. For useful general discussions of "accommodation," see Ryken, *Apocalyptic Vision*, 7–33; and Patrides—both chapter 1 of *Milton and the Christian Tradition* and "Accommodation" in *A Milton Encyclopedia*.

18. See Swaim, *Before and After*, 170–71, on Raphael's repeated parenthetical asides that signal the difficulty of comparing the unknown with the unknown.

19. See Johnson, "Life of Milton," 464–65.

20. As Swaim puts it: "Raphael supplies Adam with vicarious equivalents of experience that will not compromise his innocence" (*Before and After*, 19).

21. Swaim voices this truism thus: "As the prelapsarian universe is unified

and continuous, the postlapsarian is divided and fragmented" (*Before and After*, 56). Kierkegaard directs Miltonists to think about how this commonplace refers not simply to the external world but to how fallen humans know that world.

22. See Lewis, "Eros" in *Four Loves* (131–60), for a modern treatment of the problem of keeping erotic love subordinate to spiritual love of God—a problem that entered the Renaissance most forcibly through Plato's *Symposium*.

23. By the same token, Satan toxifies morally positive terms, such as *league* and *amity* (see 4.375–76).

24. Cf. Grossman: "For the first time, Eve begins to fashion herself as an object of her own and Adam's contemplation, planning her appearance and calculating the effects she will promote (9.816–30). Thus her alienation from providential order is immediately read as a division within the self. . . . In the same passage, Eve begins to use the 'fallen conditional' construction that characterizes Satan's speech" (*"Authors to Themselves,"* 145).

25. See Goffman, *Presentation of Self*, for a classic study of human behavior as seen through the metaphor of theatrical performance.

26. This view of the Fall's noetic effects is propounded by Ramism. Summarizing Ramist theory, Perry Miller wryly observes: "The fall of man had amounted in effect to a lapse from dialectic; the loss of God's image . . . was simply the loss of an ability to use the syllogism" (*New England Mind*, 111). My argument about the Fall's epistemological consequences in *Paradise Lost* counters such reduction, whether Ramistic or Platonic; hence, it differs from both Swaim (*Before and After*, 133–44) and Samuel (*Plato and Milton*, 101–29). See Bennett, *Reviving Liberty*, for a deeply informed discussion of Milton's understanding of "right reason." Bennett's discussion of Milton's antinomianism also points to an area of broad similarity with the author of *Fear and Trembling*.

27. As Shawcross aptly notes, the myth of "exodus also underlies the Platonic myth of the cave" (*Mortal Voice*, 123). Thus, one can understand Michael's "purging" of Adam's eyes (11.412–22) or the Lord's "clearing" of fallen humanity's darkened senses (3.188) in a prophetic or Platonic fashion. For Hebraic and Hellenic concepts are conflated in these images of purgation, as they are when the narrator implores God to purge his sight, as Michael purges Adam's vision: ". . . there plant eyes, all mist from thence / Purge and disperse, that I may see and tell / Of things invisible to mortal sight" (3.53–55), or when he pleads "What in me is dark, / Illumine, what is low raise and support" (1.22–23).

Nevertheless, I believe we misrepresent Milton to interpret him exclusively or mainly through a Platonic filter (see Samuel, *Plato and Milton*, for the most comprehensive treatment). The blindness Milton most fears is spiritual rather than intellectual; the enlightenment he most desires comes only through holiness and purity. Hence, Milton's famous dictum that "he who would not be frustrate of his hope to write well hereafter in laudable things, ought him selfe to bee a true Poem" enacts a fundamentally prophetic gesture. Similarly prophetic is his bid to have "all utterance and knowledge" enriched by the Holy Spirit, just as God sent down "his Seraphim with the hallow'd fire of his Altar to touch and purify the lips" of the prophet Isaiah (*CP*, 1.890, 821; Isa. 6:1-7; see also the "Nativity Ode," line 28).

28. The young Milton, author of "Comus" and "Of Education," may have felt more sanguine about the power of education to "repair the ruins" of the Fall (*CP*, 2.366) than the mature Milton, who has witnessed the perversity of his people "chusing them a captain back for *Egypt*" against his repeated warnings (*CP*, 7.463). Bennett suggests that Milton learns that "teaching cannot cure moral blindness," citing his remark in *The Christian Doctrine* that although "a true knowledge of God" is needful for faith, "the seat of faith is not really the intellect but the will" (*Reviving Liberty*, 172; cf. *CP*, 6.476).

29. This chapter has stressed the difference between Greek and Christian modes of knowing God. A fine discussion of this subject is to be found in Boman, *Hebrew Thought*. See also Verdenius, "Plato and Christianity," for a more general discussion of the incompatibilty between Platonism and Christianity.

5

Temptation by Anxiety

"Ye Shall Be as Gods": Anxiety in Eve's Temptation

Much more than carnal appetite tempts Milton's Eve and Adam to taste the prohibited fruit. In addition to being an attractive, savory-smelling food (9.730–43), the fruit also constitutes a "pledge" (3.95), "sign" (4.428), "memorial" (*CP*, 6.352) "of their [Adam and Eve's] obedience." The interdicted tree serves as "freedom's necessary other" (*CA*, 39n), conspicuously defining the limit or boundary in Paradise against which innocent creatures can assert their freedom from God, as well as, of course, prove their free fealty to God. Upon the fruit, consequently, devolves the special aura of the taboo, perhaps best described by Satan's provocative apostrophe in Eve's dream: "O Fruit Divine, / Sweet of thyself, but much more sweet thus cropt, / Forbidd'n here" (5.67–69); and by Eve's similar sentiments just before eating the fruit in Book 9:

> but his forbidding
> Commends thee more, while it infers the good
> By thee communicated, and our want:
> For good unknown, sure is not had, or had
> And yet unknown, is as not had at all.
>
> (753–57)

Offering occasion for deviation, the fruit tempts Adam and Eve to cross a boundary and explore the unknown—like the poem's arch-explorer, Satan; it tempts them to reject faith and take experience as their guide (9.807–8, 988). The fruit thus betokens the possibility for unknown possibilities—even for infinite possibility, for first through Satan's suggestion and then again in Eve's rhetoric to Adam, tasting the fruit promises to make humans "as Gods"! (9.708–32, 865–77). Hence, although without question Milton's protagonists are tempted by a "definite choice" (*CD*, 55) to eat or not to eat the fruit, the concrete, delimited object of

their choice is suffused with significance beyond itself. It therefore awakens anxiety. How anxiety figures in the Temptation, especially of Eve
but also of Adam, is the subject of this chapter.

The fact that Milton's Eve, whom I shall consider first, experiences
anxiety far more conspicuously than does his Adam reveals something
essential about how the poet differentiates their two falls: Eve's fall
enacts a reaching after freedom, Adam's marks the denial of freedom.
Anxiety is foregrounded in Eve's transgression and masked in Adam's.
Let me, however, be very clear about one point from the start. By emphasizing Adam's and Eve's anxiety over unknown possibilities rather
than desire for a known outcome, I do not mean to imply that physical
desire plays no role in the Temptation as Milton imagines it. Far from
it. Obviously the Temptation in *Paradise Lost* proceeds in part by means
of sensuous desire for a delicious fruit. This is particularly true of Eve's
temptation. Satan's rich description of the fruit to Eve is calculated to
appeal to her senses of taste, sight, and smell:

> I chanc'd
> A goodly Tree far distant to behold
> Loaden with fruit of fairest colors mixt,
> Ruddy and Gold: I nearer drew to gaze;
> When from the boughs a savory odor blown,
> Grateful to appetite, more pleas'd my sense
> Than smell of sweetest Fennel, or the Teats
> Of Ewe or Goat dropping with Milk at Ev'n,
> Unsuckt of Lamb or Kid, that tend thir play.
> To satisfy the sharp desire I had
> Of tasting those fair Apples, I resolv'd
> Not to defer; hunger and thirst at once,
> Powerful persuaders, quick'n'd the scent
> Of that alluring fruit, urg'd me so keen.
>
> (9.575–88)

Similarly, Eve is urged to eat the fruit by the powerful persuasion of
keen appetite:

> Meanwhile the hour of Noon drew on, and wak'd
> An eager appetite, rais'd by the smell
> So savory of that Fruit, which with desire,
> Inclinable now grown to touch or taste,
> Solicited her longing eye.
>
> (9.739–43)

Clearly appetite for a delicious object constitutes a principal motivation
for the Fall in *Paradise Lost*.[1]

It should be remembered, however, that Eve's sensual desire for the fruit is not directed toward a known good. Since she has never eaten fruit from the Tree of the Knowledge of Good and Evil, Eve must infer its deliciousness from its beauty and smell, as well as from the testimony of the serpent; she must imagine its flavor in the absence of actual knowledge by tasting. Furthermore, unlike a brute snake, who supposedly eats the fruit merely to "satisfy the sharp desire" of physical appetite alone, Eve is also tempted by words "replete with guile" yet ringing in her ears about the powers of this "God-like food" (9.733, 717). Thus the fruit grows "inclinable" to her not only by its sensuous appeal to nose and eye but also by the attraction of sweet yet fearful, unimaginable possibilities it adumbrates in her mind's eye. As a door to divinity, the fruit tempts by means of what Kierkegaard calls "the anxious possibility of *being able.*" But exactly what it is she is able to do, Kierkegaard continues, the first sinner would have no clear conception (*CA*, 44). Similarly, Milton's Eve has no real understanding of what tasting the fruit will allow her to do or be, in its promise to make her as God. Eating the forbidden fruit, therefore, becomes not simply an act of gratifying physical appetite (an act Milton calls "neither good nor evil" [*CP*, 6.352]), nor merely a choice to do something quite specific (that is, eat a fruit), although it is both of these. More important, eating the fruit is a leap by which Eve intends to go beyond herself (see *CA*, 62); through tasting, she hopes to attain a new order of being.

A key paragraph likening anxiety to dizziness provides Kierkegaard's most detailed account of the psychology of temptation by anxiety. As such, it offers a suggestive text for looking at Milton's Eve:

> Anxiety may be compared with dizziness. He whose eye happens to look down into the yawning abyss becomes dizzy. But what is the reason for this? It is just as much in his own eye as in the abyss, for suppose he had not looked down. Hence anxiety is the dizziness of freedom, which emerges when . . . freedom looks down into its own possibility, laying hold on finiteness to support itself. Freedom succumbs in this dizziness. Further than this, psychology cannot and will not go. In that very moment [that is, the moment of the fall or leap] everything is changed, and freedom, when it again rises, sees that it is guilty. Between these two moments [that is, innocence and guilt] lies the leap, which no science has explained and which no science can explain. . . . Anxiety is a feminine weakness in which freedom faints. Psychologically speaking, the fall into sin always takes place in weakness. But anxiety is of all things the most selfish [egotistical], and no concrete expression of freedom is as selfish as the possibility of every concretion. This again is the overwhelming factor that determines the individual's ambiguous relation, sympathetic and antipathetic. In anxi-

ety there is the selfish infinity of possibility, which does not tempt like a choice but ensnaringly disquiets with its sweet anxiousness. (*CA*, 61)

We may extrapolate from this passage how Kierkegaard would characterize the fall of Eve. Kierkegaard suggests that the Woman might be tempted not simply by the sensual appeal of a savory fruit but by the allure of her own possibility for possibility that the fruit betokens. Wavering between desire and dread with regard to the taboo, she becomes entangled in anxiety's characteristic sympathetic antipathy. When she does at last yield, the decisive instant paradoxically seems at once self-assertive and passive, egotistic and impotent. Moreover, her leap into sin itself constitutes an incommensurable rupture in the psychological process that leads up to it. The unfallen Eve approaches the abyss of freedom with a vertiginous sense of possibility. The fallen Eve rises from her fall to discover herself guilty and everything changed. But the instant of her leap (that is, sin itself) cannot be penetrated with full consciousness or explained by the psychological determinants that precede it.

Let me apply Kierkegaard's model of temptation by vertiginous freedom to both of Eve's temptations in *Paradise Lost* — that is, her dream-temptation in Book 4 and her daylight temptation in Book 9. First, the dream-temptation.[2] In Eve's dream, the crisis occurs in a moment of psychological collapse, brought on by extreme, dizzy anxiety. Her "fall" itself seems to involve the momentary loss of consciousness, from which Eve rises to find herself compromised. But what actually takes place in the decisive instant of choice is not clear. In fact, nothing is more striking about Eve's dream-temptation than the impenetrability of its climax. Led to the furthest edge of freedom's yawning abyss, as the incubus presses the forbidden fruit provocatively against her lips, Eve trembles in dizzy anxiety. Suggesting Eve's dreamlike paralysis, Eve's language lingers over the fruit held against her lips, as though she feels frozen, mesmerized by the temptation:

> So saying, he drew nigh, and to me held,
> Even to my mouth of that same fruit held part
> Which he had pluckt; the pleasant savory smell
> So quick'n'd appetite, that I, methought,
> Could not but taste. Forthwith up to the Clouds
> With him I flew.
>
> (5.82–87)

But does Eve or doesn't she eat the fruit? No one, apparently not even she, can say. The caesura between "I, methought, / Could not but taste" and "Forthwith up to the Clouds" is surely among the most charged, teasing lacunae in the entire epic. Rather than openly choose to eat, Milton's Eve seems to faint in acute horror and excitement—a dizzy, "feminine" swoon. This is followed by a heady, elated flight. Her "high exaltation" (5.90) may suggest a psychological condition equivalent to anxiety—an egoistical sensation of the possibility for unimagined freedom ("every concretion"). Or perhaps her flight symbolizes avoidance of completion, a common feature of anxiety dreams in which flying also is associated with the sensation of being without support and fear of falling. In any case Milton, like Kierkegaard, imagines Eve's temptation as suffused with dizzying, hypnotic anxiety that seems to transfix and draw her, almost against her will, toward the taboo ("I, methought, / Could not but taste"). Then, precisely at the fatal instant of crisis, there is a gap in which we momentarily lose touch with Eve's consciousness—as if she either cannot or will not take full consciousness of the instant, or leap. "Further than this, psychology cannot and will not go."

Although Adam exonerates Milton's Eve from any blame, and despite her uncertainty about whether or not she ate the fruit (if only in a dream), Eve somehow still feels guilty. Two tears well up and fall from her eyes, "the gracious signs of sweet remorse / And pious awe, that fear'd to have offended" (5.134-35). That Milton introduces nascent remorse in unfallen Eden is consistent with the stunningly latitudinarian nature of his Garden. *Paradise Lost* allows for knowledge about good *and* evil, erroneous judgment and deception, personal disagreements and disputation, and even sex—all within the bounds of innocence and bliss. Like Kierkegaard, Milton also recognizes that innocence is beset by the burden of anxiety. Edenic anxiety is not a "troublesome burden, no suffering that cannot be brought into harmony with the blessedness of innocence" (*CA*, 42), but it is a burden nevertheless, and one that, according to Kierkegaard, can come to feel much like guilt even before the innocent being becomes guilty (*CA*, 75).

In fact, however, so long as the innocent individual communicates with sin only as an anxious possibility—that is, "dreamingly" according to the symbolism employed by both Milton and Kierkegaard—no actual guilt is possible. Dreaming knowledge of evil remains qualified by existential ignorance. In ignorance, evil tempts not as a clear choice sinfully to desire a known good (*concupiscientia*) but as a focal point for the sensation of possibility (*angst*). The psychology of anxiety is less straightforward and more ambiguous and deeply dialectic than that of concupiscence (*CA*, 40). Anxiety entails "an ambiguous relation" to an imperfectly understood object, a relation "both sympathetic and antipathetic" (*CA*, 61).

In Eve's dream, the fruit becomes the focus of just such an admixture of sympathy and antipathy according to anxiety's distinctive dialectic. Eve is powerfully drawn by the fruit's "pleasant savory smell"; indeed, she confesses that in sleep the interdicted tree appears exceptionally attractive, "much fairer to my Fancy than by day" (5.53). Yet she is also horrified, almost sickened, at the prospect of transgression. Aghast, Eve beholds her guide violate the taboo: "mee damp horror chill'd / At such bold words voucht with a deed so bold" (5.65–66); relieved, she awakens from her nightmarish fantasy: "O how glad I wak'd / To find this but a dream!" (5.92–93). In short, in her dream Eve neither abhors nor yearns for the fruit. Rather, consonant with Kierkegaardian anxiety, she feels both emotions simultaneously. Her words at the crisis, "I, methought, / Could not but taste," betray anxiety's ambiguous filiation of reluctance and desire, sympathy and antipathy.

Eve's waking temptation equally bears comparison to Kierkegaardian anxiety. Once again, the fruit appeals to her imagination as to her senses. She calls it "intellectual food" that will "feed at once both Body and Mind" (9.768, 779) and apostrophizes it in a speech reminiscent of Satan's in her dream: "but his [God's] forbidding / Commends thee more, while it infers the good / By thee communicated, and our want" (9.753–55). The fruit promises her a chance to venture "higher than [her] lot" (9.690), a chance to explore the most unimaginable and infinite possibility for the self: Godhood! As she contemplates the dizzy prospect of becoming a "Goddess humane," her gaze "Fixt on the Fruit," Eve seems again to be hypnotized by the fruit (9.732, 735). She is in a state of high arousal from the serpent's words, "impregn'd / With Reason" (9.737–38). This is indeed a dizzy moment, for her eye is being drawn ever deeper into the yawning abyss of her own possibility for possibility—indeed, for infinite possibility.

But still Eve hesitates. Even in this moment of high excitement, tottering on a precipice, suffused with anxiety's sympathetic antipathy, Eve remains "yet sinless" (9.659). With these words, the narrator tactfully marks off the final moments of Eve's colloquy with the serpent. The poet's intent, I believe, is to disallow the reader from concluding that Eve decides to eat (thus committing the sin of concupiscence) before she actually eats. Milton is quite scrupulous about this point.[3] He strongly implies that Eve does *not*, in fact, fall before she falls by sinfully lusting after the fruit before she actually ate it. Like Kierkegaard, the poet wants to preserve the paradoxical truth of his source: that "sin came into the world by a sin," specifically the sin of disobedience. There is only one way Adam and Eve could disobey, for they were enjoined by only one interdiction, and that is not to eat the fruit.

Clearly, Eve's actions immediately prior to eating are crucial in determining her ethical status. So it is vital to examine carefully the last unfallen thing Eve does, which is to make a speech, a sort of soliloquy addressed initially to the fruit but eventually to herself. During her soliloquy at the tree, even while articulating all the reasons she has to eat the fruit, Eve has not yet decided to transgress. Rather, she is engaged in persuading herself to transgress and not in justifying a decision that she has already made. The rhetorical model is that of the deliberative soliloquy—an explicitly provisional, self-reflective, tentative mode of discourse. Her internal debate is punctuated by numerous interrogatives signaling her indecision even as they move her argument toward a decision. Likewise her final words, which take the reader up to the very moment of choice, recall the tentative syntax of her dream. Instead of the triple hesitation registered in "I, methought, / Could not but taste," Eve now puts to herself the negative question, "what hinders then / To reach and feed at once both Body and Mind?" (9.778–79). Nothing hinders her, of course; she retains her freedom to eat or not eat. But even to answer the question "nothing hinders" affirmatively is not yet to decide positively "I will!" By such means, Milton refuses to let the first sin arrive before the act of transgression.

Furthermore, he heightens the impression that anxious hesitation—sympathy and antipathy—extends through the actions that lead to Eve's taking her first bite by connecting her soliloquy to her fatal deed with a present participle: "So *saying*, her rash hand in evil hour / Forth reaching to the Fruit, she pluck'd, she eat: / Earth felt the wound" (9.780–82; my emphasis). The participle *saying* invites the reader to imagine Eve's deliberation proceeding through the act of her picking the fruit and right up until the very moment of eating it. Is Eve's will free when she eats? Yes, unquestionably. Yet it is not indifferent but utterly enmeshed in anxiety. Concurring "with Leibniz that a completely indifferent will (*æquilibrium*) is an absurdity and a chimera," Kierkegaard early asked himself, "In what relationship does the will stand to the last act of the understanding?" (Introduction, *CA*, vii).[4] The answer to this question led him to explore anxiety in Eden, as it led Milton to portray, trembling before the tree, a woman whose "last act of understanding" is thoroughly entangled in anxiety's sweet thrall.

Eve's behavior at the tree might be compared to that of a child who finds herself alone with a forbidden sweet. Such a child may never actively decide to eat before she eats. Instead she begins the process that will culminate in an irreversible act without fully resolving to disobey: each successive step is always only provisional; at any moment (she presumes), she could reverse the process and remain "yet sinless." She merely unwraps the candy (no sin here!), holds it, feels its texture, examines its color. All the while her eye is being drawn deeper and deeper into the abyss. Then she smells the sweet, passes it in front of her lips. Suddenly she finds she has tasted it—almost without her ever having made a conscious, irrevocable choice and despite her partial reluctance to sample the candy when she first unwrapped it for contemplation.

This account of the psychology of sin does not deny a role to rational reflection in the decision. As Ib Ostenfeld observes, "Reflection plays a part in and contributes to the direction of the leap. But the leap itself is by nature what Kierkegaard describes as a moment of discontinuity beyond the scope of reflection." Lucid reflection is followed by a "gap during which the individual momentarily abandons himself, 'lets things slide,' even though he has later to confirm the decision as his own."[5] Kierkegaard's psychological model of temptation could apply to any number of sins, including sexual transgression. Such transgressions often occur, psychologically, between reluctance and desire. In many cases the transgressor does not choose to transgress and then commit the deed, in a simple linear fashion. Rather, the sinner commits the fatal act even while he or she is toying with the possibility of doing it or not. The sin thus occurs almost (but not quite) unconsciously, almost (but not wholly) by letting go rather than by choosing. Thus Kierkegaard characterizes the passage from innocence to guilt as both a leap (suggesting a self-assertive, upward reach for greater freedom) *and* as a swoon (suggesting a sort of collapse under the extreme anxiety of possibility itself). Similarly, he says that "the fall into sin always occurs in impotence" and yet "is at the same time the most egoistic thing" (*CD*, 55). The leap occurs just outside the threshold of reflection. For this reason sin often brings us face to face with startling new revelations about ourselves, leading us to cry, "What have I become!" One rises from the leap as from a faint to discover that "everything has changed" for one is suddenly guilty (*CA*, 61). Yet we now recognize that our preliminary actions had been moving toward this new painful reality and feel guilty for them too.

Likewise Milton's Eve: anxious indecision characterizes her decision up to the very instant of disobedience; further than this "psychology cannot and will not go." True, her moment of transgression feels somewhat like a deliberate choice, but in other ways it resembles a fainting swoon from which she rises to discover that "everything is changed." Indeed, the whole of her life prior to sin now seems to have been leading to this cataclysm: "The Fall must have the effect of revising our notion of the events preceding it, of causing us to see them in relation to itself."[6]

Yet if sin initially "takes place in weakness" (*CA*, 61), sinning releases

within Eve a surging sensation of power, comparable to the heady exaltation of her dream-flight and reminiscent of Kierkegaard's assertion that
the leap, which occurs in impotence, is also "the most egotistic thing"
(*CD*, 55). Similarly, Eve feels "hight'n'd" after eating the fruit, as she
had in her dream-temptation, but this time "as with Wine" (9.793). She
is drunk with the sense of elation that typifies the breaking of a taboo,
intoxicated by the "dizziness of freedom" (*CA*, 61). In this particular
transgression, moreover, Eve's violation is specifically a reaching out for
infinite, absolute freedom—"ye shall be as Gods" (9.708). It is a way of
indulging her appetite for pure potentiality. Eve's ego is distended in a
heady, dizzy, expansive sensation of the "possibility for every concretion" (*CA*, 61). In this frame of mind, any limit whatsoever, however
minimal—such as the forbidding of a single tree—feels oppressively burdensome. Hence God, formerly praised as author of "this one, this easy
charge" (4.421), is felt by sinful Eve to be "Our great Forbidder" (9.815).
Tasting the fruit becomes a gambit by which Eve seeks to become empowered with total freedom, without constraint or limit; "for inferior,"
she asks, "who is free?" (9.825).

Because the fruit seems to promise just such freedom, it becomes the
focal point of anxiety. Both Milton and Kierkegaard imagine how such
anxiety might accumulate and intensify until it, not mere unmitigated
bliss, becomes the chief characteristic of Eden. For both authors the
fruit becomes the focus of disturbing dreams. For both, anxiety casts
its sweet and dreadful fascination upon Eden—and especially upon the
Woman, who seems peculiarly alive both to sensuousness and freedom
("spirit"). Yet for neither Milton nor Kierkegaard does this anxiety constitute itself a sinful motive for evil. Rather, anxiety describes the ambiguous, elastic determinant from which sin breaks forth as a free leap—a
leap related to but ultimately incommensurable with the psychological
condition that precedes it.[7]

"What Seem'd Remediless":
Anxiety in Adam's Temptation

Adam's temptation and fall is notably unlike Eve's in many respects.
Although Eve tries to beguile Adam with the promises of greater knowledge ("opener eyes") and divinity ("growing up to Godhead"), Adam
does not transgress primarily in order to gain knowledge or to be as God
(9.875–77). Nor does his transgression feel like a heady assertion of
freedom, as does Eve's. The psychology of Adam's sin is quite dissimilar

to that of Eve. Consequently, the passage in *The Concept of Anxiety* on the dizziness of freedom that typifies Milton's Eve has little application to his Adam. Adam experiences no protracted period of deliberation comparable to Eve's temptation at the tree. Instead, as soon as he learns of his beloved wife's transgression, he immediately resolves to eat the fruit. The conversation that intervenes between his resolution to sin and his physical act of disobedience does not, apparently, deeply engage the question of whether or not he will eat the fruit. Rather, it celebrates his gallant decision to die for love, if he must, with erring Eve. It is as if Adam bypasses the self-conscious moment of choice that so occupies Eve, in effect short-circuiting any anxious awareness of his freedom. Because Adam avoids thinking about his freedom to act, it is not surprising that his psychological condition during temptation should display none of the reeling sensation of freedom that characterizes Eve's fall.

Yet even so, there remain a few similarities between Adam's fall and Kierkegaard's description of vertiginous anxiety. Like Eve, Adam speaks warmly of the "inducement strong" figured in a fruit that might make them "be Gods, or Angels Demi-gods" (9.934-37). Also like Eve's, Adam's sin unleashes an egoistic sensation of divine power within him: he too feels intoxicated by sin "As with new Wine"; he too feels "Divinity within [him] . . . breeding wings" (9.1005-11). In addition, Milton characterizes Adam's sin as the result of "feminine weakness," as does Kierkegaard in the passage on anxiety (*CA*, 61). In *Paradise Lost*, both the narrator and the Son label Adam's sin effeminate, unmasculine submission: Adam is "fondly overcome with Female charm" (9.999); he is rebuked for uxoriousness: "Was shee thy God, that her thou didst obey" (10.145). These sexually coded judgments suggest a Miltonic equivalent to Kierkegaard's assertion that "psychologically speaking, the fall into sin always occurs in weakness" — or, elsewhere, "feminine weakness" (*CA*, 61).

However, unlike Milton's Eve, who is anxiously aware of her freedom during the Temptation, Adam presumes that his freedom evaporated with the choice of his wife. Thus his decision, though forthright, seems weaker than Eve's for he presumes (or pretends) he has no choice in the matter. Ironically, that very morning in the separation scene Adam had championed free choice to his wife, warning her that man's real danger lies within because "Against his will he can receive no harm" (9.350). Yet Adam now shows himself remarkably unwilling to look within himself, where the real danger lies. Rather than assume responsibility, he speaks as if his choice has been made for him by the choice of his wife, as if his fate is set and his fall is (in Arnold Stein's language) "as good as done" the moment Eve tells him of her "adventurous" deed:

> some cursed fraud
> Of Enemy hath beguil'd thee, yet unknown,
> And mee with thee hath ruin'd, for with thee
> Certain my resolution is to Die.
>
> (9.904–7)

One might easily think that Adam sins the moment he "resolves" to die with Eve. To take this position, however, one must either accept Adam's dubious claim that his fatal act is no longer free but inevitable, or concede that his professed willingness to sin is itself already a sin, whether or not he follows through with the deed. Both arguments strike me as highly questionable. Nevertheless, even so staunch an opponent of a fall before the Fall as Wayne Shumaker concedes to Millicent Bell that Adam sins when he here resolves to cast his lot with Eve.[8] Perhaps. But I suspect that Milton would be very uncomfortable with this extrapolation of inward moral culpability before any decisive outward act, especially since he has been so scrupulous in Satan's and Eve's falls to make sin coincident with visible disobedience and not to permit sin to arrive, as it were, before its enactment. After all, not until Adam eats the fruit does Earth tremble in her entrails and utter a second groan (9.1000–1001).

Could it be that Adam's freedom and its attendant anxiety lie hidden by self-deception during his temptation? *The Concept of Anxiety* defines a type of anxiety that may shed light on Adam's existential position during the few moments before he eats the fruit. Adam's condition resembles that of the later individual who "confounds himself with the race and its history" (*CA*, 73). That is, living amidst a "more" in which sinfulness is so pervasive in the environment, so seemingly inevitable historically, some people feel that "possibility is lost before it has been" (*CA*, 91). This phenomenon, Kierkegaard suggests, is particularly characteristic of paganism, which lacks a proper understanding of time and eternity because it lacks the concept of the "instant" vital to comprehending the true relationship among past, present, and future. As a result, paganism conceives of the future as already belonging to the past and expresses this understanding by means of the concept of fate.

By paganism, Kierkegaard almost always has in mind Greek culture, the most sophisticated pagan culture he knows. To the Greeks, Kierkegaard argues, time opens up backward: "For the Greeks, the eternal lies behind as the past that can only be entered backwards" (*CA*, 90; cf. 88–92). To understand this suggestive remark, one might think of Oedipus. Unbeknownst to him, his fated crimes of killing his father and marrying his mother lie in the past from the start of the drama. Oedipus moves forward into the future by going backward, discovering that he had been guilty of parricide and incest all along. In an even deeper sense, his guilt lies in the past even before he commits his appalling crimes. It is all over as soon as the oracle utters the word of doom — and even before, to the extent that one's fate is decreed from eternity and lies beyond the will even of the gods. When Greek oracles foretell the future, they are in a profound sense reading what is already past. Fate effectively empties the future of possibility, thus essentially reducing the future to the past. As Kierkegaard remarks, "If there is no moment [that is, "instant"], the eternal appears behind as the past" (*CA*, 90); thus for the pagan, what is fated to be is always, somehow, already immutably over and past.

This is not true in the Judeo-Christian view — at least not for Kierkegaard nor for Milton (cf. *PL* 3.111–23). This is why Bell is wrong to account for the Fall in *Paradise Lost* in terms of an Aristotelian recognition scene — as if the very deed that broke time in two according to Judeo-Christian tradition were no more than Oedipus's discovery of his prior evil: "The technical Fall is not the sudden entry of Sin into the guileless heart, but the bursting forth of human, fallible nature into the external act which forces it to recognize itself for what it is."[9] Kierkegaard would consign this reading of the Fall to a paganized version of Christianity. For paganism as well as for "its repetition within Christianity" (as per Bell's interpretation of *Paradise Lost*), there is "merely quantitative determination from which the qualitative leap of sin does not break forth" (*CA*, 93). Yet if there is no leap or instant, there is no genuine distinction between past or future. Rather, the future is already past because everything is "as good as done" from the start.

Hence, Kierkegaard's saying that paganism enters eternity backward. So, too, would Milton's Adam as he succumbs to fatalism. Tellingly, as soon as Adam hears of Eve's sin, he starts talking about himself as a victim of fate. Vanished is his former rhetoric of heroic free will. Suddenly, though his future still remains open and the very moment of decision is upon him, Adam begins to think of himself as a creature of circumstance and his fall as good as done. His discourse invokes a concept that previously has had no place in his bold language of free will and that had been characterized by Milton as part of the logic of hell: "Fixt Fate" (2.560). Adam forgets what Raphael has taught him, that what God wills is fate (7.173) — and what God wills for his human creatures is freedom untinged by the "least impulse or shadow of Fate" (3.120).

Adam's first thoughts concern, innocently enough, how Eve's fall is now irrevocably past. This is, of course, beyond question. Yet this thought leads Adam erroneously to think of his own (still future) deed as equally in the past, as he begins to confound his individual existence with the historical process of the race: "But past who can recall, nor done undo? / Not God Omnipotent, nor Fate" (9.926-27). This is the language of a man who is starting to enter time backward, who would convert the future into the past in order to avoid the anxious freedom of the present. Because what's done cannot be undone, Adam has begun to think of the past as necessary, forgetting that the past might have been otherwise. "To view the past as necessary is to regard the future as closed and freedom as illusory," writes Mark Taylor of Kierkegaard's interpretation of historical necessity, for "the predication of necessity to any part of the historical process dissipates genuine becoming."[10] Similarly, a few lines later, Adam succumbs to the sensation that his decision to eat the fruit—still to be acted upon in the future—is irrevocably doomed: "However I with thee have fixt my Lot, / Certain to undergo like doom" (9.952-53). Again, Adam's language conspires to convert the future into the past: note the preterit "have fixt," the deterministic term "certain," and the fatalist diction "Lot" and "doom." Yet Adam's doom is not certain until and unless he makes it so by violating the prohibition against eating the fruit.

Conspicuously absent from Adam's speeches is a proper consciousness of his own free will. Therefore, what must be constantly asked of Adam's language as he announces his decision is, What is being repressed? Where is freedom? Kierkegaard would demand that any reading of Adam's fall confront these questions. He would not let Adam sink into utter "spiritlessness" of the nonhuman world, as Adam commences to do when he first hears of Eve's sin:

> amaz'd,
> Astonied stood and Blank while horror chill
> Ran through his veins, and all his joints relax'd;
> From his slack hand the Garland wreath'd for *Eve*
> Down dropp'd, and all the faded Roses shed:
> Speechless he stood and pale.
>
> (9.889-94)

For Kierkegaard knows that even though freedom seems to be excluded by spiritlessness, anxiety lies in waiting, "hidden and disguised" (*CA*, 96). Unlike the fallen garland, Adam cannot sink into vegetal existence, however enervated he may feel, because he is human and hence still free. God will call Adam into account; he will remind Adam of the freedom from which he averted his gaze as, during his temptation, he conceived himself as the victim of fate because of the actions of his wife: "Was shee thy God, that her thou didst obey / Before his voice" (10.144–45). God's queries reinstate Adam's action under the repressed categories of obedience and choice.

So, to return to the question: Does Adam sin when he announces, "Certain my resolution is to Die"? No, quite clearly what Milton intends to display here is not a boldly sinful resolution but instead what Michael will later call "Man's effeminate slackness" (11.634). It makes better sense to think of Adam as suffering from spiritlessness than from sin. His existential position is comparable to that of a pagan who presumes, erroneously, that his future is already behind him. As for Kierkegaard's "subsequent individual," so for Milton's Adam: the "future seems to be anticipated by the past or by the anxiety that the possibility is lost before it has been" (*CA*, 91). But the possibility of reversing his slide toward sin is not lost until he eats the fruit. Adam's eating of the fruit is never "as good as done before" it actually *is* done, nor do I think Milton would have admired criticism of the poem that accepts Adam's feeble fatalism.[11] Rather, in his final unfallen dialogue with Eve, Adam manifests the psychology of an individual who would repress his consciousness of freedom by deploying the language of fate. Yet in spite of his fatalism, Adam cannot enter time backward, nor fob nontransferable responsibility onto another, nor sink to the level of the nonhuman like the fallen, faded roses, nor permanently elude anxiety, for even in the repression of freedom, "anxiety is nevertheless present, except that it is waiting" (*CA*, 96) — waiting to be brought into the open by the dread voice of God. Thus for Milton's Adam, just as for his Eve, the Temptation has anxious dimensions: the difference is that Eve's temptation foregrounds freedom while Adam's conceals it and represses its attendant anxiety.

Notes

1. Burden's "The Provocative Fruit" in *The Logical Epic* (124–49) gives a good account of the role of innocent sensuous desire in the Temptation and Fall.

2. The best discussion of Eve's dream to date is to be found in McColley, *Milton's Eve*, chapter 3. For a brief discussion of the dream in the literary tradition of anxiety dreams, see Weidhorn, "Anxiety Dream."

3. Gallagher, in *Milton, the Bible, and Misogyny*, 74–84, 93–96, supplies closely reasoned corroboration of my position on Eve's prelapsarian sinlessness. Though I formulated my views independently of Gallagher's, our arguments about Eve's innocence are equally uncompromising and often overlapping.

4. The full quotation may be found in Kierkegaard, *Journals and Papers*, 2.1241.

5. Ostenfeld, *Søren Kierkegaard's Psychology*, 25.

6. Savage, "Freedom and Necessity," 299.

7. It should be plain how strongly I take exception to Broadbent's casual use of Kierkegaard to talk about anxiety in *Paradise Lost*: "He [Milton] makes Adam and Eve move from careless innocence in Book IV towards a point at which they have to make a decision. This point lies in an area of acute anxiety *which is already sin*, properly considered—here Milton agrees with Kierkegaard" (*Some Graver Subject*, 198; my emphasis). Wrong. Milton and Kierkegaard insist that the point of anxiety is decidedly *not* sin.

8. Shumaker, "Notes," 1187.

9. Bell, "Notes," 1188.

10. Taylor, *Journeys to Selfhood*, 128.

11. A few critics resist Adam's fatalistic view that his sin is sealed when he resolves to cast his lot with Eve. In his chapter on "The Fall of Adam," Burden calls attention to the fatalism of Adam's rhetoric, describing his state of mind in terms of the stoic wisdom of Hell (*Logical Epic*, 172–77). Objections raised by Lewis and Fish against Waldock are also very much to the point; Lewis and Fish both contend that Adam's inability to see a way out of his predicament is no reason for his joining Eve in sin (Lewis, *Preface*, 127; Fish, *Surprised by Sin*, 261–72).

II

Anxiety and the Actuality of Sin

6

Anxiety and Remorse

"From Deep to Deeper Plung'd": Anxiety about Evil

"O Conscience, into what Abyss of fears / And horrors hast thou driv'n me; out of which / I find no way, from deep to deeper plung'd!" (10.842–44). These are the final cries from Adam's remorseful lament that splits the "still Night" after the Fall. Similar words introduce Satan's lament atop Mt. Niphates: "Now conscience wakes despair / That slumber'd, wakes the bitter memory / Of what he was, what is, and what must be / Worse" (4.23–26). Clearly, both Man and Devil have consciences; both experience the pangs of remorse. But within this similarity remains a crucial difference: Conscience plunges Adam and Eve deeper and deeper into regret for evil until remorse finally gives way to genuine self-reproach and repentance. Satan, by contrast, attempts to turn his conscience inside out. Thus his lament, which begins expressing anguish for evil, ends explicitly beyond remorse, embracing evil: "Farewell Remorse: all Good to me is lost; / Evil be thou my Good" (4.109–10). These contrasting existential positions may be summarized as follows: for Milton's human sinners, evil always remains evil—that which they loathe; for Milton's demonic sinners, evil becomes defined as good—that which they love, or at least attempt to love.

These different responses to sin may be seen equally in another example. After a very brief moment of intoxicated excitement, Adam and Eve abhor their transgression. From then on, they find sin repugnant—an offensive new reality about themselves that they seek to cover up with fig leaves or otherwise annul by means of the numerous denial strategies making up the end of Book 9 and much of Book 10. Satan, by contrast, lusts after and ravishes Sin because, as his daughter later reminds him, Sin figures forth an enticing new image of himself: "Thyself in me thy perfect image viewing / Becam'st enamor'd" (2.764–65). As his "perfect image," Sin discloses to her father a new, deeply seductive possibility for the self—namely, to be Satan or "Adversary." Far from constituting an embarrassing or offensive self-revelation, Sin embodies an attractive

123

double, the object of his narcissistic lust. Unlike Milton's two human sinners, Satan never ceases trying to love sin. Never mind for now that he is disgusted by Sin's "execrable" shape when he first sees her at the gates of hell (2.681ff.). This response simply gives the lie to Satan's spurious boast of power to turn the moral world topsy-turvy, demonstrating that though the Fiend may make love to Sin, he cannot, finally, always love it. Nevertheless, demonic existence founds itself on the impossible enterprise of loving evil and loathing good, while human existence is characteristically governed by precisely the reverse imperative — however imperfectly each achieves its telos.

Kierkegaard subsumes these human and demonic responses to sin under the rubrics "anxiety about evil" and "anxiety about good," respectively. At first it may seem odd that anxiety exists at all after one has sinned, since up to now anxiety has been described only with respect to the responses of unfallen individuals to their possibility for sin. Chapter 4 of *The Concept of Anxiety*, "Anxiety of Sin," begins by acknowledging the initial novelty of the idea of guilty anxiety, given that the previous chapters treat exclusively anxiety before the leap: "As soon as the leap is posited, one would think that anxiety would be canceled, because anxiety is defined as freedom's disclosure to itself in possibility. . . . However, this is not the case." For the guilty individual, sin has become an actuality, to be sure, "and so it would seem that possibility is annulled along with anxiety" (*CA*, 111). Yet because guilty individuals still can and do experience the sensation of freedom (or possibility) with respect to actuality, they still suffer from anxiety. Sinners might, for instance, fantasize about how they could have acted otherwise in the past, or how they may yet act differently under similar circumstances in the future. Because possibility continues to surround even so concrete an actuality as personal sin, so too, does anxiety, whose phenomenology Kierkegaard traces beyond the leap into "freedom's psychological attitudes toward sin" concretely posited after the Fall (*CA*, 118).

As a particularly disturbing kind of actuality, personal sin is likely to provoke some sort of denial or, in Kierkegaard's Hegelian terminology, "negation": "Since sin is an unwarranted actuality, it is also to be negated. This work anxiety will undertake. Here is the playground of the ingenious sophistry of anxiety" (*CA*, 113). The characteristic human response to actual sin is to attach possibility to the obtrusive, illegitimate new actuality. The object of anxiety is thus no longer "nothing" but evil concretely posited by sin; hence Kierkegaard's label, "anxiety about evil." A common name for anxiety about evil is remorse (*CA*, 113–18). Remorse, in the sense of regret, not repentance,[1] is considered a form of anxiety because it defines the way one's sense of possibility engages the monstrous actuality of personal sin. In remorse, the imagination (which in innocence had been in communication with sin vis-à-vis the "possibility for possibility") now directs its limitless inventiveness upon sin as a concrete actuality. Thus the mood of reflection becomes subjunctive: "if only I had . . .," "what if I hadn't . . .," "perhaps I might . . ." The possibilities of remorse are endless, for here as elsewhere anxiety has infinite resourcefulness. Anxiety's "sophistry has a way of perpetually picking up a particular point and perpetually varying it" (*CD*, 101). This indeed offers a wide "playground of the ingenious sophistry of anxiety" (*CA*, 113).

Kierkegaard identifies three movements within anxiety about evil: (1) remorse over "the actuality of sin," oriented toward the past, (2) remorse over "the further possibility of sin," oriented toward the future, and (3) insane remorse, or the sorrow over sin that always lies in advance or in retrospect of sin, but always arrives a "moment too late" (*CA*, 115). Insane remorse is best seen in those addicted to compulsive vices rather than in Adam and Eve, in whom sin has not yet hardened into habit. Therefore, unlike the addict, they do not repeatedly fall victim to a vice, such as drugs, drink, or debauchery, all the while upbraiding and condemning themselves for the very weakness they are about to indulge or to which they have just succumbed. Adam's and Eve's remorse in *Paradise Lost* does, however, follow anxiety's double preoccupation over sin as an avoidable past cataclysm and as a future possibility.

Book 9 ends with Milton's fallen protagonists trying to come to terms with the disquieting actuality brought about by their recent transgression. Yet neither secluded groves nor fig-leaf girdles successfully shield them from the obtrusive actuality of evil: "thir shame in part / Cover'd, but not at rest or ease of Mind" (9.1119–20). So they assuage their consciousness of personal guilt by bitter recriminations, seeking to transfer blame to each other. The mood of their "mutual accusation" is emphatically past subjunctive. At first, however, their reflections do not take up the question "if I had not" but "if *you* had not . . ." "Would thou hadst heark'n'd to my words, and stay'd / With me," remonstrates Adam to his spouse, "we had then / Remain'd still happy, not as now, despoil'd / Of all our good, sham'd, naked, miserable" (9.1134–35, 1137–39). Eve retorts in kind. She challenges Adam's self-serving assumption that had he been with her during the Temptation he would have discerned the serpent's fraud, and she asserts that neither of them would have fallen if only Adam had more resolutely refused her permission to work alone: "Hadst thou been firm and fixt in thy dissent, / Neither had

I transgress'd, nor thou with mee" (9.1160–61). And so the reproaches go, the mood of argument clearly being past subjunctive *contrary to fact*. Yet the gnawing reality of sin endures all such evasions.

Since the possibilities for second-guessing each other and themselves are illimitable, Book 9 well concludes: "and of thir vain contést appear'd no end" (1189). Remember, anxiety about evil possesses a sophistry of "perpetually picking up a particular point and perpetually varying it" (*CD*, 101). Yet, with respect to the concrete fact of sin, anxiety enjoys only hobbled freedom. Adam and Eve may unleash their minds in free-wheeling flights of imagination about how it might have been otherwise, but at any moment their flights of fancy may be brought low to earth by the intrusion of cold, hard knowledge of actual guilt. Kierkegaard draws a metaphor for anxiety's hobbled freedom from Mozart's *Don Giovanni*: "While the actuality of sin holds one hand of freedom in its icy right hand just as the Commandant held Don Giovanni, the left hand gesticulates with delusion, deception, and the eloquence of illusion" (*CA*, 113). Likewise, though Adam's and Eve's accusations and self-reproach in books 9 and 10 are often distinguished by eloquent illusions, always the crippling actuality of nontransferable guilt holds them fast in its icy right hand, insisting that each alone bears the blame.[2]

Especially fallen Adam, or "Adam Agonistes" as John Spencer Hill called him,[3] entertains several eloquent fantasies that seek to subdue the "unwarranted actuality" (*CA*, 113) of sin through reimagining the past. One such illusion occurs when, like a petulant child (10.762), he blames God for creating him: "Did I request thee, Maker, from my Clay / To mould me Man" (10.743–44). By cursing his creation (10.853), Adam indulges the ultimate fantasy of the past-subjunctive contrary to fact — that it would be better never to have been created. This being patently impossible (not to say self-contradictory), Adam yearns for the next best alternative: immediate annihilation. If he cannot entirely write himself out of the script, perhaps he can at least be allowed a swift and permanent exit (10.771–82, 854–56), for the only future he can imagine is one robbed of hope by his acute "sense of endless woes" (10.754).

Adam's and Eve's remorse, as per Kierkegaard's schematization, directs itself to the future as well as to the past. However, their anxiety over the consequences of evil assumes a somewhat different configuration from that which Kierkegaard imagines. For Kierkegaard, anxiety about evil (as does all anxiety) concerns itself principally with one's *own* predicament before God and not with events external to oneself. Thus, to sorrow "aesthetically" over the sinfulness of humanity at large is to indulge in false sympathy for "those poor sinners" while ignoring one's own fallibility; true sympathy demands absolute existential identification with other sinners, remembering that there but for the grace of God go we all (see *CA*, 38, 119–20). Milton's human protagonists, by contrast, are anxious as much or even more about the consequences of sin for their posterity as for themselves (10.725–29, 818–24) — a measure of Milton's healthier sense of the value of other people.[4] Nothing so forcibly expresses Adam's and Eve's remorse for generations yet unborn as Eve's proposals of celibacy and suicide (10.979–1005). By such means would she obstruct the future "consequence of sin" for others.

Yet in addition to this anxiety about their children, Milton's Adam and Eve are also anxious about the consequence of sin for themselves. They suffer from the fear of being forever immobilized by guilt. Worse than any concrete, limited penalty God has pronounced, says Adam, is the superadded "sense of endless woes" (10.754). The future opens underneath him as a fearful "abyss of fears and horrors": "Into what Abyss of fears / And horrors hast thou driv'n me; out of which / I find no way, from deep to deeper plung'd" (10.842–44). Similarly, Kierkegaard observes that remorse makes the future seem to fall away beneath the sinner as a vast gulf, for "no matter how deep an individual has sunk, he can sink still deeper, and this 'can' is the object of anxiety" (*CA*, 113). For Kierkegaard, the sinner founders in the future owing to his or her sense of it as a chasm yawning wide open upon the possibility of what further evil he or she may yet fall into. For Milton, Adam feels engulfed by a future that seems to offer nothing but endless guilt. In either case, anxiety of evil possesses the power to foreclose the future in advance: "anxiety sucks out the strength of repentance and shakes its head" (*CA*, 116).

In any of its manifestations, anxiety about evil is intensely enervating. Milton's Adam delivers his rueful soliloquy "outstretcht" on the "cold ground," oppressed by the "damps and dreadful gloom / Which to his evil Conscience represented / All things with double terror" (10.848–50). In his grief, he has "lost the reins of government, and . . . has retained only the power to grieve" (*CA*, 115). His remorse, however, "cannot cancel sin, it can only sorrow over it"; it "cannot make him free" (*CA*, 115, 116). Anxiety about evil provides no avenue out of guilt, only a cul-de-sac that constantly throws one back upon the painful actuality of sin. The only remedy for remorse is faith: "The only thing that is truly able to disarm the sophistry of sin is faith, courage to believe that the state [of sin] itself is a new sin, courage to renounce anxiety without anxiety, which only faith can do" (*CA*, 117).

Faith similarly holds the key to escaping from remorse in *Paradise*

Lost, though by "faith" Milton and Kierkegaard designate somewhat different accomplishments. The "courage to believe" of which Kierkegaard speaks refers to the rare and paradoxical achievement of an Abraham, Knight of Faith in *Fear and Trembling*. To become like Abraham, "it takes a paradoxical and humble courage to grasp the whole temporal realm now by virtue of the absurd" (as Abraham does when he receives Isaac back with joy); "this is the courage of faith."[5]

Perhaps the remorse-slaying faith exhibited by Milton's Adam and Eve does not qualify as technically absurd according to Kierkegaard's special definition of the absurd. That is, their faith does not straddle both sides of an absolute contradiction between the temporal and eternal. Nevertheless, their faith does entail considerable absurdity—such as the folly of hoping for forgiveness without positive evidence that mercy is even possible, and the paradox of prevenient grace. In *Paradise Lost*, too, faith requires that one swim in deep waters, leap into a void. Moreover, before Adam and Eve are able to exercise faith unto prayer, each must find the courage "to renounce anxiety" of evil—that is, all the vain strategies of denial—and admit responsibility for sin. Adam says:

> all my evasions vain
> And reasonings, though through Mazes, lead me still
> But to my own conviction: first and last
> On mee, mee only, as the source and spring
> Of all corruption, all the blame lights due.
>
> (10.829–33)

Similarly, Eve says to Adam:

> both [of us] have sinn'd, but thou
> Against God only, I against God and thee,
> And to the place of judgment will return,
> There with my cries importune Heaven, that all
> The sentence from thy head remov'd may light
> On me, sole cause to thee of all this woe,
> Mee mee only just object of his ire.
>
> (10.930–36)

Eve's magnanimous, Christlike offer prepares Adam to think about formerly unrecognized hints of mercy in God's response to their disobedience. Suddenly, what before seemed unendurable now seems full of hope. Without any knowledge of the Atonement, without any promise of grace to rely on, Adam finds hope, paradoxically, in his punishment: in the obscure prediction of vengeance upon the serpent adumbrated by the protoevangelium; in the surprising delay of promised death; in the mildness both of the manner in which the Lord decreed their sentence and of the curse itself (which fell on him "aslope" and "glanc'd on the ground" [10.1053–54] — that is, "cursed be the ground for thy sake"). To a cynical, unbelieving heart, such evidence as this provides scant reason for hope. Indeed, to hope for forgiveness based on such faint hints would be mad, absurd, folly. But by the end of Book 10, Adam and Eve are prepared to indulge in the folly of faith. They are prepared to believe that for God nothing is impossible — the essence of Kierkegaardian faith — including the miracle of mercy.

Given how little reason they have to hope for such mercy, their petitionary prayer demonstrates something like Kierkegaard's "courage to believe." But their belief is not simply the product of what Kierkegaard would call "purely human courage."[6] In *Paradise Lost*, the courage that disarms remorse is specifically extrahuman, God-inspired courage flowing from prevenient grace. Book 10 ends with Adam and Eve's prayer for forgiveness; Book 11 begins:

> Thus they in lowliest plight repentant stood
> Praying, for from the Mercy-seat above
> Prevenient Grace descending had remov'd
> The stony from thir hearts, and made new flesh
> Regenerate grow instead.
>
> (11.1–5)

The contrition that in Book 10 seemed a human accomplishment, an act of courage, becomes in Book 11 also a divine gift. Both Kierkegaard and Milton, then, see faith as the key to escape the Sisyphean cycles of remorse. But *The Concept of Anxiety* suggests that the self is empowered to disarm anxiety about evil if only it will exercise "courage to renounce anxiety without anxiety" (*CA*, 117). *Paradise Lost* acknowledges that the courage thus to renounce anxiety is something given as well as something grasped.

"Farewell Remorse": Anxiety about the Good

Kierkegaard identifies a species of postlapsarian anxiety that is the exact inverse of remorse (or, anxiety about evil); this he labels, logically enough, "anxiety about the good," or "the demonic."[7] Whereas human sinners, like Milton's Adam and Eve, respond to evil with anxiety, the demonic discovers anxiety in the good — meaning "the restoration of freedom, redemption, salvation, or whatever one would call it" (*CA*, 119).

Anxiety about the good thus describes a morally upside-down universe, a world in which sin has acquired such naturalized citizenship that it is regarded as the normal, legitimate condition of the self, while salvation appears to be a foreign, unwarranted, profoundly threatening possibility.

For the Miltonist, Kierkegaard's description of the demonic could hardly fit *Paradise Lost* more neatly. It is a commonplace that Satan and his legions attempt to fashion a morally topsy-turvy kingdom. The text enacts this in countless details — the most obvious, perhaps, being the construction of Pandemonium as a parodic heaven (see 2.267ff.). At the heart of this and every demonic enterprise lies the deep heresy that the rebel angels can themselves legislate the moral conditions of the universe by sheer fiat. None of Satan's claims to the power to redefine good and evil is so open, perhaps, as the ringing peroration with which he concludes his Mt. Niphates soliloquy: "So farewell Hope, and with Hope farewell Fear, / Farewell Remorse: all Good to me is lost; / Evil be thou my Good" (4.108–10). The terms of Satan's leave-taking here are precise, according to a Kierkegaardian diagnosis of anxiety of the evil. If the Devil truly could make evil his good and good his evil, then he would indeed be beyond remorse, for sin would hold no anxiety for him but would constitute a legitimate rather than "unwarranted" actuality.

He would not, however, be free from anxiety. Another "evil" could still occasion anxiety — namely, the "evil" of salvation; that is, actual good. Kierkegaard's analysis of this anxiety supplies a shrewd psychological profile for all Milton's demons. In fact, Kierkegaard's discussions of "the demonic" in *The Concept of Anxiety* and *The Sickness unto Death* offer so many illuminating congruencies with Milton's characterization of Satan and his fellows that one wonders how for so long they have been largely overlooked by Miltonists. I shall attempt to remedy this oversight here and in the next chapter.[8]

Satan's Mt. Niphates speech, which informed Milton's thinking about Satan from the time of an earlier tragic prototype of the epic, defines the *locus classicus* in *Paradise Lost* for the demonic, both demonic anxiety and (as we shall see in the next chapter) demonic despair. In this speech, Milton captures the essential nature of the Satanic condition. Satan's comments are so quintessentially demonic because they reveal him choosing again to be himself, the Devil. In so doing, he exposes the impossible contradictions upon which he painfully tries to found his existence.

Satan's anxious self-revelations on Mt. Niphates are provoked by the good — figured first by the sun, which reminds him of heaven, and then by the most deeply disturbing good of all, the prospect of salvation. Salvation constitutes an unwarranted actuality for Satan comparable to sin for Adam and Eve. His soliloquy is marked by anxiety's defining dialectic of sympathy and antipathy; his words disclose a longing to change, yet "the possibility of true change is what Satan's soliloquy specifically denies."[9] His opening apostrophe begins by sounding like a panegyric to the sun's resplendence ("O thou that with surpassing Glory crown'd"), but admiration quickly degenerates into execration ("how I hate thy beams," 4.32, 37). And so throughout the soliloquy: Satan's rhetoric registers anxiety's dialectic of longing and loathing, sympathy and antipathy — especially with respect to the possibility of redemption:

> is there no place
> Left for Repentance, none for Pardon left?
> None left but by submission; and that word
> *Disdain* forbids me, and my dread of shame
> Among the Spirits beneath.
>
> (4.79–83)

Kierkegaard asserts that the demonic is drawn out into the open when it is touched by the good, as Satan is when he is struck by the beauty of the sun: "the demonic . . . manifests itself clearly only when it is in contact with the good" (*CA*, 119). Based on New Testament accounts of Christ's contact with evil spirits, Kierkegaard's remark suggests unrecognized analogues between Satan's soliloquy and biblical exorcisms. The sun extorts unwelcome clarity from Satan about his relation to a good God in the same way that Jesus coerces unwilling testimony from the devils in the Gospels (see Matthew 8:29; Mark 5:7; Luke 4:34; Luke 8: 28). Similarly, Satan's encounters with any other beauty in Eden cast out the despairing devil from behind his mask of imperviousness to all that is good. Incited by contact with such "goods" as Adam and Eve's love (4.358ff.), fair Eden (9.99ff.), and the lovely Eve (9.444ff.), Satan's self-revelations bring unwelcome truths and dark lies to the light of day: "Ay me, they little know / How dearly I abide that boast so vain" (4.86–87). These contacts with the good exorcise the true Satan from his many disguises.

His self-revelation on the Assyrian mount functions as an exorcism not only for us as readers but also, we later learn, for Uriel, God's sentinel on the sun (4.569–71). After Uriel rallies his fellow angels, Satan is quite literally "touched by the good" in the form of Ithuriel's spear when the fiend sits crouched "squat like a toad" at Eve's ear. In this instance, the analogy to a New Testament exorcism seems particularly close, though here a fiend is cast out of a bestial shape rather than into one. In the Gospels, Christ's very presence or touch is enough to bring forth an unclean spirit railing in a loud voice, "Let us alone; what have we to do with thee, thou Jesus of Nazareth? art thou come to destroy us? I know thee who thou art; the Holy One of God" (Luke 4:34). Similarly, Satan bursts up from his toad-like squat to his defiant guise as "grisly King" because, we are told, "no falsehood can endure / Touch of Celestial temper, but returns / Of force to its own likeness" (4.811–13): "abasht the Devil stood, / And felt how awful goodness is, and saw / Virtue in her shape how lovely, saw, and pin'd / His loss" (4.846–49). Like an unclean spirit, Milton's Satan also trades defiance with the good angels. But unlike his New Testament counterpart, he insists they acknowledge his identity rather than vice versa: "Know ye not mee?" (4.828).

Like the searing self-revelations provoked by the sun, Satan's confrontation with the good angels (and, indeed, his encounters with the beauty of Eden, Eve, and so forth) show him to be terribly anxious about the good. "Lives there who loves his pain?" he asks the angel guard, "Who would not, finding way, break loose from Hell" (4.888–89). Yet he himself has claimed to be just such a one who loved the pain of hell more than the blessedness of heaven. Nevertheless, goodness, beauty, the prospect of salvation, and like "goods" continue to hold sway over Satan against his will. They call forth his most strenuous negation, just as does evil for human sinners. They become the object of demonic anxiety.

In several encounters with the good (such as upon Mt. Niphates, at the tip of Ithuriel's spear, in the presence of Eve's or Eden's beauty), Satan is visibly out of control. Although he claims absolute power to determine his response to the world, the beautiful and the good force him into shapes, admissions, and admiration he would not choose, if he could. Goodness compels the devil to respond as he does. Kierkegaard's analysis of demonic anxiety predicts this bondage; he observes that the demonic is not in bondage to sin but stands in an "unfree relation to the good" (*CA*, 119). Truly Satan's soliloquies in books 4 and 9 disclose a being more indentured to defiance of God than enamored of the pleasures of evil. By his final soliloquy, he admits that he has lost all joy in rebellion, which offers him at best nothing but momentary "ease / To my relentless thoughts" (9.129–30). Yet even in full consciousness of his wretchedness, Satan cannot repent, for, as he admits earlier, he can respond to God's grace only with resentment. Consequently, even if God were to offer pardon, he would rebel again: "therefore as far / From granting hee [God], as I from begging peace" (4.103–4).

Satan's unfree relation to the good stands as a painful hidden irony within his supposed freedom. "The mind is its own place, and in itself / Can make a Heav'n of Hell, a Hell of Heav'n" (1.254–55), vaunts Satan in Book 1. But the Satan of Book 4 knows he has power to achieve only the latter (that is, make of heaven a hell), for "within him Hell / He brings" (4.20–21). So within demonic freedom lurks bondage with respect to the good. Satan cannot *not* respond to God except with anxiety, for God constitutes an authentic alternative source of being and truth, one that debunks the demonic presumption that one can be one's own author of meaning. Therefore, Satan is trapped within his own infinite but abstract freedom — a freedom that is unfree to respond to the good, God, and hence the world apart from self with anything but denial. According to Kierkegaard, the consequence of this is not simply anxiety but (as I shall discuss in the next chapter) "demonic despair."

Satan's freedom, then, is really unfreedom in relation to the good. For true freedom, both Kierkegaard and Milton agree, requires the "restoration of freedom" with the Power that posited the self (see *SD*, 14 and passim). Short of admitting that God and a divinely created world constitute components of his contingency, Satan must remain confined in his own hellish self ("Which way I fly is Hell; Myself am Hell," 4.75), absurdly trying to impose his own willful meaning upon good and evil (4.110), love and hate (4.69–70), despair and hope (1.190–91), up and down (2.5–6), and so forth. To maintain the illusion of self-sufficiency, Satan must expend enormous energy in "negating" or denial. One of the demonic's deepest denials has to do with the nature of freedom and unfreedom itself. In anxiety about good, "freedom is posited as unfreedom, because freedom is lost. Here again freedom's possibility is anxiety" (*CA*, 123). In his soliloquy Satan makes this movement typical of demonic anxiety by defining the liberty of heaven as bondage to a "debt immense of endless gratitude, / So burdensome, still paying, still to owe" (4.52–53). Thus Satan posits God's service (freedom) as servility (unfreedom), and self-slavery as freedom.

To the degree that he can live in such absolute self-sufficiency, the Devil would radically shut himself off from outside influence and into his own fantastical, infinite self. For Kierkegaard, too, the demonic is isolated by its *det Indesluttede* — "shut-upness" (*CD*, 110) or "inclosing reserve" (*CA*, 133) — "unfreely disclosed."[10] Demonic shut-upness describes an existential closing-off of self: "The demonic does not close itself up with something, but closes itself up within itself" (*CA*, 124). That is, the demonic's self delimits the boundaries of his prison; as the narrator in *Paradise Lost* shrewdly remarks of Satan, "nor from Hell / One step no more than from himself can fly / By change of place" (4.21–23). This secret existential hell remains closely shut-up within Satan until encounters with the good bring it out into the open and the demonic is "unfreely disclosed."

However, the demonic keeps its unfreedom and despair (the miserable facts of its inwardness) to itself, while assuming outwardly an air of indifference or defiance. Kierkegaard's remarks about "inclosing reserve" recall Milton's Satan in the first glimpse we get of him rousing his compeers upon the Stygian lake. "What though the field be lost?" he exclaims,

> All is not lost; the unconquerable Will,
> And study of revenge, immortal hate,
> And courage never to submit or yield:
> And what is else not to be overcome?
> That Glory never shall his wrath or might
> Extort from me. To bow and sue for grace
> With suppliant knee, and deify his power
> Who from the terror of this Arm so late
> Doubted his Empire, that were low indeed,
> That were an ignominy and shame beneath
> This downfall.

$$(1.105–16)$$

The stoic courage and magnificent defiance of this speech are most impressive; what is more, they are meant to impress. Satan's rhetoric, like his tears later (1.620), is manufactured for public consumption. But however much Satan has come to believe his own propaganda about making God doubt his empire, deep inside he knows his defiance is hopeless. For God is God, whether or not in contrite submission Satan "deifies" him by recognizing the Almighty for what he is. Capping Satan's first speech, the narrator discloses the secret despair Satan keeps in close reserve, even from his followers: "So spake th' Apostate Angel, though in pain, / Vaunting aloud, but rackt with deep despair" (1.125–26).

By his public bluster and bravado in books 1 and 2, Satan keeps his despair and anxiety tucked away in close reserve until the soliloquy of Book 4. He cannot share his doubts even with his closest comrades. Rather, he tells his troops, "our better part remains / To work in close design, by fraud or guile" (1.645–46). Satan does not concede that "close design" governs his relationship to his coconspirators as well as to God. Only in his private soliloquy can he reveal the hidden despair he vigilantly masks from the fallen angels,

> whom I seduc'd
> With other promises and other vaunts
> Than to submit, boasting I could subdue
> Th' Omnipotent. Ay me, they little know
> How dearly I abide that boast so vain,
> Under what torments inwardly I groan
> (4.83–88)

Inclosing reserve isolates the demonic from his fellows, despite his posture as a comradely *bon amie*. Who and what the demonic is manifests itself only by contact with the good.

In addition to "inclosing reserve unfreely disclosed," the demonic is "the sudden": "The sudden is a new expression for another aspect of inclosing reserve. When the content is reflected upon, the demonic is defined as inclosing reserve; when time is reflected upon, it is defined as the sudden" (*CA*, 129). Kierkegaard's linkage between these purportedly symmetrical manifestations of the demonic is not entirely clear in *The Concept of Anxiety*. Milton's Satan, however, may help clarify what Kierkegaard intended. In *Paradise Lost*, as we have seen, Satan is isolated, cut off, dis-integrated from others by his close reserve; this is how Satan looks if we reflect upon the content of his personality. If we reflect upon how his character manifests itself in time and space, Satan's actions also look dis-integrated; his movements are sudden, discontinuous, shifting, and unstable. Similarly, Milton's hell pulsates with erratic energy, while his heaven stands stately and serene.

This difference conforms to Kierkegaard's observations that "sin comes into the world as the sudden," and likewise "the demonic is the sudden," while "the good signifies continuity, for the first expression of salvation is continuity" (*CA*, 32, 129, 130). It follows from Kierkegaard's definition of the demonic as anxiety of the good that the devil would dread continuity, for continuity expresses salvation. The demonic, therefore, expresses itself by means of the "negation of continuity [which] is the sudden" (*CA*, 129). "At one moment it is there, in the next moment it is gone, and no sooner is it gone than it is there again, wholly and completely. It cannot be incorporated into or worked into any continuity" (*CA*, 130). This interpretation of suddenness unfolds possible psy-

chological significance to the rapid discontinuities that typify Milton's
Satan, who though forever changing yet remains always the same. In
Paradise Lost, heaven and the Divine have a fixity and serene stasis that
contrasts sharply with the restlessness and frenetic bustle of hell and
with the volatility of Satan. The well-known Satanic degradation into
cormorant, toad, and serpent recounts only a few of his abrubt Protean
metamorphoses. Along the way toward infiltrating the serpent, for example, he rapidly assumes several other bestial forms:

> Then from his lofty stand on that high Tree
> Down he alights among the sportful Herd
> Of those fourfooted kinds, himself now one,
> Now another, as thir shape serv'd best his end.
> (4.395–98)

Kierkegaard's analysis of the sudden suggests that Satan's Protean habit
of suddenly altering his appearance expresses more than a tactical need
for disguises. It attests deep anxiety about continuity itself; it manifests
demonic rejection of the idea of permanence figured in heaven. The
sudden exhibits a certain spiritual restlessness in Satan's self and the
dis-integration of the demonic self from all fixed frames of reference.

The sudden also describes Satan's habitual mode of locomotion just
as it does his Protean shapes. Note that in his initial plunge into the
Garden, Satan abruptly "alights" down, his action like that of the beasts
among whom he cavorts. His transmogrifications ("now one, now another") seem not only strange but quirky and erratic. Similarly, Satanic
flight on his own wings is a conspicuously graceless action: he soars off
the lake, "incumbent on the dusky Air / That felt unusual weight"
(1.226–27), and through Chaos "Flutt'ring his pennons vain" (2.933).
Such fitful, animal-like movement is precisely the way, Kierkegaard
opines, an actor might best express Mephistopheles on stage: "Mephistopheles must walk as little as possible"; rather, he should leap in such a
way as to remind one of "the leap of the bird of prey and of the wild
beast" (*CA*, 132). At one point we observe Milton's Satan choose an
animal-like leap specifically because it expresses his opposition to the
divine order, which the poet represents as "bounds," comparable to the
Kierkegaardian term "continuity." Satan bounds over the boundary wall
of paradise "in contempt," and in so doing imitates the action of a
"prowling wolf" and then the cormorant (4.180–96). He leaps again when
he literally comes into contact with the good in the point of Ithuriel's
spear. Milton's simile suggests a connection between the sudden Satan's
demonic anxiety of the good:

> up he starts
> Discover'd and surpris'd. As when a spark
> Lights on a heap of nitrous Powder, laid
> Fit for the Tun some Magazin to store
> Against a rumor'd War, the Smutty grain
> With sudden blaze diffus'd, inflames the Air:
> So started up in his own shape the Fiend.
> Back stepp'd those two fair Angels half amaz'd
> So sudden to behold the grisly King.
>
>   (4.813–21)

Numerous other instances of Satan's sudden transformations and movements could be adduced. But "I shall not pursue this any farther" because "the principal thing is to have my schema in order" (*CA*, 137).

Satan's readiness to adapt his appearance to any shape whatsoever, no matter how degrading, argues for a certain emptiness in his self — a self in which inheres no form firm enough to resist transmutation, a self so fluid that it can dissolve itself in river mists (9.75, 180).[11] Perhaps Satan's volatility and formlessness express, then, Kierkegaard's third characteristic of the demonic: it is not only "inclosing reserve" and "the sudden" but also "the contentless, the boring" (*CA*, 132). Perhaps it is easier to see how Milton's Satan could be considered contentless (since he has no content to his self except that which he arbitrarily wills) than it is to detect how he is boring. Indeed, as one of the most compelling antiheroes in all of English literature, Satan hardly seems a good candidate for "the boring." Yet, as C. S. Lewis reminds us, great literary characterizations, such as Milton's Satan or Austen's Miss Bates or Meredith's Sir Willoughby, may be interesting to read about and at the same time boring to be.[12] Insofar as Satan actually succeeds in being the kind of monomaniacally self-sufficient individual he desires to be, his life would indeed be monotonous, for, by definition, he could only see, feel, hear, understand life in the way he wants; he could never be surprised, never learn from experience, never grow.

Up to this point I have discussed anxiety about good only with reference to Satan, Milton's preeminent demon. But Milton populates hell in *Paradise Lost* with many minor demons who share their leader's demonic anxiety. The last section of Kierkegaard's chapter on anxiety about good discusses the way the demonic attempts to evade the good by repressing "inwardness"; this section catches the ambiance of Milton's minor demons in Pandemonium. For example, consider the following "general observations"; these remarks could easily have been written with the likes of Mulciber, Mammon, and (especially) Belial in mind: "The demonic is able to express itself as indolence that postpones thinking, as curiosity that never becomes more than curiosity, as dishonest self-deception, as effeminate weakness that constantly relies on others, as superior negligence, as stupid busyness, etc." (*CA*, 138). Milton's demons also variously exhibit indolence, curiosity, self-deception, mindless bustle, and so forth. What is more, the purpose of either demonic indolence or bustle, indeed of every seemingly serious enterprise in Milton's hell, is to insulate its inhabitants from the painful reality of their God-relationship. Hell's magnificent building projects, great debates, heroic games, and exploring expeditions are all diversionary tactics; all are designed to take the mind off the point of hell: damnation.[13]

The escapism of Milton's lesser demons, of course, mirrors that of countless demonic denizens of our modern wasteland, the personality-types Kierkegaard no doubt had most in mind when he described the demonic. Kierkegaard saw the modern age as everywhere conspiring to avoid consciousness of the anxious possibility of salvation by losing itself in trivial pursuits; that a game by this name should have become so popular would have amused, but scarcely surprised, the author of *The Present Age*. Demonic strategies for avoiding "inwardness" (roughly meaning consciousness of one's existential predicament before God) are manifold. Kierkegaard categorizes these avoidance strategies in three active/passive pairs: Inwardness may be excluded by "unbelief — superstition," "hypocrisy — offense," or "pride — cowardice" (*CA*, 144–45). The last tandem perhaps best applies to Pandemonium. It suggests an underlying likeness beneath the supposedly rival proposals Moloch and Belial put forward in the great debate: both "open war" and "ignoble ease and peaceful sloth" are similarly beside the point since both strategies demonically evade the inward truth of damnation, compensating for lack of inwardness by outward shows of defiance or indifference, respectively.

Both proposals fundamentally lack seriousness — as do all hell's projects — for inwardness is the enabling condition of "seriousness." Indeed the two terms are nearly synonymous, both having to do with a proper concern for one's own salvation (or more largely stated, self) in respect to any other object of one's attention (see *CA*, 146). As an image of a life that has lost seriousness, Kierkegaard cites the following lines by Macbeth, uttered just after Duncan's murder:

> From this instant
> There's nothing serious in mortality:
> All is but toys: renown and grace is dead,

The wine of life is drawn, and the mere lees
Is left this vault to brag of.
(*CA*, 146; cf. *Macbeth* 2.3.92–96)

Kierkegaard sees *Macbeth* as the tragedy of a man who slays his own inwardness as he murders others, a man who drifts farther and farther away from self-knowledge as he wades deeper and deeper into blood. For one who has lost inwardness and its corollary, seriousness, "all is but toys," says Kierkegaard, echoing Ecclesiastes' "all is vanity."

Lacking inwardness, however, an individual tries to become serious about his toys: "Someone is in earnest about the national debt, another about the categories, and a third about a performance at the theater, etc." (*CA*, 149–50). The effect of becoming serious "at the wrong place" is comic if viewed from an eternal vantage: "everyone who becomes earnest at the wrong place is *eo ipso* comical, even though . . . the opinion of the age may be exceedingly earnest about it" (*CA*, 150; cf. 133). No English writer knows better than Milton the humor of misplaced seriousness. The demonic sections of *Paradise Lost* contain some of the greatest sustained mock-heroic verse in the language before Pope.[14] Milton's God is an ironist; he laughs at the Satanic rebellion, for it is quite literally ridiculous. We, too, are meant to enjoy the parodic hilarity of Pandemonium—with its moral and spatial inversions that make the highest and best in hell the lowest and worst in truth (hence, Satan is "by merit rais'd / To that bad eminence" [2.5–6]); with its massive building projects led by a crookbacked architect who could find nothing greater to admire in heaven than its gold-paved streets; with its great debates, staged to provide the illusion of parliamentary participation but really little more than puppet politics, a distraction from despair; with its tournaments, oratory, philosophy, and exploration. Pandemonium gets serious all right, but in the wrong places.

For me, the most delicious instance of misplaced seriousness in Pandemonium is demonic philosophy and theology. After the great debate, the devils divide up according to their diverse interests. Some participate in "Olympic Games," some in military drills; others set off to explore hell's uncharted territories, while yet "others more mild" sing of their heroic deeds and battles, complaining "that Fate / Free Virtue should enthrall to Force or Chance" (2.546–51). The terms of their songs, as well as the description of all these activities, are drawn from classical literature.[15] The devils re-create (or, from the perspective of the poem, create for the first time) the world of Greek and Roman epics; their debates even occur on hell's equivalent of the Areopagus—a fitting allusion to Paul's sermon about the unknown god in Acts 17. Philosophy and speculative theology are the highest achievements of Milton's proto-classical Pandemonium, as they were of ancient Athens (remembering, of course, the inversion of values that always obtains in hell — the higher, the lower):

> Others apart sat on a Hill retir'd,
> In thoughts more elevate, and reason'd high
> Of Providence, Foreknowledge, Will, and Fate,
> Fixt Fate, Free will, Foreknowledge absolute,
> And found no end, in wandering mazes lost.
>
> (2.557–61)

Here is seriousness egregiously misplaced. For what could be further from the point than to speculate in hell about God and truth all the while ignoring one's existential relation to the topics of discussion? Goaded by hell to repent, the demons instead talk theology. Such God-talk, however, serves only to distract them from thinking seriously about their concrete, existential relationship to God — namely, their sin-induced damnation:

> Of good and evil much they argu'd then,
> Of happiness and final misery,
> Passion and Apathy, and glory and shame,
> Vain wisdom all, and false Philosophie:
> Yet with a pleasing sorcery could charm
> Pain for a while of anguish, and excite
> Fallacious hope, or arm th' obdured breast
> With stubborn patience as with triple steel.
>
> (2.562–69)

Like Milton, Kierkegaard knows all about the "pleasing sorcery" of false philosophy. He knows that the demonic is perfectly capable of theoretical speculation about Deity. Yet, lacking inwardness, the demonic does theology in order to avoid reflecting seriously on God. Theology supplies the demonic with a subtle escape from the searing consciousness of its own existential relationship with God. Such is its dread of a living God that the demonic empties the term of life, reducing the Word to dead letters on the page, a mere cipher for the Good rather than a being who thunders down from Sinai and whispers across Galilee insisting that we answer his voice with our lives. Thus the demonic drowns out God, ironically, with theology.

Kierkegaard also knows that philosophy cannot wholly silence the stirrings of eternity, nor can theology satisfy the thirst for the divine any more than a book on human relationships can substitute for a lover, for to reiterate: "Whoever loves can hardly find joy and satisfaction . . . in preoccupation with a definition of what love properly is. Whoever lives in daily and festive communion with the thought that there is a God could hardly wish to spoil this for himself, or see it spoiled, by piecing together a definition of what God is" (*CA*, 147). In a similar vein Kierkegaard writes:

> With what industrious zeal, with what sacrifice of time, of diligence, of writing materials the speculators in our time have wanted to produce a complete proof of God's existence. . . . The demonstration of the existence of God is something with which one learnedly and metaphysically occupies oneself only on occasion, but the thought of God forces itself upon a man on every occasion. What is it such an individuality lacks? Inwardness. (*CA*, 140)

However assiduously they busy themselves with learned proofs of God's existence, demonic metaphysicians cannot avoid an even more anxious question of existence: namely, the issue of their own existence before a living God.

The thought of God, inwardly grasped, undercuts every demonic evasion and denial—even the high self-deception of theology—while self-forgetful demonic seriousness serves but to awaken divine laughter: "Whoever has not become earnest about this [himself], but about something else, something great and noisy, is despite of all his earnestness a joker, and though he may deceive irony for some time, he will, *volente deo* [God willing], still become comical because irony is jealous of earnestness" (*CA*, 150). Likewise the metaphysical speculations of Milton's devils about fate and free will, good and evil, and so on summon forth the spirit of irony that attends misplaced seriousness. God's laughter in *Paradise Lost* implicitly exposes to ridicule not simply the War in Heaven but *every* demonic enterprise. None of hell's grand and noisy projects can avoid appearing absurd *sub specie aeternitatis*. Hence, demonic individuals remain in such "terrible haste" to avoid eternity. They "preach the moment" and throw themselves into the present, although there is no escape from eternity—neither by "mockery," nor by "prosaic intoxication with common sense," nor by "busyness," nor by "enthusiasm for the temporal" (*CA*, 152). There is no Lethean stream by which the demonic can become oblivious to the anxious consciousness of eternity, salvation, God—in short, to the good.

Kierkegaard concludes his chapter on anxiety of the good by alluding to the River Lethe in order to contrast Greek and Christian views of immortality. The one posits oblivion, symbolized by the River Lethe, at the threshold to immortality; the other imagines eternity opening up with the total recollection of Judgment Day (*CA*, 153–54). In a striking coincidence of insight and imagery, Milton also concludes his depiction of Pandemonium with an account of the discovery of the River Lethe. Since hell contains the rest of the classical world, it is not surprising that its demon explorers discover the "silent stream / Lethe the River of Oblivion" as well (2.582–83). What is surprising is that they cannot drink from its anesthetizing stream. Lethe flows through hell, it appears, in order to mock its pretense to forgetfulness, to show that hell cannot forget — try as it might — what it is. Therefore, every demon must periodically cross the "Lethean Sound" to endure the icy torment of a "frozen continent," but none can drink from the Lethe and thus "with one small drop to lose / In sweet forgetfulness all pain and woe / All in one moment" (2.604, 587, 607–9).[16]

To forget all pain and woe, of course, has been the intent of Pandemonium from the start. This final image of Pandemonium confirms that all of hell's efforts to numb itself against what it is are vain. The fate of its explorers represents that of all hell's enterprises: that which had begun with the appearance of purposeful, serious activity dissolves in confusion, in the restless, meaningless motion of a classical hell:

> Thus roving on
> In confus'd march forlorn, th' advent'rous Bands
> With shudd'ring horror pale, and eyes aghast
> View'd first thir lamentable lot, and found
> No rest.
>
> (2.615–18)

Having set out in an effort that denies that hell is hell, they discover the landscape intractably hellish:

> through many a dark and dreary Vale
> They pass'd, and many a Region dolorous,
> O'er many a Frozen, many a Fiery Alp,
> Rocks, Caves, Lakes, Fens, Bogs, Dens, and shades of death,
> A Universe of death, which God by curse
> Created evil, for evil only good.
>
> (2.618–23)

The fate of this band of explorers comments ironically on the false heroics of another explorer, to whom the poem immediately returns.[17] Though this adventurer will escape hell geographically, he will not in fact escape hell any more than did his band of lesser devils. Satan will also yearn for a Lethean opiate to make him forget what and who he is but will not find it. Nevertheless, in despair he will continue his quest, making believe that good is evil but ever anxious about genuine good, which at any moment can expose the truth of his eternal condition "before God," turning to mockery of the grand schemes about which he tries to be so serious. Behind every demonic enterprise one hears faint echoes of divine laughter, for anything other than repentance is ridiculous.

So why does hell persist in its evasive strategies? The same reason we all do, to the degree that we, too, share the demonic predicament. We dread the possibility of salvation even more than we dislike the disturbing actuality of sin. We "are not willing to think eternity earnestly but are anxious about it, and anxiety can contrive a hundred evasions. And this is precisely the demonic" (*CA*, 154).

Notes

1. The Lowrie translation preserves this distinction between remorse and repentance; the Thomte translation does not.

2. Nietzsche makes a similar point about the will's hobbled freedom with respect to the past, except he identifies the resulting mood as melancholy rather than anxiety: "Willing liberates; but what is it that puts even the liberator himself in fetters? 'It was'—that is the name of the will's gnashing of teeth and most secret melancholy. Powerless against what has been done, he is an angry spectator of all that is past. The will cannot will backward; and that he cannot break time and time's covetousness, that is the will's loneliest melancholy" ("Of Redemption," in *Thus Spoke Zarathustra*, 139).

3. Hill, *Poet, Priest, and Prophet*, 144.

4. One of the more frequently noted weaknesses in Kierkegaard's philosophical writings (in contrast to his edifying discourses) is the lack of human reciprocity. This is typified by the relationship between the Knight of Faith and the object of his infinite concern. The Knight simply projects infinite passion upon his object; Isaac (Regine) has no say in the affair at all. Hardly a relationship, if you ask me. (For more on this, see Croxall, *Kierkegaard Commentary*, 219ff.). Whatever may be said against Milton's views about women, he feels deeply the importance of reciprocity. Indeed, spiritual mutuality is the crowning glory of marriage; its absence is the grounds for divorce.

5. Kierkegaard, *Fear and Trembling*, 49.

6. Ibid.

7. This section and chapter 7 focus on the Kierkegaardian "demonic." Kierkegaard studies have paid too little attention to the "demonic." Lapointe's 1980 international bibliography, for example, lists only three articles and one short

French monograph (Drolet, *Le Démoniaque chez S. A. Kierkegaard*) on the subject. True, critics occasionally make reference to the demonic in connection with a particular work in which it appears, but they rarely discuss the demonic as a single coherent psychological type. By linking the demonic in *The Concept of Anxiety* and *The Sickness unto Death*, I intend to suggest that the Kierkegaardian demonic does indeed constitute a coherent personality—one that finds a close literary analogue in Milton's Satan.

8. Broadbent alludes, without elaboration, to Kierkegaard's concepts of demonic anxiety and demonic despair in connection with Milton's Satan (*Some Graver Subject*, 76–78). Broadbent's slender comments, however, do little to clarify these concepts in Kierkegaard or apply them to Milton.

9. Hunter, *Paradise Lost*, 90.

10. See *SD*, 73, for further discussion of "inclosing reserve" and the demonic. McCarthy has offered "closed-in-ness" as a more literal, if more awkward, transliteration of *det Indetsluttede* (*The Phenomenology of Moods*, 44).

11. See Svendsen, *Milton and Science*, 105–13, for a discussion of Satan and the imagery of mists.

12. "The Hell he [Satan] carries with him is, in one sense, a Hell of infinite boredom. Satan, like Miss Bates, is interesting to read about; but Milton makes plain the blank uninterestingness of *being* Satan." The tediousness of Satan's life derives from his "monomaniac concern with himself" (Lewis, *Preface*, 102).

13. Lewis, *Preface*, 104–7; Stein, *Answerable Style*, 43–45. Lewis argues that the debate in Hell is an escape from the unspoken alternative: repentance. Stein suggests that escapism underlies all Hell's projects: "Pandemonium, sports, song, philosophy—these can suspend hell, can charm, excite, arm; but hell remains hell" (44).

14. "The first scenes in Hell seem to me the most successful examples in English of serious mock-heroic" (Summers, *Muse's Method*, 41). The nature and extent of Milton's comic irony in the demonic sections of his poem is a much-debated topic— especially since Stein argues that the War in Heaven is "epic farce" (*Answerable Style*, 17–37). Summers summarizes the issue more justly when he says that the war is absurd to God, heroic to the good angels, and tragic to the fallen angels (122). I also admire Shawcross's balanced disposition of the whole vexed issue of the comic elements in *Paradise Lost* (*Mortal Voice*, 84–90).

15. As Hunter remarks, "Their recreations, like their architecture and their institutions are modelled on those of a Greek city-state: competitive sports, mimic battles, verse-readings, philosophic debates, walking tours of the region" (*Paradise Lost*, 142).

16. Stein applies this same interpretation to the Lethe in Hell: "Hell *is* ultimately real and external—not just a base for operations for elsewhere, and not to be turned into a materialistic heaven either by act of will (Satan's) or by an act of salesmanship (Mammon's) that makes mind a partner of place by becoming place. This is not sufficient oblivion for the damned mind; it wants Lethe" (*Answerable Style*, 45).

17. For a discussion of Satan as antihero, see Shawcross, *Mortal Voice*, 35–38.

7

Demonic Despair

"Myself Am Hell": Demonic Sickness unto Death

No sooner is Satan "hurl'd headlong flaming" to hell than he escapes from the "Stygian flood" and thence from hell itself. By this act, Milton's Satan appears successfully to evade his punishment. Yet no matter how far Satan may distance himself from hell geographically, he can never elude damnation spiritually: for though Milton's hell is a place, it is even more essentially a condition of the demonic self. As the narrator shrewdly remarks upon Satan's arrival on earth: "for within him Hell / He brings, and round about him, nor from Hell / One step no more than from himself can fly / By change of place" (4.20–23). In like fashion, we learn out of Satan's own mouth, "Which way I fly is Hell, myself am Hell" (4.75). Hell is Satanic selfhood; its boundaries and contours are defined by the self Satan fashions for himself. Hence, there are few lurid scenes of corporal torture in Milton's inferno, as compared to Dante's, for damnation in *Paradise Lost* is primarily an inward condition.[1] This internalization of hell forms a crucial plank in the poem's theodicy. By fixing hell in Satan's psyche, Milton defines Satan's punishment as not, principally, something God does to the Devil but rather something Satan does to himself, thereby softening the notion of a vindictive God. Milton thus partially displaces crudely physical and punitive conceptions of hell with the hell of despair. He depicts despair, in turn, as the inexorable consequence of the demonic mode of existence.

That is to say, Milton characterizes hell as existential. The concept of an existential hell obviously predates Sartre and the modern period. It predates even Milton, as these lines from Marlowe's Mephistophilis attest: "But where we are is hell, / And where hell is there must we ever be" (1.5.125–26; see also 1.3.76–80).[2] Faustus's skepticism about the existence of hell reminds us that beginning in the late sixteenth century and culminating in eighteenth-century deism, the Western world became increasingly dubious about the existence of a literal hell and about the doctrine of eternal damnation.[3] Just before the Enlightenment denuded the afterlife of hell, the Renaissance peopled the stage with figures suffering the pangs of hell in this life; tragically hardhearted sinners like Macbeth discover the hell of the mind, the hell of sin-begotten despair. Milton's treatment of damnation surely owes something to both these intellectual currents. By making Satan's suffering at once profoundly psychological and largely self-induced, Milton's hell seems to anticipate the torrent of skepticism soon to engulf the doctrine of hell; by conducting a probing inquiry into the spiritual condition of the hardened heart, Milton's hell draws on and immeasurably deepens a great tradition in English tragedy.[4]

Milton's exploration of Satan's existential hell belongs among the greatest depictions of the devil and hell in world literature. Milton's Satan has rightly attracted constant and repeated evaluation. It is therefore with no little trepidation that I excavate again this well-worked vein in Milton studies. Yet despite all that has been written about Milton's Satan, significant new insights into his malaise are available from Kierkegaard, whose analysis of "demonic despair" in *Sickness unto Death* (*SD*, 42; cf. 72–75) often seems as if it were penned specifically with the existential position of Milton's Satan in mind.[5]

A Kierkegaardian analysis of Milton's Satan rewards Milton criticism and Kierkegaard studies alike. Kierkegaard's diagnosis of demonic despair supplies Miltonists with a coherent profile of Satan's pathology; Milton's rich characterization of Satan furnishes Kierkegaardians with a full-bodied, compelling prototype of the Kierkegaardian "demonic." More important, analyzing Satan's "sickness unto death" provides both groups with a powerful antidote against misreading the nature of Miltonic and Kierkegaardian individualism. The ensuing argument defends Milton against misappropriation by his Romantic heirs and Kierkegaard against the same by his Existentialist successors. Yet I want to acknowledge at the outset that such widespread and persistent misreadings as these must be grounded in half-truths.[6] Though not, as William Blake charged, "of the Devil's party without knowing it,"[7] Milton was surely wrestling demons within himself in his great portrait of Satan. Likewise, Kierkegaard was doubtless battling his own demons in his analysis of demonic despair.[8] What Gregor Malantschuk said of Kierkegaard's relation to Romanticism applies equally as well to Milton: "Kierkegaard is also able to recognize his own romantic tendencies, and therefore his criticism of this movement in its various formations must be regarded as a showdown with himself."[9] Through Satan and through the demonic, Milton and Kierkegaard variously exorcise the demon excesses of their own individualism.

Sickness unto Death is an unusually systematic document among Kierkegaard's pseudonymous works. The text's taxonomy of despair is suited to classify a great array of psychological configurations. Every configuration flows out of the notoriously complex, but precise, definition of the self enunciated in the first paragraphs (Miltonists, hold onto your hats!):

> A human being is spirit. But what is spirit? Spirit is the self. But what is the self? The self is a relation that relates itself to itself or is the relation's relating itself to itself in the relation; the self is not the relation but is the relation's relating itself to itself. A human being is a synthesis of the infinite and the finite, of the temporal and the eternal, of freedom and necessity, in short, a synthesis. A synthesis is the relation between two [R_1]. Considered in this way, a human being is still not a self.
>
> In the relation between two, the relation is the third as a negative unity, and the two relate to the relation and in the relation to the relation; thus under the qualification of the psychical the relation between the psychical and the physical is a relation. If, however, the relation relates itself to itself, this relation is the positive third, and this is the self [R_2].
>
> Such a relation that relates itself to itself, a self, must either have established itself or have been established by another.
>
> If the relation that relates itself to itself has been established by another, then the relation . . . is yet again a relation [R_3] and relates itself to that which established the entire relation.
>
> The human self is such a derived, established relation, a relation that relates itself to itself and in relating itself to itself relates itself to another. (*SD*, 13–14)

Obviously, a full explication of this labyrinthian definition lies beyond the scope of this study. However, the diagram on page 148 and a few brief comments might let a little light into the thicket of relationships that constitute the Kierkegaardian self.[10]

Kierkegaard regards the self as a relational activity ("the relation's relating") occurring within three enveloped relationships, which I have designated R_1, R_2, and R_3. This "thoroughly relational"[11] activity is generated initially from the fact that the self is a synthesis of mated opposing potentialities: finite-infinite, temporal-eternal, necessity-freedom (R_1). These "constituents" or "factors" of existence correspond roughly to the body-soul (or mind) dichotomy.[12] The factors form the ground of human existence, but merely having these potentialities is not yet to be a self (or "spirit"), properly understood. Rather, to be a self (or "spirit") is to relate to the synthesis (R_2). This is necessarily a psychic activity, and in this sense Kierkegaard privileges the mind. But note that the self is not simply mind or consciousness (as it is for Idealists from Plato on); it is a relation to body-mind "under the qualification of the psychical." Yet even

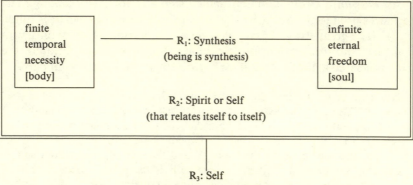

this relation does not exhaust the relational activities of human existence, for to discover oneself as a self or spirit is to recognize that the self must have either constituted itself or been constituted by another. Because the "human self is such a derived, established relation," it must not only relate itself to itself but "in relating itself to itself relate itself to another" (R_3) — subsequently described as "the power that established it" (*SD*, 13–14).

Despair, or "the sickness unto death," describes the disequilibrium resulting from countless ways of getting these relationships wrong. Demonic despair describes the sickness of the "infinite self" (*SD*, 68–72), or the self that tries to found its existence on the factors on the right in the diagram. Put another way, such a self presumes it can create itself through sheer will. Kierkegaard divides his study according to these two ways of looking at despair. He first classifies despair according to misrelations of the three paired factors, considering each pair separately. He then looks at despair "as defined by consciousness," which means as a function of how one wills or does not will to be oneself. Let me briefly illustrate possible failures for each of the three paired factors and then offer a sketch of despair "as defined by consciousness."

Freedom-Necessity. Some are in despair owing to lack of freedom. These regard themselves to be the victims of necessitarian powers, such as fate, environment, history, and so forth. The impossibility of hope for such individuals needs no elaboration. Others, however, suffer from despair for just the opposite reason: a lack of necessity. These individuals champion their power to choose their lives, to be the captains of their fate, the shapers of their destiny. They, too, are in despair. For the self is a very concrete thing — with concrete physical characteristics, a specific past, definite aptitudes, and so forth. Those lacking necessity flounder in a sea of possibility, as the self becomes more and more abstract the more they emphasize its power to transcend necessity.

Eternal-Temporal. For some unstated reason, Kierkegaard fails to analyze this pair. But it is possible to conjecture what the lack of eternity and the lack of temporality would entail. To lack eternity would be to try to live wholly in the present, a manifestly impossible task as the present describes an infinitely receding vanishing point, while consciousness necessarily spans past (by recollection) and future (by anticipation). Were this not so, we could neither speak nor understand the simplest sentence; language would splinter into meaningless syllables of sound and time, signifying nothing.[13] Nevertheless, many people do attempt to immerse themselves in the moment, only to discover that they are inescapably eternal beings who can never achieve perfect, nonreflective immediacy. Others would try to immerse themselves in the eternal, denying that they are time-bound beings, located in a particular moment in history, unable to live in the past except through memory or the future except through imagination. To opt for either temporality or eternity is to choose despair, for the human mode of selfhood is defined by the paradoxical conjunction of "eternity-temporality."

Infinite-Finite. Some are in despair by "becoming completely finitized, by becoming a number instead of a self, just one more man" (*SD*, 33). These lose themselves in "the public," though it is more correct to say they never acquire a self to lose, so void is their existence of genuine passion, risk, and individuality. Their despair derives from a "lack of infinitude." Yet others suffer despair from "lack of finitude." This sort make too much of the mind's impressive powers of transcendence. Realizing that human existence cannot be confined merely to the finite space our bodies occupy, these poetic souls equate the self with man's freedom to range in the "zodiack of his own wit" (Philip Sidney). Such souls "dwell in Possibility," understanding that

> The Brain — is wider than the sky —
> For — put them side by side —
> The one the other will contain
> With ease — and You — beside —
> (Emily Dickinson)

and that "Stone walls do not a prison make" (Richard Lovelace). Yet, since brains have heft and stones possess formidable mass (as Dr. Johnson graphically demonstrated when he refuted Bishop Berkeley's idealism by kicking a rock), those lacking finitude are also in despair.[14]

The whole truth about human existence is that it is paradoxically dual. Constrained by our finitude, temporality, and necessity to share a common world, we are also empowered by transcendence to inhabit worlds as infinite and various as the imagination itself. Robert Herrick's marvelous epigram on dreams recognizes this duality: "Here we are all, by day; By night w'are hurl'd / By dreames, each one, into a sev'rall world."[15] The truth is even stranger than this: even by day we dwell in our secret several worlds even while sharing one common world. Accordingly, from Kierkegaard's view, Hedonists, Stoics, Fatalists, Transcendentalists, and most Christians—indeed, all existential positions but one—fail to resolve the contradictory potentialities of the self.[16] Hence, the title of one chapter: "The Universality of This Sickness (Despair)" (*SD*, 22–28).

In the second section of *Sickness unto Death*, Kierkegaard pursues the same analysis of despair, only this time not by dissecting the factors but by looking at selfhood holistically according to three "aspects of consciousness." In ascending order of consciousness, these are the despair that is unaware of having a self; the despair of not willing to be oneself; and the despair of willing to be oneself. The first form of despair attends the nonreflective condition typified by mass culture. Unless the self escapes the crowd, it remains virtually unconscious of itself as a self—that is, as an autonomous individual. In this case, the self never even rises to the consciousness of its despair but exists in a condition of "spiritlessness."[17] The second form of despair is also passive, but self-consciously so. A "despair of weakness," the "despair of not willing to be oneself" occurs when one identifies the self with the limiting factors on the left side of the diagram of page 148—necessity, temporality, finitude. The third form of despair, by contrast, equates the self with the expansive factors on the right side of the diagram—freedom, eternity, and infinity—and also denies R_3 by presupposing that the self is wholly self-constituted. For this despair, called "defiance," "there must be consciousness of an infinite self" (*SD*, 67–68) as "the self in despair is restlessly and tormentedly engaged in willing to be itself" (*SD*, 73). Kierkegaard brands this last, "most intensive" form of despair "the devil's despair" or "demonic despair" (*SD*, 42, 72–75).

Aptly enough, demonic despair is the malady that best applies to Milton's Satan, who consistently lays impressive claims to own an infinite self. According to *Sickness unto Death*'s schema, Satan's existential position can be looked at in two ways. From the perspective of the "factors," Satan's sickness springs from his choice to embrace only the infinite, eternal, and free potentialities of his being, while denying their corollaries: the finite, the temporal, and the necessary. Or, from the perspective of self-consciousness, Satan's despair arises from his absolute defiance. In defiance, the demonic attempts to detach himself from contingency and arrogate to himself the power of self-existence (*SD*, 68); that is (to adopt Kierkegaardian language), the demonic wills to be himself by himself, without reference to the power that constituted the self; he is the self-made man manifested in "demonic ideality" (*SD*, 72). "With all his power," however, the self-made demonic cannot "break the despair by himself and by himself alone — he is still in despair and with all his presumed effort only works himself all the deeper into deeper despair" (*SD*, 14).

Since "factors" and "consciousness" present two ways of talking about the same existential movements, I shall subsume demonic defiance in my "factor analysis" of Satan's sickness. Together, defiance and the lack of necessity-temporality-finitude constitute the despair of the infinite self, which I discuss in the next section. Then in the third section, I examine one aspect of Satan's consciousness: his despairing relation to beauty.

"Not to Be Chang'd by Place or Time": Satan's Despair and the Infinite Self

When Satan first takes possession of hell, he simultaneously lays claim to an infinite self. In the most famous lines from this speech, Satan explicitly denies finitude, temporality, and necessity:

> Farewell happy Fields
> Where Joy for ever dwells: Hail horrors, hail
> Infernal world, and thou profoundest Hell
> Receive thy new Possessor: One who brings
> A mind not to be chang'd by Place or Time.
> The mind is its own place, and in itself
> Can make a Heav'n of Hell, a Hell of Heav'n.
> (1.249–55)

"Place" and "Time" correspond neatly to finitude and temporality in Kierkegaard's scheme, while the entire discourse stands in massive opposition to the third element of Kierkegaard's triad, necessity:

> What matter where, if I be still the same,
> And what I should be, all but less than hee
> Whom Thunder hath made greater? Here at least
> We shall be free; th' Almighty hath not built

> Here for his envy, will not drive us hence:
> Here we may reign secure, and in my choice
> To reign is worth ambition though in Hell:
> Better to reign in Hell, than serve in Heav'n.
>   (1.256–64)

This is the utterance of one who would make a choice out of a necessity. The rivalry with God that energizes this discourse ultimately emanates from Satan's boast to possess the same kind of being as God: that is, a being that is the source of its own being, a sovereign self empowered to deploy the language of divine *fiat* as if his word could will the world into existence: "Be it so, since he / Who now is Sovran can dispose and bid / What shall be right" (1.245–47). All Satan's projects *qua* Satan depend on this illusion of the infinite self.

Though they form a single, coherent syndrome, for purpose of analysis let us inspect Satan's denials of temporality, finitude, and necessity separately. First, temporality. The infinite self denies its temporality by arrogating to itself the a priori, uncreated self-existence of God, the source of being. Like Pride in *Dr. Faustus*'s pageant of the Seven Deadly Sins, the infinite self "disdain[s] to have any parents" (2.1.116).[18] Or as Kierkegaard remarks: "He wants to begin a little earlier than do other men, not at and with the beginning, but 'in the beginning'"; that is, he regards his genesis as Genesis, as if he begins time rather than begins in time. The infinite self "wants to create itself," "to fashion out of [his concretion] . . . such a self as he wants"; "he does not want to put on his own self, to see his given self as a task — he himself wants to compose his self by means of being the infinite form" (*SD*, 68). Denial of temporality results ineluctably in despair. Why? The eternizing self has no way of reintegrating itself back into time (the corollary pole of its existence), nor into the concretions that define its temporal existence. Because "his concrete self . . . certainly has necessity and limitations, is this very specific being with these natural capacities, predispositions, etc." (*SD*, 68), the infinite self's mode of existence must be essentially negative. To will to be in this way is to will to dispose oneself of whatever lies beyond will. But much resists assimilation by the will, including the stubborn fact of the self's temporality. In this existential contradiction lurks despair.

Consonant with this diagnosis of the infinite self, Milton's Satan proves to be profoundly seduced by the fantasy of self-creation.[19] His debate with Abdiel brings to light this heretofore hidden demonic heresy. Satan regards his beginning as in fact The Beginning. Although Satan's claim to be God's rival has always rested on this presumption of self-existence, the demonic denial of temporality remains only implicit until Satan is provoked by Abdiel's assertion that the creature owes its creator loyalty: "As by his Word the mighty Father made / All things, ev'n thee, and all the Spirits of Heav'n" (5.836–37). To which, Satan scornfully responds:

> That we were form'd then say'st thou? and the work
> Of secondary hands, by task transferr'd
> From Father to his Son? strange point and new!
> Doctrine which we would know whence learnt: who saw
> When this creation was? remember'st thou
> Thy making, while the Maker gave thee being?
> We know no time when we were not as now
> Know none before us, self-begot, self-rais'd
> By our own quick'ning power.
>
> (5.853–61)

This is the utterance of one unwilling to "attire himself in himself," as Lowrie's translation puts it; of one "not willing to begin with the beginning but 'in the beginning'" (*SUD*, 202). Like Marlowe's Pride or Dickens's Bounderby, the self-made man must deny his paternity through oedipal rebellion.[20] To be "self-begot" is ultimately to will oneself out of history.

Yet, although Satan proclaims, "We know no time when we were not as now," of all the characters in the poem he undergoes the most metamorphoses over the course of time, at least in appearance. Satan's constant self-refashionings enact another sort of negation characteristic of the infinite self: the denial of finitude. Incessantly refashioning his outward self, Satan displays contempt for the finite boundaries imposed by the somatic element of his self, whatever these may be for a spirit being. In a curious way, Satan is a dualist; he must disparage externality in order to champion his free subjectivity. Hence, his rhetoric constantly evokes attitudes familiar through Stoicism — a philosophy of heroic denial Milton faults implicitly through the figure of Satan and rejects outright through Jesus in *Paradise Regained* (4.300–308) and in *The Christian Doctrine* (2.10).[21] Similarly, Kierkegaard says: "If a generic name for this despair is wanted, it could be called stoicism" (*SD*, 68).

The infinite self presumes it "can dispose of itself or . . . create itself" at any moment (*SUD*, 201). What is lacking is the finite, or "the limiting factor"; instead, the self has only the infinite, or "the expanding factor. Infinitude's despair is therefore the fantastical, the limitless" (*SUD*, 163). Satan's Protean nature discloses a being seduced by infinitude's dream of ever more fluid, fantastical, expansive self-representations. No single, fixed form can contain the Devil. At last, shapelessness itself becomes his chosen shape: "In with the River sunk, and with it rose / *Satan* involv'd in rising Mist" (9.74–75). Twice more before the Temptation, Milton associates the Tempter with mists and vapors (9.158–59, 180). No doubt Milton has many motives for these identifications, but among their other purposes the vapors serve as emblems of Satan's would-be infinite self – a self desperately committed to an expansive and fluid mode of selfhood.

Satan's fluid self-representations are not merely accidental to his status as a spirit being but expressive of a specifically demonic condition, for though both good and bad angels possess malleable spirit bodies (1.423–31), only the Devil undergoes so many Protean changes.[22] Unlike Satan, the faithful angels and God enjoy a certain fixity of form. The unfallen angels appear more at ease with their contingent, created selves – and hence with their harmoniously ordered world. By contrast, the Devil's volatility as well as hell's frenetic energy betray unease of fragmented selves – like that of the unconverted Augustine, whose "heart is restless until it find repose in thee [God]" (*Confessions*, Book 1).

Because the infinite self undertakes to deny its finitude, its existential hell must be sufficently concrete to remind the self that the mind is not utterly its own place. That is to say, even an existential hell must be partly external. The "physical" punishments of Milton's hell are precisely adjusted to the demonic's spiritual predicament: his "lack of finitude." Finite impediments serve as divine correctives against the illusions of the would-be infinite self. For those with eyes to see, Milton's hell is full of concrete reminders of what it is: "A Dungeon horrible" burning with "penal fires" (1.61, 48); yet everywhere the damned are engaged in willful self-deception. They conspire to blind themselves to the nature of hell and regard it as a rival kingdom, or at least a "safe retreat" (2.317). Therefore, God must deny the damned what they most desire, which is to drown consciousness of despair in Lethean oblivion (2.604–9). So periodically the fallen angels must be forced to "feel by turns the bitter change / Of fierce extremes" between fire and ice (2.598–99). This reality-therapy jolts them with painfully concrete reminders of their finitude. Similarly, once a year the fallen angels are forced to appear outwardly to be what they are inwardly: they are enclosed in the form of serpents and compelled to chew fruit that turns to ashes in their mouths (10.504–77). This is done in order "to dash thir pride" (10.577).

Through such punishments, God reminds the fallen angels of that which they would fain forget: "the limiting factor," their finitude. These punishments guarantee that, try as they might to equate their being with mind, the demons will inevitably collide against their finitude. Like hell's band of explorers, sooner or later the demonic self will run up against "Rocks, Caves, Lakes, Fens, Bogs, Dens, and shades of death" (2.621). Such intractable features of the landscape are potentially educative, even redemptive; finitude could teach the demonic of the illusory nature of its definition of freedom. But the demonic prefers to cling to the fantasy that the mind is its own place, though to do so is despair, rather than admit that the self is constituted by the finite along with the infinite.

The infinite self defines itself as absolute freedom, pure possibility. In fact, however, its self breaks down over the "lack of necessity," the third missing factor in the Kierkegaardian triad. Kierkegaard's images for this despair recall Satan's journey through Chaos in *Paradise Lost*. Without necessity, Kierkegaard writes, the "self becomes an abstract possibility; it flounders in possibility"; also, "eventually everything seems possible, but this is exactly the point at which the abyss swallows up the self" (*SD*, 36). These descriptions remind us of the dark abyss that nearly engulfs the antihero of *Paradise Lost*—the "vast vacuity" of Chaos (2.932). Satan flounders in anarchic possibility as he journeys into the dark realm where Chaos and "Sable-vested Night" "hold / Eternal Anarchy" (2.962, 895–96). Regina Schwartz has recently illuminated the subtle meanings of this mysterious realm in Milton's epic.[23] In addition to the purposes of Chaos she describes, I should like to suggest that Chaos serves another use: it exposes Satan's need for a ground of being besides his will.

Satan's journey through Chaos betrays just how vulnerable he himself is to randomness, accident, and chance—that is, to the very anarchic world of Lucretian atomism to which he would reduce the universe as an agent of uncreation (2.890–910).[24] Ironically, Satan shows himself unable to act in a realm that lacks necessity, a world of sheer possibilty. He tumbles awkwardly down into Chaos, "Flutt'ring his pennons vain plumb down he drops / Ten thousand fadom deep" (2.933–34). Satan is helpless in a realm of actual anarchic freedom. That he escapes from the abyss at all is only "by ill chance" (2.935)—and the high permission of Providence (2.1025). This dependency undercuts his boast of absolute autonomy. Had he truly been autonomous, the Devil could master *all* conditions upon which his identity depends. Chaos reveals that Satan's identity depends on his having firm ground beyond the self. Satan's inability to cross Chaos on his own debunks the Devil's fallacious claim to will the conditions of his existence. God, who embodies genuine self-existence, has nothing to fear from Chaos and Night, for although they are "eldest of things" (2.962), He is elder yet. He is the ground of being.

As Creator, God draws from "the Womb of nature" "his dark materials to create more Worlds" (2.916). It is otherwise for the blasphemous self-creator, who cannot bear to acknowledge creaturely dependency. Yet though "he wants to tear his self away from the power that established it" (*SD*, 20), he requires such a power, however unwelcome, to ground his self. Ironically Satan's journey through Chaos makes clear that he needs necessity as an enabling condition of freedom. Without necessity, there is no place for the self to stand, so a vast vacuity opens underneath the self, an "Illimitable Ocean, without bound, / Without dimension, where length, breadth, and highth, / And time and place are lost" (2.892–94). The echoing of "time and place" mocks Satan's earlier boast to author his own time and place. In an actual void, Satan flounders. Therefore he flees this realm without limit or bound or dimension, the narrator wryly observes, "glad that now his Sea should find a shore" (2.1011).

It becomes increasingly clear, as Satan departs from Chaos, that the Devil desperately needs a shore—some stable ground beyond naked will upon which to stand.[25] Because he "lacks necessity," Satan is free only to exercise his will upon the world, but not to accept it. "What is missing" from such freedom, Kierkegaard notes, "is essentially the power to obey, to submit to the necessity in one's life, to what may be called one's limitations" (*SD*, 36). Milton signals this deficiency of demonic freedom in countless ways. Perhaps the most obvious occurs when he describes Satan's first entrance into Paradise. The Devil breaks into Eden by leaping over the wall rather than passing through the gate. Of this act the narrator comments: "Due entrance he [Satan] disdain'd, and in contempt, / At one slight bound high overleap'd all bound / Of Hill or highest Wall" (4.180–82). Milton thus makes Satan's entrance into Eden iconographic of a transgressive nature. Satan defines himself as the foe to boundaries and limits; he breaks them at every turn. The play upon "bound" as leap and as limit enacts in brief one of the largest philosophical questions of *Paradise Lost*: the nature of freedom.

For Milton, authentic freedom is enabled by proper limits. His model is temperance, which designates a class of freedom that is specifically "within bounds" (7.120). The poet repeatedly celebrates this ideal as the only "true liberty" (12.83; see 11.530–34, 804–7). For Satan, by contrast, freedom is incompatible with limits. He aptly becomes an ensign for Chaos, for his mode of freedom is fundamentally at odds with order; it would return the world to randomness (see 2.871–1009). Charged with breaking "the bounds [God] prescrib'd" (4.878), Satan hears in "bounds" only its oppressive sense of binding (see 4.877–901) and hurls back this revealing retort at the obedient angel who apprehends him: "when I am thy captive talk of chains, / Proud *limitary* Cherub"; "thou with thy Compeers, / [art] Us'd to the yoke" (4.970–71, 974–75; my emphasis). Satan regards all service as servility and every limit as a provocative limitation because for him freedom signifies, precisely, the illimitable.

Consonant with this mentality, Satan teaches Eve to view the limits of Paradise as reprehensible restrictions upon her freedom. Imagining Eden not as an enclosed space that allows a fullness of action and joy (cf. 4.410–38) but as a "narrow circuit" (9.322), Eve seems especially susceptible to the Satanic seduction of the fantasy of infinite freedom as she leaves Adam. After her fall, Eve maligns God as "Our Great Forbidder" (9.815), even though nothing was forbidden in Eden except eating the fruit of a single tree. She has learned to frame her accusation of God in Satan's idiom of infinite, unsatiable desire. Created with minds capable of imagining infinite possibilities, human beings may regard any limit whatsoever, even so small as a single prohibition, as oppressive. "For inferior who is free?" (9.825), fallen Eve remarks. This is the central question of the infinite self. The answer is that no one is absolutely free in the sense presupposed by the question, for existence is founded on the paradoxical synthesis of necessity-freedom. Human possibility always occurs within boundaries; freedom always emerges in a world. Therefore everyone's life, however lofty, furnishes occasion for the complaint "inferior who is free?" for human existence is constituted by powers beyond the self. In Milton's universe, Woman can reasonably feel herself impaired because she is unequal to Man; Man can imagine himself unfairly created lower than the Angels; an Angel like Satan can regard himself insufferably below the Son; the Son could choose to feel himself intolerably subordinate to the Father.[26] Or each can find in finitude blessed fullness.

Any hierarchical principle, any limit whatsoever, threatens the self that defines its freedom by the denial of necessity. For the infinite self no space is so vast, no kingdom so ample, that it offers no occasion for envy. Yet, ironically, envy itself signals that the self is not absolute, as it presumes to be. Thus Satan both envies divine infinitude and, in effect, denies the possibility of envy by claiming infinity for himself. Demonic envy gives the lie to Satan's professed Godlike ability to subsume time and place into his mind. Because he is not God, he cannot will the conditions of his existence; they exist apart from his will. In the attempt lies despair.

Satan makes a game effort to promote his mode of selfhood, especially in his public speeches of books 1 and 2. And doubtless he is somewhat taken in by his own attitudinizing. But beneath the public bravado lies the "infinite despair" he admits to only in solitude (see 4.31–114; 9.99–178). In these soliloquies we see that Satan is punished *by* his sinfulness more than *for* it. Satan damns himself. Yet short of repentance, he cannot do otherwise, for "every human life is religiously designed" (*CA*, 105): it either rests paradoxically in providence or lives in despair. Satan chooses despair. His is an existential hell, literally a hell born out of his mode of selfhood.

Surely this view of damnation constitutes a major plank in the scaffolding of Milton's "great argument." Both *Paradise Lost* and *Sickness unto Death* portray hell as a condition of a self that the demonic tries to fashion by itself alone but that constantly collides against the fact of its creaturely status. Such a self, Milton and Kierkegaard agree, suffers from a sickness unto death. What is more, there is no exit from such despair short of reconstituting the self. As long as the Devil holds fast to the self he chose when the Light-bearer (Lucifer) became Adversary (Satan) he will never escape hell "no more than from himself can fly / By change of place" (4.22–23). The only exit from hell and despair is to abandon this demonic self and reintegrate himself with the power that posited him: God. But this is precisely what the demonic — whether devil or human — defiantly refuses to do. Above all else, Satan clings fast to the fantasy of the infinite self, though such a self defines the very boundaries of hell. He prefers his punishment to forgiveness, as he admits on Mount Niphates. For like Captain Ahab, his monomaniac sense of himself as a victim provides a ready excuse to cling to his hatred and his defiance, upon which his whole identity now rests: "now he would rather rage against everything and be the wronged victim of the whole world . . . and it is of particular significance to him to make sure that he has his torment on hand and that no one takes it away from him" (*SD*, 72).

"Though Terror Be in Love and Beauty": The Ontological Terror of Beauty

Observing Eve just before his final assault, Satan momentarily hesitates, confessing that "She [is] fair, divinely fair, fit Love for Gods, / Not terrible, though terror be in Love / And beauty, not approached by stronger hate" (9.490–92). Here and elsewhere (for example, 4.355–56) Satan cowers at beauty. Because beauty normally is thought to evoke desire rather than dread, one may wonder why Satan is so concerned to keep up his guard; why the need to overwhelm beauty with "stronger hate," especially as beauty ordinarily is regarded to be wholly subjective. In this section I argue that Satan's terror is ontological, rooted in a profound misunderstanding of the nature of genuine subjectivity and individualism; that in Satan's terrified response to beauty we observe manifestations of a consciousness gripped by demonic despair; that Satanic individualism suffers from a pathological inability to connect to, much less to love, the non-self. Satan's deficiency anticipates modernism's perennial problem with the "other." A Kierkegaardian critique of Satan's despairing response to beauty thus serves to critique not simply Milton's demon but similarly mistaken modern conceptions of the self, especially as it has been defined since Descartes reoriented Western thought along a sharp subject-object axis.[27]

But before attempting a Kierkegaardian diagnosis, let me first look more closely at the symptoms of Satan's sickness as they manifest themselves in his response to beauty. Satan's confession of terror at the sight of Eve follows immediately upon his being struck "stupidly good" in Eve's presence. Of this moment, the narrator says:

> Her graceful innocence, her every Air
> Of gesture or least action overaw'd
> His Malice, and with rapine sweet bereav'd
> His fierceness of the fierce intent it brought:
> That space the Evil one abstracted stood
> From his own evil, and for the time remain'd
> Stupidly good, of enmity disarm'd,
> Of guile, of hate, of envy, of revenge.
>
> (9.459–66)

Eve's beauty is demonstrably powerful here—powerful enough to overawe and disarm the Evil One. Yet Eve's loveliness terrifies Satan, I submit, not simply because it manifests her moral superiority (which it does) but because it signals the sheer, stubborn ontological presence of an "other" whose existence stands plainly apart from ego and will.[28] Eve's comeliness is terrible because it is God-given; her beauty attests the even more terrible beauty of the Lord who fashioned her. To recognize Eve for what she is (namely, beautiful) is to concede that the other (and, by implication, the world) is *not* merely what one wills it to be. Here lurks the deepest terror of beauty for Satan. Beauty signals ontological otherness; it makes conspicuous Eve's alterity and marks her participation in an order that is manifestly not self- but God-fashioned.

To succumb to beauty's charm is to be drawn out of (literally, *abs tractus*) one's subjective world.[29] Thus the otherness of beauty necessarily imperils Satan's subjectivist fantasy that reality is an extension of his mind.

To argue that beauty is at once powerful, and powerful because it is *not* wholly subjective, flies in the face of commonplaces, for conventionally beauty is regarded as both fragile and subjective: Its "action," Shakespeare says, "is no stronger than a flower" (Sonnet 65); its very existence is said to reside solely in the "eye of the beholder."[30] But Milton attributes both strength and autonomy to beauty. Eve's beauty commands Satan's grudging admiration as tribute due to an imperious sovereign power. Milton's diction lays particular stress upon beauty's coercive power: Eve "overawes," "abstracts," "disarms," and strips Satan of fierceness with "rapine sweet" and "sweet compulsion." She immobilizes and enervates her adversary, momentarily mesmerizing him with wonder at her irresistible grace. Having been thus thrown off balance, the Devil must willfully reassert control over his mind, which he had proclaimed to be its own place: "Thoughts, whither have ye led me," he remonstrates, "with what sweet / Compulsion thus transported to forget / What hither brought us" (9.473–75).

Satan's stupefaction here enacts a common aesthetic experience. We duplicate Satan's wonder whenever we are swept off our feet by love, or struck dumb by a resplendent landscape, or poem, or symphony, or building. Most people rather enjoy such sensations. Yet our language implies that intense aesthetic exhilaration marks a condition of acute vulnerability, tinged with pain. For although normatively it is a point of praise to call a landscape "breathtaking," a symphony "moving," a painting "captivating," a poem "stunning," an aria "ravishing," and so forth, these terms acknowledge the terror of beauty, which evidently possesses fearful power to work its will forcibly upon ours.

Satan, whose mode of existence is defined by absolute self-control, thrills to beauty like the rest of us (9.468). But he also trembles in terror at the loss of control attending his rapture. He sees Eve as unwittingly reversing her rape, ravishing her would-be ravisher with "rapine sweet" and "sweet compulsion" by her loveliness. She thus allures Satan toward the good just as he will tempt her toward evil—the good here being simply to relent and enjoy God's gracious creation, a prospect Satan's identity as Adversary makes him regard first with terror and then denial. Nor can he ever wholly relax and delight in natural beauty, for he poses as one who himself determines the goodness and beauty by fiat:

Is this the Region, this the Soil, the Climate. . . .
That we must change for Heav'n; this mournful gloom
For that celestial light? Be it so, since he
Who now is Sovran can dispose and bid
What shall be right.

(1.242, 244–47)

Such a "sovran" cannot simply let the world be, either by accepting its pain or by welcoming its surprising graces. He must be ever vigilant to filter experience, rather than simply feel it; he must dominate nature, rather than participate creatively in it.

In his proud independence, Satan becomes a paradigm of radical individualism, or what a recent examination of American culture usefully labels "ontological individualism."[31] Satan depicts, unalloyed, the myth of the self-made man, as I have already discussed at length. Not situated in place and time, the self must constantly invent itself out of its mind. Satan's claim to possess such freedom presupposes two dubious premises that were to become common after Descartes: (1) the sharp rift between subject and object, and (2) the priority of subject to object. In this view, "being" is located in a mind not constituted by the world but itself constituting the world—a mind that is "its own place, and in itself / Can make a Heav'n of Hell, a Hell of Heav'n" (1.252–55). Satanic individualism is thus rightly called "ontological" and identified with other forms of subjectivism. For Milton's antihero tries to live out the subjectivist dream that one is god of one's own universe (now coterminous with one's mind) and hence empowered to legislate the conditions of that universe, including the nature of good and evil: "all Good to me is lost; / Evil be thou my Good" (4.109–10).

These grand claims for individual freedom are not without heroic overtones. Indeed, at least since the Cartesian revolution, they have supplied the very grist of Western heroism. We can recognize versions of Milton's Satan in both the Romantic and Existential hero; and prior to the seventeenth century, Stoicism and Pelagianism offered attractive conceptions of freedom and the self analogous to Satan's.[32] Hence, the common misreading of Satan as hero is prompted by his resemblance to many often-admired philosophies. Kierkegaard recognizes that demonic despair is "in a certain sense . . . very close to the truth" (*SD*, 67). But the illusion of absolute autonomy that these philosophies tend to underwrite is both nonsensical and pernicious: nonsensical because humans cannot create themselves *ex nihilo*, for human freedom always occurs as the unfolding of possibilities within a given world; pernicious because would-be self-fashioners sever themselves from the larger world and therefore from true freedom within that world.

Satan's encounters with Eve show how weak his battlements against God's larger world are. Satanic security, it seems, depends upon the fiction that there is no outside, that no enemy is real, that everywhere is equally heaven or hell. Similarly, his diabolic freedom depends, paradoxically, upon increasingly compulsive acts of denial, until he confesses "only in destroying I find ease / To my relentless thoughts" (9.129–30). No wonder natural beauty terrifies Satan as if it were hell's flames; beauty reminds him of the larger order within which he must try to impose his reign. And no wonder both Milton and Kierkegaard concur that ontological individualism offers not freedom but mere arbitrariness, not security but despair.

Two epic similes in *Paradise Lost* deepen the connection between Satan's false individualism and his despair. Properly, I believe, they ought to be read as companion pairs and in conjunction with Satan's stupefaction by Eve. All these passages reveal Satan's crippling inability to respond to beauty, which in turn evinces an even deeper impotence—his powerlessness to repent. The similes show Satan refusing to yield himself freely to beauty, which beckons him with healing in its wings, but preferring instead to feed his hatred and spite, cloistered in the hellish kingdom of his mind.

The first simile occurs in Book 4 just after Satan's soliloquy, significantly the longest and most complex enunciation of his despair in the poem.[33] After laying bare the existential hell Satan brings "within him . . . and round about him, nor from Hell / One step more than from himself can fly / By change of place" (4.20–23), the narrator notes that Satan flies from Mount Niphates to the Garden wall. His approach to the fragrant, fragile, delicious paradise is described in simile. First the simile's narrative link and vehicle:

> And of pure now purer air
> Meets his approach, and to the heart inspires
> Vernal delight and joy, able to drive
> All sadness but despair: now gentle gales
> Fanning their odiferous wings dispense
> Native perfumes, and whisper whence they stole
> Those balmy spoils. As when to them who sail
> Beyond the *Cape of Hope*, and now are past
> *Mozambic*, off at Sea North-East winds blow
> *Sabean* Odors from the spicy shore
> Of *Araby* the blest, with such delay

> Well pleas'd they slack their course, and many a League
> Cheer'd with the grateful smell old Ocean smiles.
>
> (4.153–65)

Several features in the vehicle bear upon our discussion. We might note, for example, the similarity between this moment and that when Satan is stupefied by Eve. In both, the Fiend seems caught off guard by a world of exquisite beauty. Like Eve, the Garden is pure, innocent, fragrant, blessed, graceful. Like Eve, Eden inspires, indeed compels, delight as it momentarily seems to master sense and heart. Milton's slow, stately verse, so rich in assonance, makes readers linger just as do the sailors, to smell the "balmy perfumes" that blow like spicy odors from the shores of Araby the blest. Moreover, the typically Miltonic exotic place-names function here not merely for sound or *copia* but to further the treatment of Satan's despair in the soliloquy. Araby is "the blest"; the sailors round the Cape of *Hope* (my emphasis). These names powerfully locate grace in the landscape, which reaches out to touch and to heal.

But such a world of "vernal delight and joy" can drive away "all sadness but despair." Satan has sailed "beyond the Cape of Hope"; hence the "grateful smell" can never cheer, however much he feels beckoned to submit himself to its beauty. He must here, as he does later with Eve, protect himself against the seductive power of such beauty. This he does in the tenor:

> So entertain'd those odorous sweets the Fiend
> Who came their bane, though with them better pleas'd
> Than *Asmodeus* with the fishy fume,
> That drove him, though enamour'd, from the Spouse
> Of *Tobit's* Son, and with a vengeance sent
> From *Media* post to *Egypt*, there fast bound.
>
> (4.166–71)

The tenor, so conspicuously ugly in contrast to the vehicle, depicts Satan converting a heavenly world into hell rather than opening himself to a world whose beauty is given by a power outside the self, and who in return for such graces invites only free gratitude. This enchanting simile powerfully interrogates Satan's mode of autonomous selfhood, and finds it wanting.

A comparable simile, aimed at the same point, introduces Satan's mesmerizing encounter with Eve in Book 9. Once again, the simile summons up a luxuriant landscape, now the pastoral world, in order to show Satan's inability to respond to its beauty. The Fiend beholds Eve,

> As one who long in populous City pent,
> Where Houses thick and Sewers annoy the Air,
> Forth issuing on a Summer's Morn to breathe
> Among the pleasant Villages and Farms
> Adjoin'd, from each thing met conceives delight,
> The smell of Grain, or tedded Grass, or Kine,
> Or Dairy, each rural sight, each rural sound;
> If chance with Nymphlike step fair Virgin pass,
> What pleasing seem'd, for her now pleases more,
> She most, and in her look sums all Delight.
>   (9.445–54)

Here, again, the simile evokes a world of natural "delight," appealing especially to the sense of smell (perhaps a function of Milton's blindness). Here, again, the simile's deliberate pace and sensuous imagery invite us to linger and revel in its pastoral richness through images strongly presaging Romantic sensibility. And here again, sadly, the simile serves to highlight Satan's obstinate imperviousness to beauty. Invited to breathe the fresh air of a summer's morn, Satan prefers the stink of sewers—just as he implicitly preferred fishy fume to the spicy odors of Araby the blest.

To resist the potentially redemptive beauty of Eve and the pastoral, Satan must mobilize enormous resources of will and call upon the mind to be its own place. Now, however, Satanic freedom is revealed to be compulsion because he seems unable to respond except by negation:

> But the hot Hell that always in him burns
> Though mid Heav'n, soon ended his delight,
> And tortures him now more, the more he sees
> Of pleasures not for him ordain'd.
>   (9.467–70)

Ironically reprising Satan's early boast to make a hell of heaven, the passage reminds us that the Demon's despair is a function of that boast. His isolation follows from his perversely negative conception of freedom—as *freedom from* rather than as *freedom to*.

By Book 9, it is evident that Satanic freedom is really slavery that entraps the self in itself. Such false freedom commits one to concentrating all one's energy upon denial of the temporal, necessary, and finite. Domination of the world, not cooperation, mutuality, reciprocity, or grateful acceptance, becomes the only mode of connecting the self to the other. The result of such absolute freedom is, paradoxically, a kind of slavery, or what Kierkegaard calls "unfreedom": "what is missing is essentially the power to obey, to submit to the necessity in one's life, to what may be called one's limitations" (*SD*, 36).

Misconstrued as possibility *lacking* a world rather than *acting on* a world,[34] Kierkegaardian freedom in fact unites possibility *and* necessity; it is at once situated and open (cf. *SD*, 36). Satan must plug his ears, close his eyes, and steel his will against beauty, for beauty reminds him of an autonomous, God-created world whose value he has not set nor can he arbitrate — a world full of being. Beauty and love, like other verities such as goodness and truth, are not simply subjective but ontologically grounded. They belong to an order we may reveal or conceal by our freedom, but never wholly invent *ex nihilo*. Freedom operates *in* a world as well as *on* one. Hence, existence is open to revelations that may surprise us, throw us off balance, as Eden and Eve do Satan.

The poem suggests that beauty could be a redemptive antidote to solipsism. Its potential to heal is witnessed by the fact that Satan comes closest to repenting when he is confronted by beauty. Note that the two soliloquies when Satan comes closest to repentance are both triggered by an encounter with beauty. The first occurs in Book 4 when Satan catches sight of the resplendent sun, which recalls heaven's holy light (31ff.); the second, in Book 9, when he contemplates this "Terrestrial Heav'n, the earth" (99ff.). In this last soliloquy, he admits: "With what delight could I have walkt thee round, / If I could joy in aught, sweet interchange / Of Hill and Valley, Rivers, Woods and Plains" (9.114–17). "If I could joy in aught." I find this the saddest, most tragic utterance in the poem. To be unable to joy in aught is an apt definition of hell — and virtually the same one Dostoevsky's Father Zossima gives in his definition of hell in *The Brothers Karamazov*: "Fathers and teachers, 'What is hell?' I maintain that it is the suffering of no longer being able to love."[35] Ironically, however, this crippling deficiency vis-à-vis the other is simply the necessary dark side of Satan's monomaniacal quest for absolute individualism.

Both Milton and Kierkegaard mightily esteem individual freedom. Milton fought for liberty all his life; Kierkegaard asked that his gravestone be inscribed, simply, "the individual." Yet neither of them advocate the individualism of pure egoism. In this way, their work contains the best critique of its misappropriation by advocates of radical individualism, such as the Romantic Shelley or the Existentialist Sartre. Like Satan, such individualists must sense a tinge of terror in beauty and love, for these messengers of grace summon us into a world not wholly of our own making, beyond lonely subjectivism and the isolated will.

No hate, however strong, can successfully oppose love and beauty. Everyone inevitably collides against a world apart from the naked ego — a world whose beauty may catch us unawares. True freedom lies not in denial and domination but in responsibly and responsively choosing to be within the possibilities of the world. To act freely, then, is not to invent the universe out of the self but, as Kierkegaard says, to negotiate the self between the poles of possibility and necessity. As Heidegger reminds us, to exist means, etymologically, to stand out (*ex sistere*) in a clearing (*Lichtung*) as it were, and within this opening, to unfold possibility into fullness (*Vollbringen*), revealing both the "there" and "being" or *Da-sein* ("being-there") of existence.[36] Existentialism so conceived is a far cry from the fantasy of absolute freedom in which humans exist lonely, isolated, detached, and adrift—presumably immune to pain but also severed from love and joy. Such stoical existence, though defiantly claimed by the demonic, is in fact humanly impossible. Because we cannot wholly will the conditions of our existence, we are necessarily vulnerable. We can be hurt. But we can also be healed, surprised by divine infusions of beauty. Such reminders from the world beyond will summon us to grace and reintegration into the ecology of heaven.[37]

Notes

1. Comparison with Dante's *Inferno* on this issue is instructive. Both Dante and Milton signpost hell as a place of despair: on the gate to Dante's inferno is written "Abandon all hope ye who enter here" (Canto 3, Ciardi trans.); in *Paradise Lost*, the narrator's first words about hell characterize it as a region "where peace / And rest can never dwell, hope never comes" (1.65–66). Likewise, the damned in both cases are doomed to be (in Hopkins's phrase) "their sweating selves" forever ("I Wake and Feel"). Dante, however, imagines this punishment as something "physically" imposed on the damned; according to the doctrine of *contrapasso* (see *Inf.* 28.142), Dante's sinners are forced to endure punishments that fit their crimes: the lustful are blown by the winds of passion, the treacherous are frozen in ice, and so on. Though *we* recognize the ways they are not truly repentant, the damned *themselves* often talk as if they would do better, given a chance, and regard their punishment as something inflicted on them from the outside. Milton, by contrast, depicts damnation as mainly an inside job. Hence, he imagines the torments of hell much less physically; his hell is more unmistakably one of despair, the denial of hope. His demons enjoy numerous opportunities to repent, but they continually re-choose to be "their sweating selves."

2. Marlowe, *Doctor Faustus*.

3. See Walker's *The Decline of Hell* for a comprehensive discussion of the controversy surrounding the doctrine of hell in the seventeenth century. Note especially the section on curative versus vindictive punishment in hell (42–51).

4. For a classic treatment of Satan and the theme of damnation in Elizabethan tragedy, see Gardner's essay of the same title.

5. Except for brief remarks by Broadbent (*Some Graver Subject*, 77–78), the relevance of Kierkegaardian despair to Satan has gone unobserved.

6. Gross has again argued this familiar point in a recent essay, "Satan and the Romantic Satan."

7. See Blake's *Marriage of Heaven and Hell*.

8. This is Lowrie's hypothesis in *Kierkegaard*, 1.126–27.

9. Malantschuk, *Thought*, 204.

10. I wish to acknowledge Hubert L. Dreyfus for suggesting a prototype of this diagram while guiding me through *Sickness unto Death*.

11. Dunning, *Kierkegaard's Dialectic*, 242.

12. The Hong translation calls these components of being "constituents"; Lowrie translates them as "factors." In my own usage, I have consistently called them "factors."

13. The classic argument that consciousness requires a synthesis of past, present, and future is found in Book 11 of Augustine's *Confessions*. Augustine uses the example of a sentence to show that human language is possible only through remembrance of past sounds and anticipation of future words. Otherwise, we would hear nothing but disjointed syllables. I have discussed this more fully in my essay "The Syllables of Time," esp. 135–39.

14. See Sir Philip Sidney's *Apology for Poetry* for the quotation about "zodiack of his own wit"; Emily Dickinson for "I dwell" and "The Brain"; Richard Lovelace's poem "To Althea, from Prison" for "stone walls . . ."; and James Boswell's *Life of Johnson* for the anecdote about Johnson's refutation of Berkeley.

15. Herrick, "Dreames," in *Hesperides*.

16. For Kierkegaard the one congruous existential position is Christianity. But by this he means a particularly daring and paradoxical mode of Christian faith, such as that exemplified by Abraham, the Knight of Faith in *Fear and Trembling*.

17. Kierkegaard's fullest discussion of spiritlessness is to be found in *The Present Age*.

18. Marlowe, *Doctor Faustus*.

19. Milton's Satan rightfully belongs in a long line of Renaissance self-fashioners. See Greenblatt's *Renaissance Self-Fashioning* and Grossman's *"Authors to Themselves."*

20. See Kerrigan for a book-length study of Freudian complexes in Milton's works. See Dickens's *Hard Times*, book 3, chapter 5 for the exposure of the "self-made Humbug, Josiah Bounderby of Coketown." In this vein, Bellah, coauthor of *Habits of the Heart*, an insightful study of American individualism, recently shared with me the story of a modern American Bounderby. Bellah's research team interviewed a car dealership owner deeply committed to the American myth of the self-made man. The businessman had become so accustomed to seeing his success through this filter that he would not admit he had inherited the dealership from his father!

21. For comments on Satanic Stoicism, see Hughes's "Myself Am Hell," in *Ten Perspectives*, esp. 154–59.

22. A final image associates river mists with the cherubim sent to guard the way back to Eden with blazing sword (12.629ff.), but the image pertains to the way the angels descend, not to their actual appearance.

23. See Schwartz, *Remembering*, ch. 1.

24. See "The Process of Uncreation" in Lieb's *The Dialectics of Creation*, 81–201, and Shawcross, *Mortal Voice*, 186n.

25. Cf. Lewis, *Preface*: "A creature revolting against a creator is revolting against the source of his own powers—including even his power to revolt" (96–97).

26. I don't mean to imply that the Son's "finitude" is exactly equivalent to that of Satan, Adam, or Eve. To do so would raise questions about Arianism that I don't insist on. My only point is that the Son's subordinate position relative to the Father, whatever that may consist of, opens up the possibility of filial envy.

27. For a general overview of the self and post-Cartesian philosophy, consult the eminently readable study by Solomon, *Continental Philosophy since 1750: The Rise and Fall of the Self*. For an essential discussion of this historical shift as applied to the nature of beauty, see the first chapter of Gadamer's *Truth and Method* (esp. "The Subjectivisation of Aesthetics"). Though Gadamer focuses on Kant rather than Descartes, his analysis illuminates the whole drift of philosophical thought from the Enlightenment on.

28. After I had written this analysis, I discovered Kerrigan's discussion of being and Eve's beauty in *The Sacred Complex* (289–93). Kerrigan calls attention to the ontological character of Eve's beauty through the words of the finest philosopher of otherness, Immanuel Levinas. According to Levinas, beauty is "the excess of being over function." My argument suggests that Satan finds Eve's beauty dreadful precisely because it conspicuously registers something like a surplus of being.

29. Ironically, because Satan's evil already involves self-abstraction, beauty's power to abstract him from evil in fact returns him to a nonabstracted self by momentarily grounding him in the world's alterity.

30. The originator of this cliché evidently is Margaret Wolfe Hungerford (Bartlett, *Familiar Quotations*). This is a surprisingly recent source. Hungerford's dates (1855–1897) remind us that the proposition that beauty is subjective may only *seem* self-evident when in fact it expresses an outlook rooted in Enlightenment thought, as Bartlett's cross-reference to David Hume's essay "Of Tragedy" illustrates: "Beauty in things exists in the mind which contemplates them."

31. Bellah et al., *Habits of the Heart*, 334.

32. See Wittreich, Brisman, and Knapp for full-length studies on Milton and the Romantics, and Thorslev for an article specifically about the appeal for the Romantics of Satan's claim to possess a mind that is its own place. Just as Satan's false heroism has antecedents in the Romantic and Existential hero, his mode of freedom also has precedents in the pseudoheroism (for Milton) of Stoicism and Pelagianism. On Satan's Stoicism, see Hughes's "Myself Am Hell"; on Satan's Pelagianism, see my essay "'Say First What Cause.'"

33. See Alpers, "The Milton Controversy," 294–96, and Stein, *Answerable Style*, 58–59, for two good discussions of this simile and despair.

34. Mackey, *Points of View*, 157. Mackey's essay "The Loss of the World in Kierkegaard's Ethics" is a highly stimulating discussion of alterity and Kierkegaard—even if, as I believe, Mackey is wrong that Kierkegaardian individualism loses the world.

35. Dostoevsky, *Brothers Karamazov*, book 6, chapter 3, section i.

36. These Heideggerian notions, developed at length in *Being and Time*, are also explained somewhat more accessibly in Heidegger's "Letter on Humanism" (esp. 193–207).

37. It is no coincidence that the poet and essayist Wendell Berry, a farmer and ecologist, should assail Shelley's misreading of Miltonic freedom and praise Milton's responsible freedom (*Standing by Words*, 35–36), for the two modes of freedom carry profound ecological implications. The one presumes the world is to be dominated and mastered by technological exploitation; the other suggests cooperation with the world.

8

Anxiety and Salvation

"Built by Faith to Stand": Saving Faith

Upon returning a manuscript copy of *Paradise Lost* to Milton, the young Quaker Thomas Ellwood reportedly quipped: "Thou hast said much here of 'Paradise Lost'; but what hast thou to say of 'Paradise Found'?" Ellwood credits his pleasantry with having inspired Milton to write *Paradise Regained*.[1] Be that as it may, his witticism suggests that Ellwood had either not read or not understood *Paradise Lost* — especially its conclusion, which explicitly moves the story from despair to hope, loss to salvation. *Paradise Lost* (never mind its sequel) coordinates Adam's transgression with Christ's triumph, developing the familiar Pauline parity between the first and second Adam. Also like Paul's epistles, the poem's conclusion stresses the need for a "better Cov'nant" of faith (12.302) owing to the insufficiency of both the Mosaic law and, more broadly, legalism. Kierkegaard's treatise on the Fall observes similar dynamics in its conclusion. Its final chapter redirects the focus from sin to salvation, particularly salvation through faith. Like Paul and Milton, Kierkegaard lays special emphasis on the inadequacy of legalism as a means of redemption. In addition, however, Kierkegaard asserts that to be saved through faith is necessarily to be educated in anxiety. He calls his final chapter "Anxiety as Saving through Faith" (*CA*, 155). In my final chapter, I, too, turn from despair in order to explore the conjunction in *Paradise Lost* and *The Concept of Anxiety* between anxiety and salvation.

From its famous first lines, *Paradise Lost* balances what one man lost against what "one greater Man" gained, according to parities prominent in Paul as well as in a long tradition of Pauline Christian commentary:

> Of Man's First Disobedience, and the Fruit
> Of that Forbidden Tree, whose mortal taste

Brought Death into the World, and all our woe,
With loss of *Eden*, till one greater Man
Restore us, and regain the blissful Seat,
Sing Heav'nly Muse.

(1.1–6)

Likewise Paul writing in the Epistle to the Romans: "For as by one man's disobedience many were made sinners, so by the obedience of one shall many be made righteous. . . . But where sin abounded, grace did much more abound: That as sin hath reigned unto death, even so might grace reign through righteousness unto eternal life by Jesus Christ our Lord" (5:19–21). For Milton and for Paul, Adamology coordinates with Christology in the inversely parallel stories "of Man" (Adam) and of "one greater Man" (Christ). According to this arithmetic of redemption, disobedience is balanced by obedience, the rule of death and sin is replaced by the reign of life and grace, perdition is preempted by salvation, the Fall parried by the Atonement, Adam answered in Christ.

Clearly, one need not await *Paradise Regained* to detect these symmetries at work in Milton's soteriology. Sounded in the opening invocation of *Paradise Lost*, the song of salvation through Christ reverberates throughout the entire epic. In books 3 and 5, for example, the Father foretells the Son's redemptive mission in considerable theological detail. In Book 6 the Son defeats the rebels and delivers the good angels on the third day of the War in Heaven, prefiguring how as Christ he will overcome death and free his human creatures on the third day. In Book 10, the Son is sent to newly fallen humanity in his role as "Man's Friend, his Mediator," "Ransom and Redeemer," "Judge and Intercessor," "Savior" (60, 61, 96, 209). Pronouncing the protoevangelium and clothing naked Adam and Eve (10.175–223), the Son obscurely figures his merciful role as the one who shall rout Satan and clothe humanity's "inward nakedness" with a "Robe of righteousness." And finally in Book 12, Christ's atonement becomes the main burden of Milton's music as Michael instructs Adam in futurity. Michael reveals to Adam that the Messiah will undo what Man has done, overcoming the Devil,

Not by destroying *Satan*, but his works
In thee and in thy Seed; nor can this be,
But by fulfilling that which thou didst want,
Obedience to the Law of God, impos'd
On penalty of death, and suffering death,
The penalty to thy transgression due,
As due to theirs which out of thine will grow.

(12.394–400)

Behind this statement lies Romans 5: one man's disobedience necessitates another's obedience; Adam's fall requires Christ's redemption. Throughout *Paradise Lost* and culminating in the final books, everything points to the Atonement.

Structurally and emotionally, redemption stands at the center of *Paradise Lost*'s final vision.[2] In the second (1674) edition, Milton divided books 11 and 12 (old Book 10) at the Flood, "Betwixt the world destroy'd and world restor'd" (12.3), as if to underscore the theme of redemption that governs the denoument's dynamics.[3] Additionally, at the numerical middle of the new final book occurs a climactic oracle of Christ. It reveals to Adam, at long last, that the focal figure of "all prophecy" is a messiah to derive from David's lineage:

> the like shall sing
> All Prophecy, That of the Royal Stock
> Of *David* (so I name this King) shall rise
> A Son, the Woman's Seed to thee foretold,
> Foretold to *Abraham*, as in whom shall trust
> All Nations, and to Kings foretold, of Kings
> The last, for of his Reign shall be no end.
>
> (12.324–30)

In the last books of *Paradise Lost*, Christ is foretold, foretold, and foretold again, as "all the Prophets in thir Age the times, / Of great *Messiah* . . . sing" (12.243–44).

These prophecies engender eager expectation in Adam, who, like Israel under the Old Testament dispensation, at first comprehends the mission of the Messiah imperfectly "by types / And shadows" (12.232–33). The emotional climax of Michael's history (and, some argue, of the entire poem) occurs for Adam when Jesus' redemptive mission of atonement is finally made plain. Then Adam rejoices to "understand / What oft my steadiest thoughts have searcht in vain" (12.376–77). Having learned of the Lord's promised victory at the end of the world, Adam is beside himself with wonder and joy. In one of the poem's most famous passages he expostulates:

> O goodness infinite, goodness immense!
> That all this good of evil shall produce,
> And evil turn to good; more wonderful
> Than that which by creation first brought forth
> Light out of darkness! full of doubt I stand,
> Whether I should repent me now of sin

By mee done and occasion'd, or rejoice
Much more, that much more good thereof shall spring,
To God more glory, more good will to Men
From God, and over wrath grace shall abound.
(12.469–78)

Adam's sentiments echo Paul: "But where sin abounded, grace did much more abound" (Romans 5:20). Tonally, Adam's talk of *felix culpa* lifts the poem from the somber, tragic notes (*PL* 9.6) occasioned by the Fall, to a mood more like the original peace and bliss of Paradise, if not more joyful.

Yet Adam's joy does not warrant attributing to the poem simplistic notions of a fortunate fall, which until Dennis Danielson's impressive critique had "become a kind of cliché of Milton criticism."[4] Adam's speech articulates neither the full nor final utterance in *Paradise Lost* about the conditions characterizing human salvation. Note, for example, how fleeting is Adam's ecstasy. Even by the end of his colloquy with Michael, Adam is much more subdued, and despite the elation he expresses in lines 469ff., Adam never fully recovers a "paradise within [himself] happier far" (12.587). This paradise remains only a bright possibility that Michael locates specifically on the horizon of Adam's expectation, a condition toward which he is urged to strive rather than a blessedness he has yet attained (12.574–87). Likewise, Michael's prophecy that "the Earth / Shall all be Paradise, far happier place / Than this of *Eden*, and far happier days" (12.463–65) similarly remains a prospect set in the future, in this case in a far distant eschatological future. Not till the end of time will the earth become a new Eden.

In the meantime, Adam and his posterity will have to live by faith amid adversity. Michael's prophecies fail to dispel fully the great grief Adam and Eve have traversed; indeed, the final vision actually alloys their tranquility with sorrow. Adam descends from the mountain of vision "greatly instructed," "greatly in peace" (12.557, 558), but such peace as he enjoys has had to be won out of deeply disturbing visions of the Lazar-house and the sad saga of fallen history, as well as out of his personal experience of alienation. Similarly, Eve awakens from her "gentle dreams" "calmed" and "composed," yet also subdued; and the archangel predicts that she will live "cheer'd" "though sad" (12.595–605).

Truly, then, Adam's outburst of joy provides neither the last nor complete measure of the text's concluding tone. Rather, the final books' tone resembles that of Shakespeare's final plays. It blends extremities of grief and joy, encompassing feelings aroused by a world ransomed and

one destroyed (cf. *The Winter's Tale* 5.1.15). Adam and Eve are cast out
of Eden exactly as per Michael's divine charge, "sorrowing, yet in peace"
(11.117), not singing "Happy Days" but wiping away "Some natural
tears" (12.645). Within the poem's final consolation, there remains ample
room for death, sickness, betrayal, heartache, and the whole gamut of
human experience as we now know it — including anxiety.

Especially anxiety, for anxiety, as we shall see, is uniquely empowered
to lead Adam and Eve to faith, and only through faith can they recover
"paradise within." "Without" they will encounter a world every bit as
adverse as ours, since the world that lies "all before them" as they leave
Eden *is* our world. As Wayne Shumaker aptly observes, the final books
turn *Paradise Lost* "homeward" (12.632), "toward Milton and his
seventeenth-century readers and toward us": "Milton sensed, as the best
writers have always done, that literature ought ultimately to reconcile
and strengthen, to return the audience to the everyday world with enhanced willingness to meet the stresses of living."[5] Another, perhaps
deeper, term for "enhanced willingness" is *faith*, the consummate consolation *Paradise Lost* has to offer either Adam and Eve or the reader.

"To the faithful," says Adam, "Death [is] the Gate of Life" (12.571).
These sentiments come near the end of Adam's second outburst of hope,
his final speech in the poem. I find this speech and Michael's exhortation
that follows it far more affecting than Adam's earlier outburst of *felix
culpa* ("O goodness infinite . . ."). Adam's final exclamation, beginning
"How soon hath thy prediction" (12.553), is quieter, less grandly cosmic,
and more firmly situated in the human than the first. The first expostula-
tion belongs to a discourse of metaphysics; the joy it anticipates pertains
to an eschatological paradise not to be realized till the end of history.
The second speech anticipates a paradise located in history and within
pitiable, fallen, recognizably human creatures, who must make their
lonely way through an alien world. This second consolation belongs to a
discourse of faith in and for the world — a faith that has made peace
with this harsh world without despising it, a faith that embraces human
experience with gratitude and hope. I quote Adam's speech at length:

> and thus *Adam* last repli'd.
> How soon hath thy prediction, Seer blest,
> Measur'd this transient World, the Race of time,
> Till time stand fixt: beyond is all abyss,
> Eternity, whose end no eye can reach.
> Greatly instructed I shall hence depart,
> Greatly in peace of thought, and have my fill

> Of knowledge, what this Vessel can contain;
> Beyond which was my folly to aspire.
> Henceforth I learn, that to obey is best,
> And love with fear the only God, to walk
> As in his presence, ever to observe
> His providence, and on him sole depend,
> Merciful over all his works, with good
> Still overcoming evil, and by small
> Accomplishing great things, by things deem'd weak
> Subverting worldly strong, and worldly wise
> By simply meek; that suffering for Truth's sake
> Is fortitude to highest victory,
> And to the faithful Death the Gate of Life;
> Taught this by his example whom I now
> Acknowledge my Redeemer ever blest.
>
> (12.552–73)

From first to last, this poised and gracious response to the divine is firmly emplaced in the human. Adam commences by specifically recognizing his human limitation and ends by taking strength from the humble example embodied in the human ministry of a suffering, meek Jesus (in contrast to the conquering, triumphant Christ who animated Adam's initial joy). As mere mortals, Adam admits, there is much we do not comprehend of "Eternity, whose end no eye can reach" (12.556). What we need, in our weakness and ignorance, is to obey, to love, to trust in God's merciful providence and to cooperate in his work of bringing good out of evil (12.559–65). Compared to the "worldly" great, strong, and wise, the faithful may seem small, weak, and foolish (12.566–69), but precisely through these despised qualities they shall prevail. This, however, does not mean the good will be successful in a superficial sense. Just the reverse. The meek and faithful will suffer and die, as did their Redeemer (whose praise constitutes the last word Adam speaks in the poem). Yet somehow, through human fortitude and divine grace, the Lord will turn defeat into victory and death into life (12.569–71).

This promise of renewed life includes, but is not limited to, hope for a "blissful eschaton" at the resurrection.[6] Hence, Adam's consolation eludes the Nietzschean critique, as William Kerrigan summarizes it, "that the postulate of a transcendent world debases and devalues this world." Adam's faith in an afterlife cannot be construed as "another of the poisons that taint this life"; nor does it denigrate this life as something to be "tolerated because of a life to come."[7] Rather, Adam learns to receive back the fallen world with love as a graced heavenly gift, as he receives Eve. Milton's theodicy succeeds in large measure not by answering all our questions or Adam's but by renewing his sense of gratitude and ours.[8] For by faith, virtue, patience, temperance, and love, *this life*—whatever its hardships—may become more abundant, even paradisal, as Michael tells Adam completing the poem's climactic concluding insight:

> only add
> Deeds to thy knowledge answerable, add Faith,
> Add Virtue, Patience, Temperance, add Love,
> By name to come call'd Charity, the soul
> Of all the rest: then wilt thou not be loath
> To leave this Paradise, but shalt possess
> A paradise within thee, happier far.
>
> (12.581–87)

Drawn from the Second Epistle of Peter (1:4–8), this sublime comfort is specifically aimed at fitting Adam to live blessedly in a fallen world. By the end of the poem Adam, like Job (and the mature Milton), has assimilated loss and is learning to trust—sometimes "in spite of" rather than "because of" life's experiences, but always with hope rather than contempt for this life. In *Paradise Lost* as in the Book of Job, "the sum / Of wisdom" (12.575–76) designates "not a speculative answer . . . but a way of consecrated living."[9] Faithfulness constitutes the knowledge that matters most to Milton, as it does to the Prophets.[10] Hence Michael exhorts: "only add / Deeds to thy knowledge answerable, add Faith" (12.581–82).

Faith in the midst of bewilderment and suffering is ever the surest—and perhaps the only—adequate human response to the dilemmas of theodicy. No explanation ever gets beyond faith; every generation begins at the same point, with faith.[11] This ancient wisdom, embedded in the Book of Job, is equally inscribed in the final vision of Milton's theodicy.[12] Only those "built by Faith to stand, / Thir own Faith not another's" (12.527–28) can hope to endure. To stand in the right relationship to God—vigilant, alert, willing, patient, obedient, faithful—is to obtain "the sum of wisdom," "the ultimate knowledge of God."[13]

Judged by this definition of knowledge, Milton as poet paradoxically shows himself to be wisest where he is least conventionally wise. Like fallen Adam or blind Samson, whose true strength lies in dependence on God, Milton as narrator stands firmest when he is most vulnerable for "man's need of God constitutes his highest perfection."[14] Accordingly, Milton never seems stronger to me than when he implores, "What in me is dark / Illumine, what is low raise and support"[15] (1.22–23). In this sense, the poet resembles his own faithful angels, whose "armor help'd thir harm" but whose vulnerability makes them invulnerable (6.656; cf. 595). Likewise, I find Milton's theodicy more convincing in its first stated purpose, to assert faith in "eternal providence," than in its second, to justify rationally the "ways of God to men" (see 1.22–26). Similarly, Milton's God feels more truly present in the poem when he is addressed than when he is pictured;[16] while *Paradise Lost* is more persuasive as a humanly situated poem by a man, like Adam, "fall'n on evil days" (7.25) than as theologically situated theodicy by a man who has all the right answers as from on high. The best consolation *Paradise Lost* offers Adam or its readers is new (or renewed) faith in the ancient hope that, though "sin is behovabil [inevitable]," through Christ "all shall be well and all shall be well and all manner of thing shall be well."[17]

"Anxiety Becomes a Serving Spirit": Saving Anxiety

Like *Paradise Lost*, *The Concept of Anxiety* stresses the need for faith in its final chapter, "Anxiety as Saving through Faith." Kierkegaard, however, links faith with anxiety. Up to this point in his treatise, Kierkegaard had examined anxiety mainly in its gloomy role as an agent of sin, remorse, and the demonic. Yet for all this, he never characterized anxiety as itself sinister but always insisted that anxiety is actually a barometer of human greatness because it measures one's susceptibility to freedom, possibility, infinitude, "spirit," and the like (*CA*, 64, 155). "[R]ightly used," Kierkegaard hinted in chapter 2, anxiety "plays another role" (*CA*, 53). In chapter 5 he explains that this beneficent role is salvific. For some people "anxiety becomes a serving spirit"; "with the help of faith, anxiety brings up the individuality to rest in providence" (*CA*, 159, 161). Anxiety readies the individual for salvation by setting in motion dynamics equivalent to those that led Paul, Luther, and countless others to the discovery that salvation comes not by the finite works of the law but by the operation of infinite grace. Likewise, according to Kierkegaard, anxiety teaches sinners to repose their hope for salvation not in finite human merit but only in an infinite divine atonement: "Therefore he who in relation to guilt is educated by anxiety will only rest in the Atonement" (*CA*, 162).

This relationship between anxiety and salvation by faith begs further clarification. Let me begin, however, by noting the obvious: the relationship between anxiety and salvation has to do with education. To be saved by faith is to be "educated by anxiety." The conclusion of *The Concept of Anxiety* is replete with references to education, specifically education by faith. Similarly, Milton concludes his work on the Fall by dealing with Adam's education, and in particular with his education in faith on Christ. In the poem's final book, for example, Adam is warned well before the Law is given from Sinai *not* to rest his hopes for salvation in the false security of legalism, for "Law can discover sin, but not remove" (12.290; cf. 409–10). Michael continues schooling Man in this Pauline truth thus:

> So Law appears imperfect, and but giv'n
> With purpose to resign them in full time
> Up to a better Cov'nant, disciplin'd
> From shadowy Types to Truth, from Flesh to Spirit,
> From imposition of strict Laws, to free
> Acceptance of large Grace, from servile fear
> To filial, works of Law to works of Faith.
>
> (12.300–306)

Adam then learns that the Law's impotence to save is figured typologically by the relation between Moses and Joshua. As Moses could bring his people to the Promised Land but only Joshua ("whom the Gentiles *Jesus* call" [310]) could lead them in, so the Mosaic law can prepare a person for salvation but only Christ is empowered to save. Through such teaching, Adam is educated in Pauline Christianity; he becomes in effect a Christian Adam, fully instructed in a covenant of spirit, freedom, grace, and faith.[18]

To be "educated by anxiety," as Kierkegaard deploys this phrase, is also to be educated in a particularly Pauline form of Christianity. It is to learn not to pin one's hopes for salvation upon legal, petty, finite differences of merit between me and thee but to accept one's guilt as infinite, requiring the infinite, superabundant grace of the Atonement. Though not presented as such, Kierkegaard's discussion of salvation in Book 5 could well serve as a gloss on Paul's soteriology:

> Whoever learns to know his guilt only from the finite is lost in the finite, and finitely the question of whether a man is guilty cannot be determined except in an external, juridical, and most imperfect sense. Whoever learns to know his guilt only by analogy to the judgments of the police court and the supreme court never really understands that he is guilty, for if a man is guilty, he is infinitely guilty. Therefore, if such an individuality who is educated only by finitude does not get a verdict from the police or a verdict by public opinion to the effect that he is guilty, he becomes of all men the

most ridiculous and pitiful, a model of virtue who is a little better than most people but not quite so good as the parson. What help would such a man need in life? Why, almost before he dies he may retire to a collection of models. (*CA*, 161)

Since human guilt reaches far beyond what can be ascertained by one's police record or by the verdict of public opinion, no one is good enough simply by being "a little better than most people." Those educated in anxiety could never think they need no help, for they are attuned to God's infinite demand, "Be ye therefore perfect" (Matt. 5:48), as well as to their own vulnerability, which is the consequence of their freedom. Educating man "according to his infinitude" (*CA*, 156), anxiety enables the sinner to relinquish every trace of Pharisaism—all the shrewd, "innumerable calculations" of finite legal merit by which we seek for security (*CA*, 160). Anxiety forces humans to find repose only in the Atonement.

Security is to be found nowhere else, according to Kierkegaard, though we thoughtlessly seek it everywhere else—in our bank accounts, in our résumés, in public approval, and in any number of other human endeavors. Were we less thoughtless, we would not grasp hold of such straws but would learn from the exacting "school of possibility" that no matter how comfortable or wretched we may be in actuality, "no one ever sank so deep that he could not sink deeper": "But he who sank in possibility—his eye became dizzy . . . so he could not grasp the measuring stick that Tom, Dick, and Harry hold out as a saving straw to one sinking; his ear was closed so he could not hear what the market price of men was in his own day, did not hear that he was just as good as the majority" (*CA*, 158). Thoughtless people think actuality hard and possibility light. Those schooled by anxiety, however, know that just the reverse is true. Possibility is "weightiest of all categories"; it prevents one from resting secure in any finite actuality because "terror, perdition, annihilation, live next door to every man" (*CA*, 156). To be free is to be vulnerable; it is to be "exposed to danger, not that of getting into bad company and going astray in various ways as are those educated by the finite, but the danger of a fall, namely, suicide" (*CA*, 158–59).

These sentiments should not be dismissed as morbid ruminations peculiar to a perversely "melancholy Dane." They follow directly from the basic Judeo-Christian premise of human freedom, according to which all sin becomes a kind of suicide in the sense that to sin is to succumb to self-temptation and self-destruction. Hence, the hazard against which one must be constantly on guard (and the only truly Christian tragedy) is sin. Sin may rightly be called suicide, moral suicide. Milton's Adam makes the same point when he warns Eve that their real danger always lies within themselves (9.348–49). The same idea underlies the ethics of Milton's dramatic works from *A Mask* ("Comus"), which makes sense only to the extent the dramatic question is one of seduction rather than rape, to *Samson Agonistes*, which concludes by emphasizing the protagonist's moral regeneration rather than death: "Nothing is here for tears" (1721). For Milton the most important peril is always moral. Our peril lies in how we might self-destructively abuse our freedom rather than in what others may do to us.

To believe this is to subscribe to the Christian imperative of constant vigilance—a duty seventeenth-century Puritans knew all about: "Thus we live in danger," writes John Downame, "our greatest danger being that we should feel no danger, and our safety lying in the very dread of feeling safe."[19] Christianity thus conceived offers a deeply paradoxical, anxiety-ridden path to salvation. It says to those who fear, "Fear not!" and to those who fear not, "Fear!" So no matter how you feel, you are always wrong. Anxiety is inescapable according to this religious sensibility, as countless Puritan spiritual autobiographies attest. Yet potentially, anxiety is also the Christian's serviceable ally, able to lead one from false security to the only real security: faith, grace, Atonement, the Cross. In this spirit John Donne exclaims, "Those are my best days, when I shake with fear" (Holy Sonnet 19), while Milton depicts Adam and Eve as most out of danger the more they feel endangered by the peril of misused freedom that lies within.

No critic of *Paradise Lost* is more attuned to the "dread of feeling safe" in the poem than is Stanley Fish. To the degree that the text is, as Fish argues, a complex snare cunningly constructed to disturb and disquiet its readers with their sinful potential in order finally to drive them to faith, *Paradise Lost* educates its readers in something akin to Kierkegaardian anxiety. As Fish reads the poem, the text plays a role similar to the function Kierkegaard assigns to anxiety itself. Thus to substitute "*Paradise Lost*" for "anxiety" in the following quotation from Kierkegaard is to approximate the thesis of *Surprised by Sin*:

> Anxiety . . . consumes all finite ends and discovers their deceptiveness. And no Grand Inquisitor has such dreadful torments in readiness as anxiety has, and no secret agent knows as cunningly as anxiety how to attack his suspect in his weakest moment or to make alluring the trap in which he will be caught, and no discerning judge understands how to interrogate and examine the accused as does anxiety, which never lets the accused escape, neither through amusement, not by noise, nor during work, neither by day nor by night. (*CA*, 155–56)

One need neither accept nor recapitulate Fish's argument in detail to adduce *Surprised by Sin* as furnishing a vast and intricate array of evidence that anxiety envelops the poem's protagonists and readers alike. I take as axiomatic Fish's basic contention that Adam and the reader are fitted for salvation by being entangled in redemptive anxieties.

The parallel between Kierkegaard and Fish, however, is far from exact. In fact, Kierkegaard's explanation of how anxiety operates redemptively in reader-response implicitly amends the methodology of *Surprised by Sin* — a methodology I, along with many others, find often overly ingenious and bordering on atomistic in the way it reads the text. In addition, Kierkegaard's comments on the role anxiety plays in reading may serve as a brief concluding apology for the existentialist mode of interpretation adopted by *The Concept of Anxiety* as well as by this study.

For Fish, *Paradise Lost* entangles its readers by strategically designed misreadings that serve as logical traps exposing the readers' fallibility; in this experience lies anxiety. According to Kierkegaard, by contrast, anxiety needs no such elaborate occasion. Though textual conundrums might well provoke anxiety, they are not essential. For Kierkegaardian anxiety depends more on sensibility than sense. "Take the pupil of possibility, place him in the middle of the Jutland heath, where no event takes place," writes Kierkegaard in an autobiographical vein, "or where the greatest event is a grouse flying up noisily, and he will experience everything more perfectly, more accurately, more thoroughly than the man who received applause upon the stage of world-history if that man was not educated by possibility" (*CA*, 159). Elsewhere Kierkegaard attaches anxiety explicitly to reading, but he underscores the reader's sensibility rather than the text's ingenuity. One schooled in possibility can find ample occasion for anxiety in even a simple tale of another's misfortune:

> But the individuality who is educated by possibility needs but one such story. In that very moment, he is absolutely identified with the unfortunate man; he knows no finite evasion by which he may escape. Now the anxiety of possibility holds him as its prey until, saved, it must hand him over to faith. In no other place can he find rest, for every other place of rest is mere chatter, although in the eyes of men it is sagacity. (*CA*, 158)

Fish and Kierkegaard thus concur that anxiety defines the experience of reading a text like Milton's *Paradise Lost*, but with the following difference: Fish's "harassed" reader learns insecurity primarily by means of his exceptional acuity in detecting the snares Milton supposedly lays in his verse,[20] while Kierkegaard's anxious reader is educated in anxiety principally by an extraordinary ability to identify existentially with the characters' plight.

Of the two putative readers, I suspect Kierkegaard's may be closer to Milton's imagined "fit audience" (7.31). For "fit," like "stand" and "know" and a host of other crucial Miltonic terms, no doubt carries spiritual (or existential) connotations — or so *Paradise Regained*'s delineation of the unfit reader implies. Tempted with the wisdom of Athens, Jesus responds:

> who reads
> Incessantly, and to his reading brings not
> A spirit and judgment equal or superior
> (And what he brings, what needs he elsewhere seek)
> Uncertain and unsettl'd still remains,
> Deep verst in books and shallow in himself.
>
> (4.322–27)

If this remark provides a clue as to the fitness required of the reader in *Paradise Lost*, then Milton expects from his ideal readers much more than wide knowledge or mental agility, the conspicuous attributes of Fish's imagined reader. The prerequisite of genuine fitness for Milton's readers is, first and foremost, to be deep in themselves. Without existential depth, they remain "As Children gathering pebbles on the shore" (4.330). That is, fit Miltonic readers must in some sense, like the poet himself, "bee a true poem," grasping *Paradise Lost*'s grand themes of sin and redemption by means of personal "experience and . . . practice" with spiritual realities (*CP*, 1.890).

Kierkegaard calls such fitness "the element of appropriation" (*CA*, 16), by which he means an ability to identify oneself absolutely with another's existential condition. A fit reader presumably appropriates texts as Kierkegaard does Scripture, by walking with Abraham to Mount Moriah or with Adam and Eve through Eden. Existential appropriation is to be distinguished from cheap sentimentalism, the "cowardly sympathy that thanks God for not being like such a person." "One must have sympathy," Kierkegaard explains, "however, this sympathy is true only when one admits rightly and profoundly to oneself that what has happened to one human being can happen to all" (*CA*, 54). Or again:

> Only when the sympathetic person in his compassion relates himself to the sufferer in such a way that he in the strictest sense understands that it is his own case that is in question, only when he knows how to identify

himself with the sufferer in such a way that when he fights for an explanation he is fighting for himself . . . only then does the sympathy acquire significance. (*CA*, 120)

Surely, this is the sort of sympathy that Milton brought to his reading of Genesis, as well as the kind of sympathy he invites from the reader in *Paradise Lost*. As the reader fights for an explanation of sin—be it Satan's, Adam and Eve's, or the later human family's—he is indeed fighting to comprehend himself. Sin remains unintelligible apart from one's personal experience of freedom.

"How sin came into the world," writes Kierkegaard, "each man understands by himself. If he would learn it from another, he would *eo ipso* misunderstand it" (*CA*, 51). This implies that some meanings are not available merely through decoding external signifiers, that certain human realities must be understood from the inside. Likewise, Milton's Jesus avers that without bringing a spirit "equal or superior" to the author's no one can glean true wisdom from book learning alone, adding even more radically, "And what he brings, what need he elsewhere seek"? Such sentiments tacitly sanction an existential phenomenology, expressed by the ancient maxim *unum norris omnes*: by knowing oneself, one shall have known all (cf. *CA*, 79, 183, 240).

Perhaps more than any other, this principle accounts for the myriad congruencies between *Paradise Lost* and *The Concept of Anxiety* that have been explored in this study. Although doubtless some of these correspondences are attributable to the shared scriptural and theological traditions within which each work develops, I suspect that a deeper explanation for the many subtle similarities lies in what Milton and Kierkegaard brought to the Bible and biblical commentary from their beings: namely, intimate existential knowledge of the human realities figured forth in Genesis. Milton and Kierkegaard suffused Scripture with intelligibility drawn from their personal experience of freedom, sin, guilt, repentance, faith, the demonic, despair, and so forth. They wrote of these phenomena as they knew them in their bones, especially of freedom and its concomitant anxiety. Apprehending Genesis through their own psychogenesis, Milton and Kierkegaard uncover in Eden the story of "all our woe" (*PL* 1.3).

And of our hope. For above all, Milton and Kierkegaard espied in Eden the story of human freedom. Freedom, Kierkegaard knew, laces human existence with anxiety; freedom, therefore, must have infused even Paradise with anxiety. Similarly, Milton's monumental epic meditation on the Fall insists that anxious freedom permeated human existence even in Eden. In the poem as in the treatise, sin erupts from an ambience supercharged with the heady sensation of possibility. So, too, does salvation. If possibility ensnares and beguiles Milton's Eve, it also allows her and, eventually, Adam to imagine the prospect of redemption and to exercise saving faith. Thus the very freedom that can be abused to transgress can be rightly used to seize God's saving prevenient grace. Likewise, according to Kierkegaard, the anxiety that leads to the Fall also leads the individual beyond sin to the Atonement. Hence Milton and Kierkegaard concur that the path back to paradise lies through anxiety. Rather than exorcise anxiety, paradox, pain, absurdity, or suffering, Milton and Kierkegaard bring all these elements within the compass of an existential paradise.

By the poem's final lines our eyes, like Adam's (11.411–20), have been opened to an unblinking vision of human misery, violence, and alienation. Yet even more disturbing than this spectacle is the knowledge that we share the blame for these woes insofar as by our sins, sinfulness continues to come into the world (cf. 11.515–25). Consequently, life will require of us, just as it did of Adam and Eve in Eden, constant vigilance. In respect to freedom, Milton and Kierkegaard concur that life outside the Garden will be very much as it was in Eden.

> The World was all before them, where to choose
> Thir place of rest, and Providence thir guide;
> They hand in hand with wand'ring steps and slow,
> Through *Eden* took thir solitary way.
>
> (12.646–49)

The world that lies "all before" Adam and Eve in these elegant, evocative final lines still confronts them with freedom ("where to choose"), still allows the sweet, fearful possibility for possibility and error ("wandering"), and still requires faith in "Providence." In substance if not in style, *Paradise Lost* concludes much as does *The Concept of Anxiety*: "With the help of faith, anxiety brings up the individuality to rest in providence" (*CA*, 161).

Yet there remains one notable difference, which should not go unremarked in conclusion. Milton's fallen world is somewhat less lonely than is Kierkegaard's. For Milton envisages help available from a source Kierkegaard rarely admits: another person, in this instance a spouse, with whose solace and support these primal sinners make their slow and difficult pilgrimage toward salvation. Just as Milton concedes more scope than does Kierkegaard to communal influences in bringing about human transgression, so the poet allows more support from others in the journey toward human redemption. Frail and fallible, Adam and Eve wend their way into the fallen world "hand in hand," entering their errand into the wilderness together as a family.

Nevertheless, even as partners within a reconstituted family, Adam and Eve remain, as do we all, necessarily individual sojourners. This, too, corresponds to the paradoxical double nature of human existence as simultaneously communal and individual. Fittingly, Milton's sinners leave Eden "hand in hand" *and* "solitary." The sin that has welded them together as denizens of a fallen race has also isolated them as fully differentiated individuals, forcing each to stand alone before God to answer for his or her personal actions. Fallen Adam and Eve thus depart from Eden united, but never again fully unanimous. Their passage from Paradise to Paradise promises to be slow, solitary, and because they must freely choose their way, as fraught with anxiety as their journey through Eden.

Notes

1. Ellwood, *Life*, 145.

2. The same may be said for the poem as a whole. Shawcross argues persuasively that the climactic center of *Paradise Lost* is the Son's defeat of Satan and that the Son stands in the exact middle of the poem (*Mortal Voice*, 22–32, 43). Similarly, Fish argues that "knowledge of Christ is the end of all the [poem's] . . . investigations of the nature of heroism, love, beauty, innocence, happiness. He is the measure of them all. . . . In an ultimate sense, *He* is the poem's true form" (*Surprised by Sin*, 353).

3. Summers, *Muse's Method*, 112–13.

4. Danielson, *Milton's Good God*, 202. I should note that Danielson's case against a fortunate Fall was not unprecedented. It is anticipated perhaps most trenchantly in a brief essay by Virginia Mollenkott, "Milton's Rejection of the Fortunate Fall."

5. Shumaker, *Unpremeditated Verse*, 224, 216. For other fine comments on the "homeward" movement of Milton's final books, see Summers, *Muse's Method*, 223–24, and Radzinowicz, "'Man as a Probationer of Immortality.'"

6. Kerrigan, *Sacred Complex*, 279. Because my argument partly parallels the conclusion of *The Sacred Complex* (esp. 275–86), I want to register my difference with Kerrigan. Both of us distinguish between the poem's eschatological and existential consolations; that is, between the paradise envisioned on earth at the end of time and paradise within us in time. Like Kerrigan, I am most moved by the consolation the poem offers (through faith) in and for *this* world. But unlike him, I do not intend to dismiss or disparage as "surrender to literalism" the hope offered by the promise of a Second Coming (275–76) or future heavenly bliss

(279–80), or a literal resurrection. "Unless the reader can believe or achieve the illusion of believing," Kerrigan remarks, "that the sky will one day part, and Christ, returned as judge, will reward and punish the human race, leading the just to immortal bliss, the kerygma of Milton's [eschatological] consolation is a dead letter" (275–76). These are not dead hopes for me or for Milton, who would surely concur with Paul: "If in this life only we have hope in Christ, we are of all men most miserable" (1 Cor. 15:19). I do not suggest nor does Milton require that we must choose between an eschatological and existential paradise. Both are important to the conclusion of *Paradise Lost*. However, since we can do nothing but hope for the literal renewal of Eden on earth, Milton's vision of an existential paradise moves me more. It speaks to the central purpose of Christian life as I understand it — which is the *imitatio Christi*.

7. Kerrigan, *Sacred Complex*, 279–80, 285.

8. Mackey's comments on the relation between gratitude and theodicy (*Kind of Poet*, 98–100) illuminate Adam's culminating wisdom. As Mackey reads Kierkegaard's *Edifying Discourses*, "life itself, whatever it may contain of happiness or of misery, is a gift of God . . . which man should receive with gratitude." Gratitude leaves little room for "attempts to figure out what He [God] meant by pain and evil." In fact, though it is entirely understandable that a rational creature should desire theodicy, Mackey avers that "what such a man wills is the death of God"; he would "annihilate God by reducing Him to an adjunct of man." Theodicy aims at the reduction of life into fully transparent moral categories. Our religious duty is to love God and the life we are given through "weal and woe," and to trust that all things shall ultimately work together for the good of those who love him.

9. Both citations come from commentaries on the Book of Job. Ricoeur remarks, "What is revealed [by Job] is the possibility of hope in spite of . . ." (*Essays*, 87), while Terrien concludes that the Book of Job proposes "not a speculative answer . . . but a way of consecrated living" ("Job," 902). My essay "Job and the Prophets" develops these insights further.

10. E.g., Hosea 4:1–2 and 6:6. A number of biblical studies have explored the rich significance of "knowledge" in the Hebrew Bible, especially the covenant dimensions of the term. Introductions to the topic may be found in the *Interpreter's Dictionary of the Bible* (see entries under "Knowledge" and "Righteousness in the Old Testament") as well as in Anderson's *Understanding the Old Testament*, 287–89.

11. Cf. the "Preface" and "Epilogue" of Kierkegaard's *Fear and Trembling*.

12. Kant makes this point in a trenchant little essay called "On the Failure of All Attempted Philosophical Theodicies." Kant exempts the Book of Job from failure because it does not attempt a philosophical solution. In this regard, consider Kerrigan's comment about Milton's oft-noted use of Job in *Paradise Regained*: "It is astonishing to realize that Milton the justifier turned for inspiration to the book that offers the most powerful refutation we have of the theodicial project of *Paradise Lost*. . . . Life, not doctrine, is central to the latest Milton" (*Sacred Complex*, 312n).

13. See "The Ultimate Knowledge of God," in Jacobus, *Sudden Apprehension*, 197–212. "In *Paradise Lost*," observes Jacobus, "faith, obedience, and love are the ultimate ways of truly knowing God" (197). On Milton's use of "stand" in *Paradise Lost*, see Shawcross, *Mortal Voice*, 159–65.

14. As Kierkegaard entitles a lecture in *Edifying Discourses*, 136–76.

15. See Kerrigan, *Sacred Complex*, "The Way to Strength from Weakness," for a provocative discussion of this subject. Kerrigan reminds us that an aged Milton occasionally signed his name affixing the motto "My strength is made perfect in weakness" (134; cf. Parker, *Biography*, 1.479). See also Milton's *Second Defense* (*CP*, 4.589–90).

16. This last remark was once made to me by my colleague Bruce Young.

17. From Dame Julian of Norwich; echoed in the conclusion of T. S. Eliot's *Four Quartets*. Cf. the final chorus of Milton's *Samson Agonistes*: "All is best, though we oft doubt, / What th' unsearchable dispose / Of highest wisdom brings about / And ever best found in the close" (1745–48).

18. For fuller discussions of the tradition of a "Christian Adam," see Patrides, *Christian Tradition*, 26–53, and Christopher, *Science of the Saints*, 135–46. Also, I have treated the subject briefly in "Making a Mormon of Milton," 201–2.

19. Haller, *Rise of Puritanism*, 156–57. Also cited by Fish, *Surprised by Sin*, 13–14.

20. Cf. Fish, "The Harassed Reader"—an essay later incorporated in *Surprised by Sin*.

BIBLIOGRAPHY

Milton

Alpers, Paul J. "The Milton Controversy." In *Twentieth-Century Literature in Retrospect*. Harvard English Studies 2. Ed. Reuben A. Brower, 269–98. Cambridge: Harvard University Press, 1971.

Babb, Lawrence. *The Moral Cosmos of* Paradise Lost. East Lansing: Michigan State University Press, 1970.

Barker, Arthur E., ed. *Milton: Modern Essays in Criticism*. Oxford: Oxford University Press, 1965.

Bell, Millicent. "The Fallacy of the Fall in *Paradise Lost*." *PMLA* 68 (1953): 863–83.

——. "The Fallacy of the Fall in *Paradise Lost*" in "Notes, Documents, and Critical Comments." *PMLA* 70 (1955): 1185–1203.

Bennett, Joan S. *Reviving Liberty: Radical Christian Humanism in Milton's Great Poems*. Cambridge: Harvard University Press, 1989.

Blackburn, Thomas H. "'Uncloister'd Virtue': Adam and Eve in Milton's Paradise." *Milton Studies* 3 (1971): 119–37.

Bowers, Fredson. "Adam, Eve, and the Fall in *Paradise Lost*." *PMLA* 84 (March 1969): 264–73.

Brisman, Leslie. *Milton's Poetry of Choice and Its Romantic Heirs*. Ithaca: Cornell University Press, 1973.

Broadbent, J. B. *Some Graver Subject: An Essay on* Paradise Lost. London: Chatto & Windus, 1960.

Burden, Dennis. *The Logical Epic: A Study of the Argument of* Paradise Lost. Cambridge: Harvard University Press, 1967.

Chambers, A. B. "The Falls of Adam and Eve in *Paradise Lost*." In *New Essays on* Paradise Lost, ed. Thomas Kranidas, 118–30. Berkeley and Los Angeles: University of California Press, 1971.

Christopher, Georgia B. *Milton and the Science of the Saints*. Princeton: Princeton University Press, 1982.

Cirillo, Albert R. "Noon-Midnight and the Temporal Structure of *Paradise Lost*." *ELH* 29 (1962): 372–95. (Reprinted in *Milton's Epic Poetry: Essays on* Paradise Lost *and* Paradise Regained, ed. C. A. Patrides, 215–32. Harmondsworth, Middlesex, England: Penguin, 1967.)

Cope, Jackson I. *The Metaphoric Structure of* Paradise Lost. Baltimore: Johns Hopkins University Press, 1962.

Crosman, Robert. *Reading* Paradise Lost. Bloomington: Indiana University Press, 1980.

Danielson, Dennis Richard. *Milton's Good God: A Study in Literary Theodicy.* Cambridge: Cambridge University Press, 1982.

Diekhoff, John S. "Eve's Dream and the Paradox of Fallible Perfection." *Milton Quarterly* 4.1 (1970): 5-7.

————, ed. *Milton on Himself.* 1939. Reprint. New York: Humanities Press, 1965.

————. *Milton's* Paradise Lost: *A Commentary on the Argument.* 1946. Reprint. New York: Humanities Press, 1963.

Empson, William. *Milton's God.* London: Chatto & Windus, 1961.

Evans, J. M. Paradise Lost *and the Genesis Tradition.* Oxford: Clarendon Press, 1968.

Ferry, Anne Davidson. *Milton's Epic Voice: The Narrator in* Paradise Lost. Cambridge: Harvard University Press, 1963.

Fiore, Peter A. "Augustine." In *A Milton Encyclopedia*, ed. William B. Hunter, Jr. 9 vols. Lewisburg, Pa.: Bucknell University Press, 1978-1983.

————. *Milton and Augustine: Patterns of Augustinian Thought in* Paradise Lost. University Park: Pennsylvania State University Press, 1981.

Fish, Stanley Eugene. "Discovery as Form in *Paradise Lost.*" In *New Essays on* Paradise Lost, ed. Thomas Kranidas, 1-14. Berkeley and Los Angeles: University of California Press, 1971.

————. "The Harassed Reader in *Paradise Lost.*" *Critical Quarterly* 7 (1965): 162-82.

————. *Surprised by Sin: The Reader in* Paradise Lost. 1967. Reprint. Berkeley and Los Angeles: University of California Press, 1971.

Forrest, James F. "The Fathers on Milton's Evil Thought in Blameless Mind." *Canadian Journal of Theology* 15 (1969): 247-67.

Fowler, Alastair, ed. *John Milton:* Paradise Lost. New York: Longman, 1971.

Frye, Northrop. *The Return of Eden: Five Essays on Milton's Epics.* London: Routledge & Kegan Paul, 1966.

Gallagher, Phillip J. *Milton, the Bible, and Misogyny.* Ed. Eugene R. Cunnar and Gail L. Mortimer. Columbia: University of Missouri Press, 1990.

Gardner, Helen. "Milton's 'Satan' and the Theme of Damnation in Elizabethan Tragedy." *English Studies* (New Series) 1948. Reprinted for Wm. Dawson & Sons, 1967: 46-66. Also reprinted in *Milton: Modern Essays in Criticism*, ed. Arthur E. Barker, 205-17. Oxford: Oxford University Press, 1965.

George, A. G. *Milton and the Nature of Man.* New York: Asia Publishing House, 1974.

Greenblatt, Stephen. *Renaissance Self-Fashioning: From More to Shakespeare.* Chicago: University of Chicago Press, 1980.

Greenlaw, Edwin A. "A Better Teacher than Aquinas." *Studies in Philology* 14 (1917): 196-217.

Gross, Kenneth. "Satan and the Romantic Satan: A Notebook." In *Re-membering Milton: Essays on the Texts and Traditions*, ed. Mary Nyquist and Margaret W. Ferguson, 318-41. New York: Methuen, 1987.

Grossman, Marshall. *"Authors to Themselves": Milton and the Revelation of History*. Cambridge: Cambridge University Press, 1987.

Haller, William. *The Rise of Puritanism*. 1938. Reprint. New York: Harper & Row, 1957.

Hanford, James Holly. "The Dramatic Element in *Paradise Lost*." *Studies in Philology* 14 (1917): 178–95.

———. *John Milton, Poet and Humanist: Essays by James Holly Hanford*. Cleveland: Press of Western Reserve University, 1966.

———. "The Temptation Motive in Milton." *Studies in Philology* 15 (1918): 176–94.

———, and James G. Taaffe. *A Milton Handbook*. 5th ed. Englewood Cliffs, N.J.: Prentice-Hall, 1970.

Harding, Davis. *The Club of Hercules: Studies in the Classical Background of Paradise Lost*. Illinois Studies in Language and Literature, no. 50. Urbana: University of Illinois Press, 1962.

Hill, Christopher. *Milton and the English Revolution*. 1977. Harmondsworth, Middlesex, England: Penguin, 1979.

Hill, John Spencer. *John Milton: Poet, Priest, and Prophet: A Study of Divine Vocation in Milton's Poetry*. London: Macmillan, 1979.

Howard, Leon. "'The Invention' of Milton's 'Great Argument': A Study of the Logic of 'God's Ways to Men.'" *Huntington Library Quarterly* 9 (1945): 149–73.

Huckabay, Calvin. "The Satanist Controversy of the 19th Century." In *Studies in English Renaissance Literature*, ed. Waldo F. McNeir, 197–210. Louisiana State University Studies, Humanities Series, no. 12. Baton Rouge: Louisiana State University Press, 1962.

Hughes, Merritt Y. *Ten Perspectives on Milton*. New Haven: Yale University Press, 1965.

Hunter, G. K. *Paradise Lost*. Unwin Critical Library. London: Allen & Unwin, 1980.

Jacobus, Lee A. *Sudden Apprehension: Aspects of Knowledge in* Paradise Lost. Studies in English Literature 94. The Hague: Mouton, 1976.

Johnson, Samuel. "Life of Milton." In *Rasselas, Poems, and Selected Prose*, ed. Bertrand H. Bronson, 446–69. New York: Holt, Rinehart & Winston, 1958.

Johnson, William C. *Milton Criticism: A Subject Index*. Folkestone, Kent, England: Wm. Dawson & Sons, 1978.

Kelley, Maurice. *This Great Argument: A Study of Milton's* De Doctrina Christiana *as a Gloss on* Paradise Lost. Princeton: Princeton University Press, 1941.

Kendrick, Christopher. *Milton: A Study in Ideology and Form*. New York: Methuen, 1986.

Kerrigan, William. *The Sacred Complex: On the Psychogenesis of* Paradise Lost. Cambridge: Harvard University Press, 1983.

Knapp, Steven. *Personification and the Sublime: Milton to Coleridge*. Cambridge: Harvard University Press, 1985.

Kranidas, Thomas, ed. *New Essays on* Paradise Lost. Berkeley and Los Angeles: University of California Press, 1971.

Lewalski, Barbara Kiefer. "Innocence and Experience in Milton's Eden." In *New Essays on* Paradise Lost, ed. Thomas Kranidas, 86–117. Berkeley and Los Angeles: University of California Press, 1971.

———. Paradise Lost *and the Rhetoric of Literary Forms*. Princeton: Princeton University Press, 1985.

Lewis, C. S. *A Preface to* Paradise Lost. New York: Oxford University Press, 1961.

Lieb, Michael. *The Dialectics of Creation: Patterns of Birth & Regeneration in* Paradise Lost. Amherst: University of Massachusetts Press, 1970.

———. "Milton's 'Dramatick Constitution': The Celestial Dialogue in *Paradise Lost*, Book III." *Milton Studies* 23 (1987): 215–40.

———. *Paradise Lost* and the Myth of Prohibition." *Milton Studies* 7 (1975): 233–65.

MacCaffrey, Isabel G. Paradise Lost *as "Myth"*. Cambridge: Harvard University Press, 1959.

Madsen, William G. *From Shadowy Types to Truth: Studies in Milton's Symbolism*. New Haven: Yale University Press, 1968.

McColley, Diane Kelsey. *Milton's Eve*. Urbana: University of Illinois Press, 1983.

Mills, Ralph D. "The Logic of Milton's Narrative of the Fall: A Reconsideration." Ph.D. diss., Ohio State University, 1966.

Milton Encyclopedia. 9 vols. Ed. William B. Hunter, Jr., et al. Lewisburg, Pa.: Bucknell University Press, 1978.

Mollenkott, Virginia. "Milton's Rejection of the Fortunate Fall." *Milton Quarterly* 6.1 (1972): 1–5.

Mulder, John R. *The Temple of the Mind: Education and Literary Taste in Seventeenth-Century England*. New York: Pegasus, 1969.

Murray, Patrick. *Milton: The Modern Phase. A Study of Twentieth-Century Criticism*. New York: Barnes & Noble, 1967.

Musacchio, George Louis. "Fallible Perfection: The Motivation of the Fall in Reformation Theology and *Paradise Lost*." Ph.D. diss., University of California, Riverside, 1971.

Nyquist, Mary. "Gynesis, Genesis, Exegesis, and Milton's Eve." In *Cannibals, Witches, and Divorce: Estranging the Renaissance*, ed. Marjorie Garber, 147–208. Selected Papers from the English Institute n.s. 11. Baltimore: Johns Hopkins University Press, 1987.

———. "Reading the Fall: Discourse in Drama in *Paradise Lost*." *English Literary Renaissance* 14 (1984): 199–229.

Ogden, H. V. S. "The Crisis of *Paradise Lost* Reconsidered." *Philological Quarterly* 36 (1957): 1–19.

Parker, William Riley. *Milton: A Biography*. 2 vols. Oxford: Clarendon Press, 1968.

Patrides, C. A. *Milton and the Christian Tradition*. Oxford: Clarendon Press, 1966.

_____. "*Paradise Lost* and the Theory of Accommodation." *Texas Studies in Literature and Language* 5 (1963): 58–63.

_____. "The Salvation of Satan." *Journal of the History of Ideas* 28 (1967): 467–78.

Quilligan, Maureen. *Milton's Spenser: The Politics of Reading*. Ithaca: Cornell University Press, 1983.

Qvarnstrom, Gunnar. *The Enchanted Palace: Some Structural Aspects of* Paradise Lost. Stockholm: Almqvist & Wiksell, 1967.

Radzinowicz, Mary Ann. "'Man as a Probationer of Immortality': *Paradise Lost* XI–XII." In *Approaches to* Paradise Lost. The York Tercentenary Lectures, ed. C. A. Patrides, 31–51. Toronto: University of Toronto Press, 1968.

Rajan, Balachandra. Paradise Lost *and the Seventeenth Century Reader*. 1947. Reprint. London: Chatto & Windus, 1962.

Rapaport, Herman. *Milton and the Postmodern*. Lincoln: University of Nebraska Press, 1983.

Reichert, John. "'Against His Better Knowledge': A Case for Adam." *ELH* 48 (1981): 83–109.

Revard, Stella Purce. *The War in Heaven:* Paradise Lost *and the Tradition of Satan's Rebellion*. Ithaca: Cornell University Press, 1980.

Ryken, Leland. *The Apocalyptic Vision in* Paradise Lost. Ithaca: Cornell University Press, 1970.

Samuel, Irene. "*Paradise Lost*." In *Critical Approaches to Six Major English Works: Beowulf through* Paradise Lost, ed. R. M. Lumiansky and Herschel Baker, 209–53. Philadelphia: University of Pennsylvania Press, 1968.

_____. *Plato and Milton*. Ithaca: Cornell University Press, 1947.

Saurat, Denis. *Milton: Man and Thinker*. New York: Dial Press, 1925.

Savage, J. B. "Freedom and Necessity in *Paradise Lost*." *ELH* 44 (1977): 286–311.

Schultz, Howard. *Milton and Forbidden Knowledge*. 1955. New York: Kraus Reprint, 1970.

Schwartz, Regina. *Remembering and Repeating Biblical Creation in* Paradise Lost. Cambridge: Cambridge University Press, 1988.

Shawcross, John T., ed. *Milton: The Critical Heritage*. New York: Barnes & Noble, 1970.

_____. *With Mortal Voice: The Creation of* Paradise Lost. Lexington: University Press of Kentucky, 1982.

Shumaker, Wayne. "The Fallacy of the Fall in *Paradise Lost*" in "Notes, Documents, and Critical Comments." *PMLA* 70 (1955): 1185–1203.

————. *Unpremeditated Verse: Feeling and Perception in* Paradise Lost. Princeton: Princeton University Press, 1967.

Steadman, John M. "'Man's First Disobedience': The Causal Structure of the Fall." *Journal of the History of Ideas* 21 (1960): 180–97. (Revised and reprinted in *Milton's Epic Characters.*)

————. *Milton's Epic Characters: Image and Idol.* Chapel Hill: University of North Carolina Press, 1959.

Stein, Arnold. *Answerable Style: Essays on* Paradise Lost. 1953. Reprint. Seattle: University of Washington Press, 1967.

Summers, Joseph H. *The Muse's Method: An Introduction to* Paradise Lost. 1962. Reprint. New York: Norton, 1968.

Sumner, Charles R., trans. *De Doctrina Christiana.* Vols. 14–16 of *The Works of John Milton.* Ed. Frank A. Patterson. 18 vols. New York: Columbia University Press, 1933–1934.

Svendsen, Kester. *Milton and Science.* Cambridge: Harvard University Press, 1956.

Swaim, Kathleen M. *Before and After the Fall: Contrasting Modes in* Paradise Lost. Amherst: University of Massachusetts Press, 1986.

Tanner, John S. "Anxiety in Eden: Eve's Dream and the Psychology of Sin in *Paradise Lost* and *The Concept of Anxiety.*" *Literature and Belief* (1987): 41–48.

————. "Making a Mormon of Milton." *BYU Studies* 24.2 (1984): 191–206.

————. "'Myself Am Hell': Milton's Satan and Kierkegaardian Demonic Despair." *Encyclia* 60 (1983): 77–89.

————. "The Ontological Terror of Beauty in *Paradise Lost*: A Perspective from Kierkegaard." *Phenomenological Inquiry* 13 (1989): 155–68.

————. "'Say First What Cause': Ricoeur and the Etiology of Evil in *Paradise Lost.*" *PMLA* 103 (1988): 45–56.

Thorslev, Peter L., Jr. "The Romantic Mind Is Its Own Place." *Comparative Literature* 15 (1963): 250–68.

Tillyard, E. M. W. *Milton.* 1930. Rev. ed. 1951. New York: Collier Books, 1967.

————. *Studies in Milton.* London: Chatto & Windus, 1951.

Van Doren, Mark. *The Noble Voice: A Study of Ten Great Poems.* New York: Holt, 1946.

Waldock, A. J. A. Paradise Lost *and Its Critics.* 1947. Reprint. Cambridge: Cambridge University Press, 1966.

Weidhorn, Manfred. "The Anxiety Dream in Literature from Homer to Milton." *Studies in Philology* 64 (1967): 65–82.

Wilkenfeld, Roger B. "Theoretics or Polemics? Milton Criticism and the 'Dramatic Axiom.'" *PMLA* 82 (1967): 505–15.

Willey, Basil. *The Seventeenth Century Background.* 1934. Reprint. Garden City, N.Y.: Doubleday, 1953.

Williams, Arnold. "The Motivation of Satan's Rebellion in *Paradise Lost.*" *Studies in Philology* 62 (1945): 253–68. Reprinted in *Milton: Modern Judgements,* ed. Alan Rudrum, 136–50. Nashville, Tenn.: Aurora Publishers, 1970.

Williamson, George. "The Education of Adam." Reprinted in *Milton: Modern Essays in Criticism*, ed. Arthur E. Barker, 284–307. Oxford: Oxford University Press, 1965.

Wittreich, Joseph Anthony, Jr. *The Romantics on Milton: Formal Essays and Critical Asides*. Cleveland: Press of the Case Western Reserve University, 1970.

Wright, B. A. *Milton's* Paradise Lost. London: Methuen, 1962.

Kierkegaard

Bibliotheca Kierkegaardiana. 16 vols. Ed. Niels Thulstrup and Marie Mikulová Thulstrup. Copenhagen: C. A. Reitzels Boghandel, 1978 – .

Carnell, Edward John. *The Burden of Soren Kierkegaard*. Grand Rapids, Mich.: Eerdmans, 1965.

Cole, J. Preston. *The Problematic Self in Kierkegaard and Freud*. New Haven: Yale University Press, 1971.

Collins, James. *The Mind of Kierkegaard*. 1953. Reprint. Princeton: Princeton University Press, 1983.

Crites, Stephen. *In the Twilight of Christendom: Hegel vs. Kierkegaard on Faith and History*. AAR Studies in Religion, no. 2. Chambersburg, Pa.: American Academy of Religion, 1972.

Croxall, Thomas H. *Kierkegaard Commentary*. New York: Harper, 1956.

_____. *Kierkegaard Studies: With Special Reference to (a) The Bible, (b) Our Own Age*. London: Lutterworth, 1948.

Drolet, Bruno. *Le Démoniaque chez S. A. Kierkegaard*. Joliette, Quebec: Centre de Diffusion Lanaudière, 1971.

Dunning, Stephen N. *Kierkegaard's Dialectic of Inwardness: A Structural Analysis of the Theory of Stages*. Princeton: Princeton University Press, 1985.

Dupré, Louis. *Kierkegaard as Theologian: The Dialectic of Christian Experience*. New York: Sheed & Ward, 1963.

Eller, Vernard. *Kierkegaard and Radical Discipleship: A New Perspective*. Princeton: Princeton University Press, 1968.

Elrod, John W. *Kierkegaard and Christendom*. Princeton: Princeton University Press, 1981.

Gill, Jerry H., ed. *Essays on Kierkegaard*. Minneapolis: Burgess Publishing Co., 1969.

Hannay, Alastair. *Kierkegaard*. London: Routledge & Kegan Paul, 1982.

Johnson, Howard A., and Niels Thulstrup, eds. *A Kierkegaard Critique*. Chicago: Regnery, 1967.

Jolivet, Regis. *Introduction to Kierkegaard*. Trans. W. H. Barber. New York: Dutton, n.d.

Kierkegaard, Søren. *Attack upon "Christendom."* Trans. Walter Lowrie. 1944. Reprint. Princeton: Princeton University Press, 1968.

_____. *Concluding Unscientific Postscript to the Philosophical Fragments*.

Trans. Walter Lowrie and David F. Swenson. Intro. Walter Lowrie.
Princeton: Princeton University Press, 1941.

_____. *Edifying Discourses: A Selection.* Ed. Paul L. Holmer. Trans. David F.
and Lillian Marvin Swenson. New York: Harper Torchbooks, 1958.

_____. *Either/Or: A Fragment of Life.* Vol. 1, trans. David F. Swenson and
Lillian Marvin Swenson; vol. 2, trans. Walter Lowrie. Rev. Howard A.
Johnson. Princeton: Princeton University Press, 1959.

_____. *Fear and Trembling: Dialectical Lyric.* Trans. with intro. and notes by
Howard V. Hong and Edna H. Hong. Princeton: Princeton University
Press, 1983.

_____. *Philosophical Fragments or a Fragment of Philosophy.* Orig. trans.
David Swenson; intro. and commentary by Niels Thurlstrup; rev. trans.
Howard V. Hong. Princeton: Princeton University Press, 1962.

_____. *The Point of View for My Work as an Author: A Report to History.*
Trans. with intro. and notes by Walter Lowrie. Rev. ed., with preface by
Benjamin Nelson. New York: Harper Torchbooks, 1962.

_____. *The Present Age.* Trans. Alexander Dru; intro. Walter Kaufmann. New
York: Harper Torchbooks, 1962.

_____. *Søren Kierkegaard's Journals and Papers.* Trans. and ed. Howard V.
Hong and Edna H. Hong. 7 vols. Bloomington: Indiana University Press,
1967–1978.

_____. *Stages on Life's Way: Studies by Sundry Persons.* Trans. with intro and
notes by Walter Lowrie. Princeton: Princeton University Press, 1940.

_____. *Training in Christianity and the Edifying Discourses Which "Accompa-
nied" It.* Trans. with intro. and notes by Walter Lowrie. Princeton:
Princeton University Press, 1967.

Lapointe, François H. *Sören Kierkegaard and His Critics: An International
Bibliography of Criticism.* Westport, Conn.: Greenwood Press, 1980.

Lawson, Lewis A., ed. *Kierkegaard's Presence in Contemporary American Life:
Essays from Various Disciplines.* Metuchen, N.J.: Scarecrow Press, 1970.

Lebowitz, Naomi. *Kierkegaard: A Life of Allegory.* Baton Rouge: Louisiana
State University Press, 1985.

Lowrie, Walter. *Kierkegaard.* 2 vols. 1938. Rev. ed. New York: Harper & Brothers, 1962.

Mackey, Louis. *Kierkegaard: A Kind of Poet.* Philadelphia: University of Pennsylvania Press, 1971.

_____. *Points of View: Readings of Kierkegaard.* Tallahassee: Florida State
University Press, 1986.

Malantschuk, Gregor. *The Controversial Kierkegaard.* Kierkegaard Monograph
Series. Trans. Howard V. Hong and Edna Hong. 1976. Reprint. Waterloo, Ontario: Wilfrid Laurier University Press, 1980.

_____. *Kierkegaard's Thought.* Trans. Howard V. Hong and Edna H. Hong.
Princeton: Princeton University Press, 1971.

McCarthy, Vincent A. *The Phenomenology of Moods in Kierkegaard.* The
Hague: Nijhoff, 1978.

Miller, Libuse Lukas. *In Search of the Self: The Individual in the Thought of Kierkegaard*. Philadelphia: Muhlenberg, 1962.

Ostendfeld, Ib. *Søren Kierkegaard's Psychology*. 1972. Trans. and ed. Alastair McKinnon. Waterloo, Ontario: Wilfrid Laurier University Press, 1978.

Roberts, David E. "The Concept of Dread: A Review Article." *Review of Religion* 11 (1947): 273–84.

Shestov, Lev. *Kierkegaard and the Existential Philosophy*. Trans. Elinor Hewitt. Athens: Ohio University Press, 1969.

Sontag, Frederick. *A Kierkegaard Handbook*. Atlanta: John Knox Press, 1979.

Taylor, Mark C. *Journeys to Selfhood: Hegel and Kierkegaard*. Berkeley and Los Angeles: University of California Press, 1980.

_____. *Kierkegaard's Pseudonymous Authorship: A Study of Time and the Self*. Princeton: Princeton University Press, 1975.

Thompson, Josiah. *The Lonely Labyrinth: Kierkegaard's Pseudonymous Works*. Carbondale: Southern Illinois University Press, 1967.

Thomte, Reidar. *Kierkegaard's Philosophy of Religion*. Princeton: Princeton University Press, 1948.

Thulstrup, Niels. *Kierkegaard's Relation to Hegel*. Trans. George L. Stengren. 1967. Reprint. Princeton: Princeton University Press, 1980.

Related Works

Anderson, Bernhard W. *Understanding the Old Testament*. 3d rev. ed. Englewood Cliffs, N.J.: Prentice-Hall, 1975.

Bellah, Robert N., et al. *Habits of the Heart: Individualism and Commitment in American Life*. New York: Harper & Row, 1985.

Berry, Wendell. *Standing by Words: Essays by Wendell Berry*. San Francisco: North Point Press, 1983.

Boman, Thorleif. *Hebrew Thought Compared with Greek*. 1960. Reprint. New York: Norton, 1970.

Bruner, Jerome. *On Knowing: Essays for the Left Hand*. 1962. Reprint. New York: Atheneum, 1971.

Cixous, Hélène. "Sorties." In *New French Feminisms: An Anthology*. Ed. Elaine Marks and Isabelle de Courtivron, 90–98. Amherst: University of Massachusetts Press, 1980.

Ellwood, Thomas. *The History of the Life of Thomas Ellwood*. Ed. C. G. Crump. New York: G. P. Putnam's Sons, 1900.

Gadamer, Hans-Georg. *Truth and Method*. 1960. 2d rev. ed. Trans. and rev. by Joel Weinsheimer and Donald G. Marshall. New York: Crossroad, 1989.

Genette, Gérard. *Narrative Discourse: An Essay in Method*. Trans. Jane E. Lewin. Ithaca: Cornell University Press, 1980.

Goffman, Erving. *The Presentation of Self in Everyday Life*. Garden City, N.Y.: Doubleday, 1959.

Heidegger, Martin. "Letter on Humanism." In *Martin Heidegger: Basic Writings from "Being and Time" (1927) to "The Task of Thinking" (1964)*, 193–242. New York: Harper & Row, 1977.

The Interpreter's Dictionary of the Bible: An Illustrated Encyclopedia. 4 vols. Ed. George Arthur Buttrick et al. New York: Abingdon, 1962.

Kant, Immanuel. "On the Failure of All Attempted Philosophical Theodicies" (1791). In *Kant on History and Religion*. Trans. Michel Despland, 291–97. Montreal: McGill-Queens University Press, 1973.

Levin, Harry. "*Othello* and the Motive-Hunters." *Centennial Review* 8 (1964): 1–16.

Lewis, C. S. *The Four Loves*. New York: Harcourt, Brace & World, 1960.

———. *Perelandra: A Novel*. 1944. Reprint. New York: Macmillan, 1965.

Marlowe, Christopher. *Doctor Faustus*. In *Christopher Marlowe: The Complete Plays*, ed. J. B. Steane. Harmondsworth, Middlesex, England: Penguin, 1969.

Miller, Perry. *The New England Mind: The Seventeenth Century*. New York: Macmillan, 1939.

Nietzsche, Friedrich. *Thus Spoke Zarathustra*. Trans. Walter Kaufmann. 1955. Reprint. New York: Vintage, 1966.

Ricoeur, Paul. *Essays on Biblical Interpretation*. Ed. Lewis S. Mudge. Philadelphia: Fortress Press, 1980.

———. "Original Sin: A Study in Meaning." In *Conflict of Interpretation*, trans. Peter McCormick and ed. Don Ihde, 269–86. Northwestern University Studies in Phenomenology and Existential Philosophy. Evanston: Northwestern University Press, 1974.

———. *The Symbolism of Evil*. Trans. Emerson Buchanan. 1967. Reprint. Boston: Beacon Press, 1969.

Rondet, Henri. *Original Sin: The Patristic and Theological Background*. Trans. Cajetan Finegan. Blackrock, Dublin, Ireland: Ecclesia Press, 1972.

Solomon, Robert C. *Continental Philosophy since 1750: The Rise and Fall of the Self*. A History of Western Philosophy, no. 7. Oxford: Oxford University Press, 1988.

Tanner, John S. "Job and the Prophets." *Cithara* 26.1 (1986): 23–35.

———. "The Syllables of Time: An Augustinian Context for *Macbeth* 5.5." *Journal of the Rocky Mountain Medieval and Renaissance Association* 8 (1987): 131–46.

Tennant, F. R. *The Sources of the Doctrines of the Fall and Original Sin*. 1903. Reprint. New York: Shocken Books, 1968.

Terrien, Samuel. "Introduction and Exegesis to Job." In *Interpreter's Bible*, 3: 877–905. Nashville, Tenn.: Abingdon, 1954.

Turner, Victor. "Betwixt and Between: The Liminal Period in *Rites de Passage*." In *The Forest of Symbols: Aspects of Ndembu Ritual*, 93–111. Ithaca: Cornell University Press, 1967.

Verdenius, W. J. "Plato and Christianity." *Ratio* 5 (1963): 15–32.

Walker, Daniel P. *The Decline of Hell: Seventeenth-Century Discussions of Eternal Torment*. Chicago: University of Chicago Press, 1964.

INDEX OF CITATIONS TO
PARADISE LOST

GENERAL INDEX

Abdiel, 11, 46–47, 152–53
Abraham, 73, 128, 167n.16. *See also* Knight of Faith
Accommodation, 41, 46, 103n.17
Adam: doubts equivalent to anxiety, 87; fatalism of, 117–19, 120n.11; as individual and race, 64n.2; language of, 82–85, 103n.14; remorse of, 126; temptation of, 114–19; theatrical self of, 99; uxoriousness of, 115
Adam and Eve: characterization of, 27, 53; knowledge of fallen realities, 71, 80–82, 85–90; mutual accusations, 125; mutual rape of, 98; posterity of, 57–62 (*see also* Original Sin); remorse of, 124–29; Satan's role in fall of, 51–57; self-tempted like Satan, 41–42
Addison, Joseph, 43
Admonition. *See* Warnings
Adversary, 48–49, 158. *See also* Lucifer; Satan
Aesthetic, 73; experience, 160; sphere of existence, 13n.24, 91. *See also* Beauty
Alienation, 173, 184. *See also* Self-alienation
Allegory, 43–44
Alpers, Paul, 169n.33
Alterity, 159, 168n.29
Ambition, 23, 28
Anderson, Bernhard W., 186n.10
Angels: cousins to humans, 57; faithful, 177; love-making, 95; rebellious (*see* Fallen angels); understanding, 80, 82; unequal to Son, 157
Angst, 50; defined, 3, 30–31
Animals: Adam's naming of, 82, 103nn.11,13; as individual agents, 55
Anticlericalism, 5
Antinomianism, 104n.26
Antipathy, 108, 110–12; sympathetic, 30, 70, 111
Anxiety: Adam's doubts as, 87; in Adam's temptation, 114–19; defined, 3, 30–31; demonic, about the good, 123–24, 129–43; determinant of sin, 28–34, 70; dreams and, 3, 50, 71–72, 110, 119n.2; in

Eve's temptation, 106–14; of lesser demons, 137–42; salvific, 177, 181; Satan's dizziness as, 44–45; Satan's wakefulness as, 49–50. *See also* Objective anxiety; Subjective anxiety
Anxiety about evil: 123–29; equivalent of remorse, 124; human response to sin, 124
Anxiety about good: demonic response to sin, 129–43; opposite of remorse, 130
Apostasy, 9–11
Appetite: 107–9; carnal, 106; for potentiality, 114. *See also* Concupiscence
Aquinas, Thomas, 103n.11
Arianism, 168n.26
Aristotelian recognition, 117
Atomism, 155. *See also* Chaos
Atonement, 128, 171–72, 177, 180, 184
Augustine: 8, 58, 59, 66n.23, 154, 167n.13; concept of inherited sin, 18, 57. *See also* Evil, Augustinian vs. Pelagian; Original Sin

Bader, Franz, 70
Beauty: antidote to despair, 165; not subjective, 161, 165; ontological terror of, 158–66; powerful, 160; Satan's despairing relation to, 151, 162–66; Satan's reaction to, 131–32, 158–66. *See also* Aesthetic
Becoming, Kierkegaard's theory of, 28–29, 31, 35
Belial, 137–38
Bell, Millicent, 23–32, 37n.32, 53, 116, 117
Bellah, Robert N., 167n.20
Bennett, Joan S., 104n. 26, 105n. 28
Berkeley, George (Bishop), 149
Berry, Wendell, 169n.37
Biology and sin, 54, 57–62, 66n.22. *See also* Original Sin
Blackburn, Thomas H., 36n.5, 103n.10
Blake, William, 146
Boman, Thorleif, 105n.29
Boundaries, 134, 136, 156. *See also* Limits
Bowers, Fredson, 21–22, 36n.5
Brisman, Leslie, 13n.24, 168n.32

Philosophy: Greek, contrasted to Christian, 8–9, 100–102, 116–17, 141–43; Hebraic vs. Greek, 13*n*.18; in hell, 7, 139–41. *See also* Plato; Theology
Plato, 8, 104*nn*.22,27, 147. *See also* Philosophy: Greek
Positivism, 29, 38*n*.52
Possibility. *See* Freedom
Powell, Mary, 4
Prayer, 94, 129
Pride, 21, 48, 50–51
Prohibition, the, 40, 70–71, 73, 81, 85, 88–89, 157. *See also* Taboo, the
Protoevangelium, 128
Psyche, myth of, 80
Psychology, 21, 30–32, 38*n*.52
Puritans, 180

Quantitative determination, 33, 58, 63–64*n*.2, 117
Quantitative "more": for Adam and Eve, 54–55; for "later" individual, 73–74, 77–78. *See also* Determinism
Quilligan, Maureen, 64*n*.6

Race, and individual, 55–57, 60
Radzinowicz, Mary Ann, 185*n*.5
Rajan, Balachandra, 36*n*.11
Ramism, 104*n*.26
Rapaport, Herman, 13*n*.18
Rape: of Adam and Eve, 98; of environment, 97; of Satan by beauty, 160
Raphael, 43, 64*n*.9, 80, 103*n*.18, 117; as historian, 45–49, 53, 65*n*.16; similes of, 85
Raphael's history, effect of, 80, 86–87. *See also* Warnings
Reader-response, 64*n*.6, 181
Reason (right), 100
Reciprocity, 143*n*.4, 164, 184
Redemption. *See* Salvation
Reflection, 113
Reichert, John, "Against His Better Knowledge," 36*n*.5
Remorse, 28, 123–29; as anxiety about evil, 124; Eve's prelapsarian, 110; for future and past, 125–27; opposite of anxiety of the good, 130
Revard, Stella Purce, 64*n*.3, 65*n*.13
Rhetoric, 98–99, 134
Ricoeur, Paul, 20, 36*n*.6, 45, 53, 55, 59, 66*n*.23, 67*n*.25, 186*n*.9
Roberts, David E., 102*n*.1
Romantic: hero, 161, 168*n*.32; individualism, 60, 146, 165; sensibility, 164

Rondet, Henri, 67*n*.25
Ryken, Leland, 103*n*.17

Salvation: ch. 8; and continuity, 135–37; demonic anxiety of, 129–31, 143; of devils, 7–8, 143; Pauline, 170–73, 177–79
Samson, 176
Samuel, Irene, 36*n*.5, 104*nn*.26,27
Sartre, Jean-Paul, 55, 145, 165
Satan: as agent of Fall, 20–21; as antihero, 144*n*.17; boring, 137; as catalyst of sin, 52, ch. 3; dissembler, 99; dualist, 153; fantasy of self-creation, 152–53; motives of, 20–21, 48–51; Mount Niphates soliloquy, 130–35, 158; Protean nature of, 136, 153–54; scriptural sources for, 64*n*.3; self-slavery, 132–33; terror of beauty, 158–66; transmogrification, 136; unable to love, 165; unable to repent, 132–33, 162; wakefulness of, 49–50. *See also* Adversary; Lucifer
Saurat, Denis, 36*n*.11
Schultz, Howard, 102*n*.8
Schwartz, Regina, 155
Scotus, Duns, 11
Self, the: as individual and race, 67*n*.31; infinite self, 148, 150–58; Kierkegaard's definition of, 147–48; reconstitution of, 44; synthesis of opposing potentialities, 147–51
Self-alienation, 97–100
Self-deception, 116
Self-determination, 51, 61–62. *See also* Freedom; Leap, the
Self-fashioning, 43, 65*n*.15, 153
Self-reflexivity, 62
Self-temptation, 41–45, 50–52, 63, 63*n*.2, 179
Sensuousness, 74, 77–78, 89; not sinful, 77. *See also* Erotic; Sex
Separation scene, 89
Serpent: identity of, 41; meaning of, 53; opposing treatments of, 39–41; role of in Garden, 35; symbolic of human capacity for language, 41
Service vs. servility, 157
Sex, 77, 110; fallen, 96, 98; unfallen, 91–96. *See also* Erotic; Sensuousness
Sexuality, 74–75
Shakespeare, 49, 160; *Henry IV*, 49; *Macbeth* 138–39, 146; *Othello*, 51; *The Winter's Tale*, 174
Shawcross, John T., 64*n*.7, 65*n*.12, 104*n*.27, 144*nn*.14,17, 185*n*.2, 187*n*.13
Shelley, Percy Bysshe, 165, 169*n*.37